*The ADHD Explosion*

# The ADHD Explosion

## Myths, Medication, Money, and Today's Push for Performance

STEPHEN P. HINSHAW

RICHARD M. SCHEFFLER

# OXFORD
UNIVERSITY PRESS

Oxford University Press is a department of the University of Oxford.
It furthers the University's objective of excellence in research, scholarship,
and education by publishing worldwide.

Oxford   New York
Auckland   Cape Town   Dar es Salaam   Hong Kong   Karachi
Kuala Lumpur   Madrid   Melbourne   Mexico City   Nairobi
New Delhi   Shanghai   Taipei   Toronto

With offices in
Argentina   Austria   Brazil   Chile   Czech Republic   France   Greece
Guatemala   Hungary   Italy   Japan   Poland   Portugal   Singapore
South Korea   Switzerland   Thailand   Turkey   Ukraine   Vietnam

Oxford is a registered trademark of Oxford University Press
in the UK and certain other countries.

Published in the United States of America by
Oxford University Press
198 Madison Avenue, New York, NY 10016

Library of Congress Cataloging-in-Publication Data
Hinshaw, Stephen P.
The ADHD explosion : myths, medication, money, and today's push for performance /
Stephen P. Hinshaw, Richard M. Scheffler.
    pages cm
Includes bibliographical references and index.
ISBN 978-0-19-979055-5
1. Attention-deficit hyperactivity disorder—Treatment—Finance.   I. Scheffler,
Richard M.   II. Title.
RJ506.H9H57 2014
616.85'8900835—dc23
2013028792

9 8 7 6 5 4 3 2
Printed in the United States of America
on acid-free paper

*To Kelly, Jeff, John, and Evan*
*To Meg and Zach*

# Contents

# *Foreword*

ADHD is the most common childhood behavioral health problem leading to medical and behavioral health interventions. In fact, one in nine children and adolescents in the United States has received a diagnosis (including nearly one boy in six), and medication treatment is initiated for the vast majority of them. As with autism, its numbers have skyrocketed in recent years. ADHD medications are the number one medicine used worldwide for behavioral problems in youth.

Impressive evidence exists that children who exhibit ADHD behavior patterns suffer many difficulties in school and community adjustment, struggling to keep up academically. They also have disproportionate rates of later problems, from car accidents to substance abuse and divorce. Moreover, problems of hyperactivity, impulsivity, and inability to concentrate that become evident in school and home settings commonly persist in later life, compounding difficulties in successful adjustment. Because these behaviors often first become problematic when children face increased school expectations and demands, requirements for attention and concentration, and expectations of discipline and conformity, some critics see the problem as one of regimented and unimaginative schools that are too rigid to accommodate the varied needs of children.

Thus, ADHD is commonly viewed as a contested behavior, not a true disorder, serving the interests of schools in their need to maintain order, the pharmaceutical industry that seeks to sell as many drugs as possible, or the varying professions and clinicians who build their practices around treatment of these children. Although there is some truth to such claims, they present an incomplete and distorted story that often trivializes the pain, disruptions, and frustrations caused by this behavioral syndrome, underestimating the large personal and social costs for the children, their families, schools, and communities. They also ignore the field's increasing neurobehavioral understanding and the effectiveness of some treatments.

This book brings together an unusual collaboration between an outstanding clinical investigator of ADHD and other behavioral disorders (as well as mental illness stigma) with a distinguished health economist who has specialized over his career in the economics of mental disorders. Thus, this book is unique in its scope and perspectives in examining the wide range of influences that shape ADHD as a medical and social problem within the United States and elsewhere. It seeks to understand the major disparities in incidence and prevalence, family recognition and help-seeking, and access to medication and behavioral treatments. In fact, the chances of receiving an ADHD diagnosis are twice as high in Southern states (e.g., North Carolina) as in the Far West (e.g., California); Southern states are also more likely to medicate the disorder. There are major puzzles to solve in relation to ADHD, and this book tackles them head-on.

While addressing the major social and cultural issues affecting ADHD, the book encompasses Hinshaw's clinical research and experience, grounding more abstract discussion in the everyday experiences of children, parents, teachers, doctors, and welfare personnel. It also benefits from Scheffler's long-standing expertise in the world of health economics and public policy. It tackles global issues, far beyond the United States, revealing that ADHD diagnosis and medications have rapidly expanded around the world. This is a book that deals simultaneously with clinical realities and social policy.

Children with ADHD come to attention through the challenges faced by parents and teachers. Estimates of prevalence vary greatly because children are often labeled on the basis of behavioral styles appraised by untrained adults and not thorough clinical evaluations. Nevertheless, such labeling has been increasing over time, and

ADHD is one of the most common diagnoses of children and adolescents as they proceed through their school experiences. How much of the expansion is a real increase in disorder, a reflection of growing definitional boundaries, a consequence of the changing nature of schooling and the focus on testing, stresses on teachers, or a response to advocacy and marketing of treatments remains a major puzzle.

Stimulants are the number-one medication class for children and adolescents, and their rates of prescription are climbing ever faster for adolescents and adults. Although still controversial, they have been useful to moderate the symptoms of ADHD. The rates of medication are huge, with more than 6% of all children receiving these medications. Ironically, combined treatments using both medication and behavioral treatment have been in decline despite their recognized value. This pattern follows trends in behavioral health care more generally, with greater dependence on pharmaceuticals and less availability of psychosocial treatments or rehabilitation, in order to contain costs.

As Hinshaw and Scheffler make clear, considerable debate continues about whether ADHD is a real disorder, a convenient way of describing some troublesome behaviors, or a reflection of our society and culture and the way we organize schools and learning. Like many other diagnoses in the *Diagnostic and Statistical Manual (DSM)* of the American Psychiatric Association, the criteria are descriptive and somewhat arbitrary, representing professional opinion and consensus. Describing disorders through checklists of symptoms can distort the complexity of clinical realities and comorbidities. From a theoretical perspective, the *DSM*'s deficiency is that it fails to describe the underlying causal patterns of disorder that link the underlying symptoms. As neuroscience continues to develop, we will inevitably need an entirely different way of characterizing disorders.

There is, of course, enormous biological variability; what we choose to view as disorder is in many ways a social construction. Most agree that one criterion for such a definition is harm: the behaviors or thoughts in question are in some significant way impairing, leading to suffering, disruptions in function, and even death. But this is insufficient for calling a troublesome behavioral pattern a disorder, because predictable responses to major losses, disaster, rejection by a loved one, or impossible expectations and stresses can also elicit parallel mood and behavior disruptions. A second criterion, perhaps not as widely agreed on, is that the thinking and behavior must be pathological—that is, a deviation from how humans have been programmed by evolution. While sensible in the abstract, this kind of determination can be hard to make.

It therefore becomes clear as to why ADHD is commonly contested. The degree to which unusual inattention, impulsivity, and hyperactivity are inherent in the person—in contrast to being induced by an over-restrictive and especially demanding environment, such as some schools—is arguable. Both internal states and the nature of the environment are relevant; remedial measures can be taken in each of these two spheres. But it is the relative balance between internal function and environmental pressures that helps us establish whether ADHD behaviors are properly seen as a disorder, whether medication is appropriate, and what other treatments are required.

One of the many attractions of this book beyond its comprehensiveness and readability is the authors' own new research and analyses, which explain significant gaps in much of the current literature and discussion. One such area involves increasing and less flexible school demands and the links between state policies on educational accountability and exit exams on the one hand, and increased identification of children with ADHD on the other. When Hinshaw and Scheffler make the provocative statement that the primary trigger of ADHD is compulsory education, they are fully aware of the heritability of the underlying symptoms and problems. Their direct implication is that ADHD reveals itself through the ever-increasing push for academic and job performance in an increasingly competitive world economy.

Other intriguing areas include sex differences in ADHD, developmental differences between children and adults, and contrasts between children in poverty and those less disadvantaged. Although ADHD is typically perceived as a problem of rambunctious boys, research suggests that the lives of girls are also often damaged by this condition. Similarly, rates are much higher among minorities than previously believed.

Thus, Hinshaw and Scheffler provide much food for thought. They present a comprehensive and far-reaching perspective and contribute new data and new insights toward understanding ADHD, its determinants, and its impact. They are clear that those with ADHD are likely to experience unnecessary suffering. They also address the far-reaching consequences of the use of medication as a performance enhancer for individuals far beyond the bounds of an ADHD diagnosis. Whatever one's expertise, it would be difficult to come away from the book without a greater understanding of ADHD and its large impact on individuals, communities, and society.

David Mechanic
Rutgers University

# Acknowledgments

The truly collaborative nature of preparing this book has been the source of great joy to us. Indeed, our passionate work to provide answers to the many puzzles underlying ADHD has depended on the dedicated contributions of an exceptional cast.

Our journey began eight years ago with grant R01 MH67084 from the National Institute of Mental Health. Joining us were Lisa Croen, Laurie Habel, Peter Levine, and Tom Ray from Kaiser Permanente, along with colleagues Tim Brown, Tim Bruckner, Brent Fulton, Tei-weh Hu, and Susan Stone from UC Berkeley. The policy-related research articles on which we collaborated whetted our appetite to go deeper.

Major support for writing this book came from an Investigator Award in Policy Research from the Robert Wood Johnson Foundation. The opportunities and resources provided by this grant were essential in launching and sustaining our work. The yearly meetings of the policy investigators, from which we received needed stimulation and feedback from esteemed colleagues, were essential in shaping and sharpening our thinking. It is hard to express the many ways in which the Foundation facilitated this work.

Other support for this book was provided by UC Berkeley's Center for Children, Youth, and Policy and the Nicholas A. Petris Center of the UC Berkeley School of Public Health.

Our editor at Oxford University Press, Sarah Harrington, has been wise, patient, and diligent in all of her efforts with us. We have dearly needed these attributes in order to bring the work to fruition. Andrea Zekus of Oxford has also provided excellent and enthusiastic support.

Katherine Ellison provided incisive commentary and editing on all aspects of the book, constantly steering us to refine our messages. Her skill and wisdom are extraordinary.

Julia Landau gave us essential feedback as well, along with specific assistance in the sections on media coverage. Shaikh Ahmad was invaluable in compiling our many citations and references and proofing the entire book. Zachary Scheffler read each page with utmost care, adding needed corrections and useful insights.

The extraordinary skills and dedication of Brent Fulton and Thanh-Tien Pham, of the Petris Center at UC Berkeley, have been essential regarding all aspects of book's preparation. Tien has been our anchor, also providing valuable assistance with tables and charts. Brent provided the major work for the Petris Working Papers and publications that we cite in many chapters of this book, analyzing complex datasets on policy-related issues surrounding ADHD. His intellectual input and wisdom are unmatched. We also thank Kati Phillips, Jessica Foster, and the excellent research assistants from the Petris research team: Jennifer Zheng, Sharanjit Sandhu, and Eunice Gopez. Susanna Visser, the lead investigator for the National Survey of Children's Health analyses on rates of ADHD and medication treatment at the Centers for Disease Control and Prevention, has facilitated our access to data from this landmark study and is a collaborator for key data analyses.

Rick Mayes, a postdoctoral scholar working with Scheffler some years back and now an established investigator, helped to inspire interest in this entire area. His publications and book (Mayes et al., 2009) are great examples of policy analysis in the field of ADHD.

In addition, we gratefully acknowledge the participants in our international workshop on ADHD, held in March 2010. American hosts included Brent Fulton, Brad Berman, Peter Jensen, Glen Elliott, Howard Goldman, and Amy Nuttbrock, along with international scholar–clinicians Heidi Aase and Arne Holte (Norway), Tobias Banaschewski (Germany), Wenhong Cheng (China), Paulo Mattos (Brazil), Florence Levy (Australia), Avi Sadeh (Israel), Joseph

Sergeant (The Netherlands), Eric Taylor (England), and Margaret Weiss (Canada).

A number of eminent colleagues took the time to provide feedback on earlier drafts of this book. We gratefully acknowledge Jose Barros, Brad Berman, Howard Goldman, Brent Fulton, Deborah Haas-Wilson, Joel Hay, David Kirp, Tom Rice, and Susan Stone. Their comments and suggestions were invaluable. Still, any errors or shortcomings remain our own.

We welcome you to the pages ahead.

# Introduction

"Drowned in a Stream of Prescriptions" read the banner headline on page 1 of the Sunday *New York Times*. The lengthy article in February 2013 detailed the harrowing story of Richard Fee, who hanged himself at age 24 after years of taking—and becoming addicted to—the stimulant medication Adderall. As a college student, Fee, like growing numbers of young adults, had begun to use the medicine on an occasional basis to help study for tests or crank out last-minute term papers. After graduation, he received prescriptions to help with medical school entrance exams. Yet, as time went on and he took ever-higher doses, Fee began to show clear signs of paranoia and psychosis, which his doctors seem to have essentially ignored. Although the *Times* clearly noted that such medications can be helpful for authentic cases of ADHD, the story portrayed a shocking lack of responsibility for Fee's growing agitation by a series of professionals who wrote cursory prescriptions with ever-escalating dosages. The reporter quoted experts who rightly questioned whether the all-too-common practice of a rushed evaluation without corroborating information beyond the patient at hand had led to a tragic instance of wrongful diagnosis.[1]

Fee's tragic story called attention to an unfolding crisis that is affecting many millions of people not only in the United States but around the world. The diagnosis of ADHD is at the center of this crisis.

Initiated as a fairly limited psychiatric condition, it has expanded to encompass our national—and increasingly global—preoccupation with academic and job-related performance in an increasingly competitive economic climate, where we all must process unprecedented amounts of information in a typical day. More and more, clinicians, teachers, parents, and coworkers confront the clinical, public health, and ethical issues related to medications as performance enhancers for individuals both with and without ADHD.

For nearly a decade, in fact, growing numbers of college (and even high school) students have been flocking to ADHD medications as study aids, obtaining pills from friends on dorm floors or even through faking symptoms. (Fee, in fact, had started using stimulants to help with academic pressures.) Peer-reviewed journal articles started reporting that as many as a fifth, a quarter, or even a third of all college students in the United States take stimulants to help with midterms, finals, or term papers. The supply of these medications was beginning to seem limitless, as their quotas—set and periodically reviewed by the Drug Enforcement Agency (DEA)—had been steadily rising to meet the demand of greater numbers of ADHD diagnoses.[2]

Yet a major surprise emerged in 2011. As record numbers of Americans went to their local pharmacies to fill prescriptions for ADHD medications, they quickly discovered that the pills had sold out. A survey by Children and Adults with Attention-Deficit/Hyperactivity Disorder (CHADD), the nation's largest ADHD self-help organization, reported that 49% of its members could not get prescriptions filled from late 2011 through the beginning of 2012. Fully 18% had needed to switch to a different form of medication. Demand was finally outpacing supply.[3]

For adults seeking the pills, their children's academic performance and behavioral problems—plus, in many cases, their own job evaluations, relationships, and safety on the road—were on the line. One adult with ADHD wrote the following:

> Been taking [ADHD medication] for over 13 years and now I can't refill my script. What am I supposed to do? Just get over it? Just suck it up, go cold turkey, and maybe I'll get my script filled in a few months? How can I keep working on dangerous equipment

with high voltage everywhere and I can't focus? How can I com-
mute 2 hours a day without falling asleep at the wheel? I feel so
alone.[4]

The outcry was strong enough that President Barack Obama issued
an executive order in November of 2011, asking the Food and Drug
Administration (FDA) to examine the issue. When the DEA subsequently raised quotas for stimulants, the crisis gradually abated as
more pills flowed to pharmacies.

The shortages revealed how dependent on ADHD medications
our society has become. They also raised the question of the numbers of pills falling into the hands of the general public. Across the
population, a few individuals are highly focused and a few (i.e.,
those who tend to get diagnosed with ADHD) have major problems in attention, time management, and self-regulation, with
the majority somewhere in between. Couldn't everyone improve
a notch or two on the continuum? The lure of improving performance and productivity in ever-more competitive school and job
environments is hard to overstate. Indeed, if medication quotas
continue to rise, once more, to meet the demand for legitimate cases
of ADHD, even more diversion to the general public may well follow suit. A key question we raise is just how much academic or
work performance enhancement our nation desires, especially from
medications with significant risk for abuse when used without careful medical supervision.[5]

Enter the national media. In early 2012, half a year after the
shortages had begun, *The New York Times* published two prominent opinion pieces in its influential Sunday Review section. The
first ("Ritalin Gone Wrong") stated that medications for ADHD
were short-term palliatives at best and that faulty, insensitive parenting was the actual cause. The second ("The Art of Distraction")
likened the use of stimulants for ADHD to binding children's hands
to stop masturbation, depriving youth of chances for creativity. If
readers were confused by the half-century-plus time warp reflected
by these opinions, who could blame them? The old-school arguments of the 1940s and 1950s—that misguided parenting was
responsible for nearly all child mental disturbances—appeared to

be making a sudden comeback, echoing earlier views that autism was caused by emotional refrigeration and schizophrenia by rejecting, hostile mothers.[6]

Is ADHD a myth, with the medications used to treat it poisons? This position centers on the contention that ADHD is a social construction, resulting from our culture's poor tolerance of youth who don't achieve optimally or adults who think outside the box. Or is the correct stance that of the advocates who claim that medication is a legitimate medical intervention for a diagnosis that is finally becoming less stigmatized and used appropriately to help millions of sufferers? Caught somewhere in the no-man's land between these perspectives was Richard Fee, who did not appear to have been legitimately diagnosable and who was lethally harmed by the easy attainability of stimulants.

## The Reality of ADHD

We take a clear stand in this book: for those affected, ADHD is all too real, producing a terrible inability to focus at just those times when attention is most needed: in classrooms, at the workplace, or when a peer, parent, or life partner is telling them something essential. Formed in biologically based differences between people, ADHD often leads to rushed, impulsive decisions and major trouble in keeping track of time and organizing priorities. It pushes individuals toward risky, sensation-seeking behavior, especially when caution may well be the best choice—for instance, when driving a car, weighing the best course of future options, choosing how many cigarettes or drinks to have, or deciding whether to send that nasty e-mail to your new boss. Major, lifelong difficulties afflict most individuals with ADHD, including academic failure, relationship problems, accidental injuries, risk for substance abuse, and a shocking propensity for self-injury and attempted suicide, particularly among girls and young women.[7]

However, as safe and effective as stimulant medications are when prescribed for legitimate cases of ADHD and carefully monitored by professionals, in the wrong hands they are far more likely to lead to abuse and addiction. One of the largest culprits of the entire controversy is our medical system's susceptibility to quick-and-dirty diagnoses, opening the door for the spread of medicines to individuals well beyond the bounds of ADHD. Along the same lines, medication is too often touted as the only viable treatment; behavioral and cognitive-behavioral approaches to intervention are often needed to boost academic and social skills.

## Essential Issues

Our book has four fundamental messages:

(1) Although often ridiculed, ADHD represents a genuine medical condition that robs people of major life chances. Its economic consequences are huge, totaling hundreds of billions of dollars annually in terms of special education services, juvenile justice and substance abuse costs, plus low work productivity and employment lapses among adults.

(2) Only diligent and thorough assessment can distinguish ADHD from other mental health conditions, chaotic home environments, or the aftereffects of maltreatment. Yet ADHD is too often diagnosed in extremely cursory fashion. This lack of careful evaluation, fueling both overdiagnosis and underdiagnosis, contributes to a national crisis. Moreover, rushed assessments and poor monitoring of medication fuel the diversion of stimulants to ever-larger numbers of the general public.

(3) ADHD medications are effective in reducing the condition's core symptoms, at least in the short run, but the most genuine gains are achieved by combining medication with skill-building approaches. Yet our health care system rarely provides this optimum combination.

(4) Rates of ADHD and medication treatment vary dramatically across states (and, for treatment, across the world), related to family and cultural values, health care systems, media portrayals and advertisements, and, in particular, variations in school policies linked to demands for achievement and performance.

## Rising Rates of Diagnosis and Expanding Treatment

The number of ADHD diagnoses in America has been climbing at a pace inviting wonder, concern, and skepticism. Three times in the past 10 years, a national telephone survey, sponsored by the Centers for Disease Control and Prevention (CDC), has randomly sampled families in all 50 states. Among the questions are whether a professional has ever diagnosed a child or adolescent with ADHD and, in cases of current diagnosis, whether the child is receiving medication. Of course, this kind of survey cannot determine the true rates of ADHD on the basis of a thorough diagnostic evaluation. But it certainly gives us an idea of what goes on in the offices of practitioners, as reported through the eyes of parents.

The results of this study—part of the National Survey of Children's Health (NSCH)—have been shocking. The percentage of 4- to 17-year-olds ever receiving an ADHD diagnosis was 7.8% in 2003. It went up to 9.5% in 2007 (an increase of 22% from just 4 years earlier). By 2011–2012, the figure had climbed to 11%.[8]

Let's ponder these figures for a moment. Even including preschoolers (for whom diagnoses are still relatively rare), the current rate is not 1 in 30, the proportion touted a few decades ago for "hyperactivity," an earlier term for the condition. It's not 1 in 20, the rate from the 1980s and 1990s regarding attention deficit disorder (ADD). It's not 1 in 15, the estimate from the turn of the 21st century for attention-deficit/hyperactivity disorder (ADHD). It is now one in *nine*, representing about 6.4 million youth in the United States.[9] Because boys are more likely to have ADHD than girls, the overall rate is around 15% for males, between one in seven and one in six. Moreover, for boys of high school age, nearly one in *five* (19%) has received an ADHD diagnosis at some point in his life.

These percentages are national averages, but individual states vary greatly. As of 2007, in North Carolina close to 16% of all children aged 4–17 had received an ADHD diagnosis. For boys above age 9 in that state, the rate hovered around 30%, an almost unbelievable one in *four* to one in *three*. The South (and Midwest) remained at the top in rates of diagnosis in the 2011–2012 survey, but in the West (e.g., California and Nevada) rates of diagnosis remain far lower.[10]

As for medication use, over two-thirds of children and adolescents with a current diagnosis of ADHD now receive medication (66% in 2007 and 69% in 2011–2012), nearly always with the class of pills called stimulants. This rate represents a steep increase from several decades ago. Indeed, after a major dip in the late 1980s following a spate of negative press, rates of treatment with medication rose dramatically in children during the 1990s, continuing through today, with the most striking increases in recent prescriptions for adolescents and adults. Another perspective is that over 6% of *all* children and adolescents in the United States are receiving ADHD medications. Regional differences prevail in this regard, too: medication rates in the South are around 50% higher than in the Far West.[11]

Geography isn't the only factor that helps determine rates of diagnosis and treatment. Social class and race also matter. For many years, ADHD was diagnosed mainly in upper middle-class, suburban youth. Yet children at or below the poverty level are now *more* likely to receive diagnoses than those from families with higher incomes. In fact, in the 2011–2012 survey, the rate of ADHD diagnoses for Medicaid-eligible children aged 4 to 17 was 14%. Although African-American rates now rival or surpass those of Caucasian youth, until recently Hispanic youth have been only about half as likely as their non-ethnic counterparts to be diagnosed with ADHD and to receive medication. Yet this ethnic group has been showing major increases of late.[12]

In probing these striking trends, we focus on factors not often considered in clinical accounts of ADHD: state laws, health insurance policies, direct advertisements of ADHD medications to consumers, media portrayals, training of professionals, and high-stakes testing in schools. Although biology plays an undeniable role in the genesis of ADHD, cultural values and social policies—tied directly to schooling, achievement, and the labor market—comprise the contexts within which biological influences reveal themselves. Overall, we provide an integrative view, blending the micro level of individuals with a macro perspective on social policy, economics, and cultural forces.

## ADHD: A Top 10 List

In the pages that follow, we state unequivocally that the core symptoms linked to ADHD became apparent to societies when children were made to attend school and perform difficult tasks that human brains and minds never evolved to do, like learning to read. In other words, compulsory education was the trigger for revealing the children's different attentional and learning styles. If compulsory education was the initial culprit, the fast-escalating rates of diagnosis and treatment we now see are linked to intense pressures for achievement and performance in the context of an increasingly competitive world economy. Thus, ADHD reveals itself in cultures and nations that place a premium on performance. In short, biology matters, but the context of today's pressured world brings ADHD symptoms to the fore. Each chapter addresses core questions linked to this overarching theme.

*1. What is the historical trajectory of ADHD as a concept and as a diagnosis? What are the actual costs of ADHD to society?*

In Chapter 1 we present a historical timeline revealing, among other things, that tensions between biological and cultural aspects of ADHD have been present for some time. We also analyze the enormous direct and indirect costs related to this condition. Throughout, we highlight how ADHD is linked to a strong societal press for achievement and performance.

*2. How do genes, biology, parenting, schools, and culture come together in explaining ADHD? What does the current science tell us?*

Chapter 2 scrutinizes scientific evidence, addressing the ways in which genetic and other biological vulnerabilities interact with contextual forces—families, schools, and the cultural at large—to produce the phenomenon of ADHD. Many critics argue that ADHD is a label often applied to youth who simply don't conform to current expectations. For those who think that this controversy is overblown, we note that in the first part of the 19th century a psychiatric label existed for slaves who desired freedom: *draeptomania*. This diagnosis specified that any slave who hoped for release from his or her benevolent masters was, by definition, mentally ill.[13] It is essential, therefore, to ensure that diagnoses aren't simply Band-Aids covering over fundamental social problems. In the case of ADHD, our strong belief is that accurately diagnosed individuals have a real disorder.

*3. How is ADHD diagnosed? Which treatments really work?*

Chapter 3 addresses the professional standards for accurate evaluations and, crucially, how often they are followed. We also address myths and facts about medication treatment and non-medication alternatives, and report on the substantial gap between real and ideal treatment practices. Although comprehensive evaluations are possible, and although treatments for ADHD (especially combinations of medication and psychosocial treatments) can and do work, clinical practice often falls far short of what is needed.

*4. How should we understand the flood of ADHD medication use in the United States? What aspects of functioning does medication actually promote? In a society obsessed with achievement, can medications help everyone?*

Chapter 4 looks at how ADHD medications affect the brain and probes their value for promoting actual academic success, beyond simply suppressing difficult behavior. We also discuss the extent to which medication might help the general population. This chapter propels us into the world of neuroenhancement, a topic mired in controversy.

*5. Amidst the continuing surge of ADHD diagnoses and medication use, why are there such discrepancies in rates throughout the United States? What roles are played by demographics, public policy, health care coverage, and—especially—schools and educational policies?*

Chapter 5 addresses the surprisingly large state-by-state differences in rates of ADHD and medication treatment. As it turns out, it is just those states with high accountability for test-score performance that have the highest rates of ADHD. In short, schooling, educational policies, and performance pressures matter.

*6. What is the link between ADHD and the economy? Can ADHD medication contribute to economic productivity and reduce the indirect costs of ADHD across a lifetime?*

Beyond individual and family treatment choices, Chapter 6 addresses whether interventions for ADHD can make a difference for our nation's economic prosperity. In the context of this era of rising costs related to treating ADHD, we discuss the potential for effective treatments to promote higher productivity and boost human capital, as well as alleviate human suffering. As our country struggles in the global economy, the stakes are high.

*7. How is ADHD portrayed in the media? Why do we now see ads for ADHD medications in magazines and online, which essentially didn't exist in the 1990s? Can such direct-to-consumer (DTC) advertising reduce stigma, provide useful information, and encourage treatment options or lead to overdiagnosis by trivializing life problems?*

Chapter 7 addresses both media depictions of ADHD and related advertisements. We dissect influential (and misleading) opinion pieces in *The New York Times;* we also probe whether advertisements fuel the ever-increasing levels of medication treatment for ADHD.

*8. What are current global and international trends regarding ADHD? How do other nations recognize and treat this condition?*

In Chapter 8 we find that other nations, especially those countries with strong academic and vocational pressures, are showing major increases in rates of diagnosis and intervention. A global perspective also highlights the vast differences in treatment strategies for ADHD around the world.

*9. What about important subgroups: preschool-aged kids, adults, girls and women, and minorities? Are ADHD and its treatment still stigmatized, particularly within such groups but also more generally?*

Chapter 9 discusses ADHD in groups other than the stereotype of the condition as a white, middle-class, male phenomenon. We also explicitly address the negative ways in which ADHD is still viewed by society—and what might be done to alter such stereotyped and stigmatizing views.

*10. Where are we headed with respect to the ADHD explosion? Will present rates of diagnosis and treatment continue to grow? What do current debates tell us about our society and how we perceive those who struggle to achieve and lead productive lives?*

In our final chapter we make explicit predictions about whether ADHD diagnoses and medications will continue to rise in popularity or instead taper off (or even decline). We provide recommendations for sound policies that might reduce suffering and boost performance and productivity as well as increase life opportunities for those with ADHD.

At the beginning of most chapters, we present a case vignette of an individual or family grappling with ADHD. These stories are based on real children and families, composited to protect individual identity. Our hope is that the underlying reality of these depictions will lift our arguments from the world of science and policy to the lived experiences of children and adults who contend with this condition.

It might help to say what we do *not* intend to cover in these pages. This book is not a treatment manual, an encyclopedic guide to all aspects of attention and impulse-control problems, a text on mental health economics and policy, a sociological treatise on the evils of labels, or a work on the biochemistry of ADHD and the medications used to combat it. Other books, and the many articles published on ADHD every year, do a thorough job of tackling those important issues.[14] In addition, this is not a book that either denies the existence of ADHD or claims that ADHD is a simple biological entity, every symptom of which is cast in stone from an individual's genes. Instead, we aim to provide a needed synthesis. ADHD is multifaceted and complex, lying at the center of a tangled web of early predispositions, family interactions, school factors, neighborhood contexts, and entire cultures, as well as relevant policies and economic realities.

As for the qualifications we bring to this task, one of us (Richard Scheffler, a health economist) has longstanding interest and expertise in mental health economics, mental health policy, health care delivery, health disparities, and public policy. He has taught health economics and public policy for over four decades. The other (Stephen Hinshaw, a clinical psychologist) has considerable experience in biological and social mechanisms of mental health problems, in longitudinal studies and clinical trials, and in the stigma that still clings to mental illness. Because Hinshaw has come to know hundreds of families who have dealt with ADHD over the years, we attempt to bring clinical urgency to the text. Although our backgrounds and training are different, the skills, approaches, and mindsets we bring to bear are complementary. We have learned a considerable amount from each other during our years of collaboration, and we have educated ourselves by engaging national and global leaders in discussions, to keep ourselves current—and honest.

ADHD has become a sounding board for key controversies surrounding normality, achievement, medicalization, stigma, and markets for medical and psychiatric treatment. It brings to the fore contentious debates about (1) who we are as adults, entrusted with raising and educating the next generation; (2) who we are as biological and social beings; and (3) who we are as a species in a time of extreme pressure to learn and achieve amidst marked technological and economic advances. We aim to clear the air of some of the most polarizing and misleading information that abounds, providing guidelines for research, practice, and public policy concerning this fascinating and clinically important topic.

In the end, our species devised compulsory education only a few generations ago, unleashing the potential for both unprecedented gains in knowledge *and* major issues in attentional control and behavioral regulation. In this era of high accountability, increased pressure for enhanced academic and economic performance, and an ever-increasing resource gap between haves and have-nots, none of the answers will be simple.

*The ADHD Explosion*

# The TNT Fueling the Explosion: Origins and Costs of ADHD

## Jose: "Immaturity that Might Last a Lifetime"

*Jose, now 5 years old, started crawling and walking early. He quickly graduated to running and has yet to slow down. Always wanting to be near the action, he has ended up causing much of the action: pulling down curtains, climbing on shelves, racing outside if the front door isn't double-locked, and opening car doors from the inside while a parent is driving. He stopped napping before he was 2, and since then he has rarely slept more than 7 hours a night.*

*Even at age 3, Jose had a limited vocabulary and his rapid speech was hard to understand. Because he was an only child, his parents (a construction assistant and a nurse) couldn't be certain whether his behavior was unusual. But then he was asked to leave his first two preschools—one for hitting peers who teased him, and the other for talking back to teachers. Each time, he cried and seemed genuinely sorry. Did he just not understand? Was he intentionally defiant?*

*He has been to the emergency room three times for falling from high places or burning himself on the stove. After one hospital stay, a county social worker visited the family, suspecting neglect, but she changed her mind after observing how hard they were trying.*

*His dad vacillates between letting him off the hook or becoming too strict. Increasingly depressed, his mom is on the verge of giving up. At times, the large extended Latino family (who initially called him "all boy" but now shows increasing concern) was able to help out. But relatives have become reluctant to provide child care because of his explosive temper when anyone tries to set a limit.*

*Nearly breaking the family's bank account, his parents enrolled Jose in a private preschool last fall. His vocabulary has improved, and he has started to read single words. But he can't follow rules, sitting for only 3 minutes at circle time before disrupting the class.*

*The principal approached the family about ADHD. They initially refused to discuss it, believing that kids with ADHD were "loco" and that medicines were for kids about to go to institutions. Reluctantly, the parents began attending a class with a group of other families, where they learned to implement a reward-and-consequence program, including a timeout corner. The psychologist consulted with the kindergarten teacher, extending the reward program to school. Jose is showing signs of progress, and his parents have hope that it will continue.*

*He still goes through his day non-stop. The pediatrician has told the family that adding medication may help. Although undecided about giving him pills, for the first time the family has a sense that they can manage their son's behavior. Representing the growing numbers of Hispanic children in the United States with ADHD, over half a million and growing rapidly, Jose's history reveals how troubling and troublesome ADHD can be from the earliest years of development.[1]*

Jose's story points out several crucial developments in the recent history of ADHD, including the surprisingly rapid increase in early detection of the condition, prior to the start of grade school. This increase may be a good thing if you believe that early diagnosis can lead to appropriate treatment before failure becomes entrenched, or a decidedly bad thing if you think that ADHD is a modern-day excuse for poor schools or insensitive parenting. The case also highlights the spread of the diagnosis to subgroups, such as those of Hispanic heritage, who previously were almost never involved with ADHD. It vividly reveals the enormous costs, both financial and emotional, to families grappling with the associated behaviors and impairments. Finally, Jose's story illustrates major controversies linked to this disorder: is it biological or social in nature? Should medications be used, especially for young children? Can and should school personnel bring up ADHD with families? We will explore these and other controversies throughout the book.

Two decades ago, ADHD achieved a significant cultural milestone when Matt Groening, creator of *The Simpsons*, listed it among his official "terms to avoid for 1994." It was a clear indication of the cultural oversaturation attained by the label.[2]

The modern era of this diagnosis began in 1980 with the term *attention deficit disorder (ADD)*, which replaced the earlier labels of minimal brain dysfunction, hyperactivity, and hyperkinetic reaction. By 1987, the official term had become *attention-deficit/hyperactivity disorder (ADHD)*.[3] Within a year, the antipsychiatry movement had mounted a vigorous campaign against nearly all mental disorders. Scientologists were instrumental in prompting a Congressional hearing on the use of Prozac as an antidepressant. Simultaneously, as part of their ceaseless crusade to discount psychiatric diagnoses in general and medications in particular, the Citizens Commission on Human Rights, a radical antipsychiatry group funded by Scientology, picketed major scientific meetings related to ADHD. A spate of negative media attention followed, and sales of ADHD medications plummeted by 30% or more within a short time.[4]

It didn't take long, however, for a combination of social forces and policy decisions, along with intensified scientific research, to bring ADHD back into ascendancy. Groening's disparaging remark was an accurate reading of the popularity of the diagnosis by the mid-1990s. The wave still hasn't crested.

We begin this book with the view that an appreciation of historical highlights might facilitate better treatments and more equitable policies related to ADHD. Indeed, understanding relevant historical background may prevent past mistakes from recurring. We then address the costs of ADHD, in particular the long-term economic consequences related to negative educational, vocational, and legal outcomes. As shown by the case of Jose, even before age 6 children with high levels of ADHD symptoms are likely to be eliminated from school programs (i.e., preschools and kindergarten), have high rates of accidental injuries, and cause considerable family stress and strife. Related expenses are often substantial: finding another pre-school (even after the deposit has been paid on the first one), dealing with emergency room costs (unless the health insurance is really good), or getting counseling for the parents to deal with the stresses of handling their errant child (and often wondering whether insensitive parenting caused the behavior in the first place).

## From Then to Now

The timeline of Table 1–1 lists a number of milestones in the history of ADHD. To be sure, the table is incomplete. A thorough timeline would need multiple entries for each year (and across recent history, for each month), turning quickly into an encyclopedia.

Across its entries, the take-home messages from the timeline are as follows.

(1) Although the term *ADHD* is relatively new, clinical descriptions of inattention and hyperactivity have been around since the end of the Enlightenment, which emphasized reason and obtaining knowledge. With the advent of compulsory education, children's behavior patterns came under increasing scrutiny, which strongly suggests that ADHD is tied to the pressure for academic performance.

(2) Official diagnoses of ADHD were relatively slow to develop. In 1952, the first edition of the American Psychiatric Association's *Diagnostic and Statistical Manual of Mental Disorders (DSM)* almost ignored all childhood disorders.[5] However, around this time "immaturity" became a term used in psychological studies to refer to problems in attention and impulse control.[6] This view was prescient, as brain imaging research has given new life to the contention that youth with ADHD actually lag in development of the prefrontal cortex (see Chapter 2).

(3) Medications for hyperactive and impulsive behaviors have been around longer than antipsychotic, antidepressant, or mood-stabilizing medicines. In fact, in the late 1930s, Charles

TABLE 1–1  Brief ADHD Timeline

* 1798. Sir Alexander Crichton, in Great Britain, writes of children with either inborn or disease-induced problems with sustained attention.[7]
* Mid-to-late 1800s. Compulsory education laws take effect in the United States. For the first time, all children are expected to be indoors, sit still, and pay attention to teachers, a policy that has the eventual effect of making attention problems as well as learning disabilities salient to all of society.[8]
* 1902. Sir George Still reports to the Royal Academy of Physicians in London on a syndrome of "volitional inhibition" leading to "defects in moral control," marked by a strongly familial pattern and presenting itself largely in boys.[9]
* 1917–1919. The world influenza/encephalitis epidemic leaves more than 60 million dead. Many survivors acquire symptoms of inattention, disorganization, impulsivity, and hyperactivity, leading to initial hypotheses of a postencephalitic brain damage syndrome.
* 1937. Charles Bradley, in Rhode Island, publishes initial accounts of the positive effects of the stimulant medicine benzedrine on motivation, learning, and behavior in children.[10]
* 1947. An influential publication appears on the "brain injured child syndrome," a term softened to minimal brain damage and subsequently to minimal brain dysfunction (MBD). A great many symptoms are attributed to MBD (99 in all), comprising nearly the entire domain of behavioral and emotional problems of childhood.[11]
* 1957. The condition called "hyperkinetic impulse disorder" is introduced as a far more specific syndrome than MBD.[12]
* 1960–1961. Ritalin, the trade name for methylphenidate since 1948 (and initially licensed in 1955), is approved for prescription by the U.S. Food and Drug Administration (FDA). It begins to be marketed heavily for youth with MBD or hyperkinetic impulse disorder (increasingly called "hyperactivity").
* 1968. The *Diagnostic and Statistical Manual of Mental Disorders* (*DSM-II*) offers a new diagnostic category, Hyperkinetic Reaction of Childhood.[13] The term denotes that the behaviors are a reaction to stress or conflict, in keeping with the predominant views favoring psychosocial causation.

(continued)

TABLE 1-1 (Continued)

* 1970. The *Washington Post* reports that between 5 and 10% of grade-school children in Omaha, Nebraska, are treated with Ritalin, fueling outrage and a federal inquiry.[14]
* 1971. Because of rampant overprescription and diversion (i.e., nonmedical use) of stimulants as diet pills and pep pills, the International Narcotics Control Board is founded, which monitors worldwide production of addictive substances.[15]
* 1975. The Education for All Handicapped Children Act (PL 94-142) becomes federal law. Schools must provide free and appropriate education for all disabled youth and must find means of accommodating children who have disabilities that impede learning and achievement. Yet because of its nature as an underfunded mandate—meaning that federal funds only partially support the stipulations—tensions soar between needed accommodations and school districts' abilities to fund them.[16]
* 1980. *DSM-III* introduces the category of Attention Deficit Disorder (ADD) as a replacement for Hyperkinetic Reaction of Childhood. ADD is proposed to come in two forms or subtypes: With or Without Hyperactivity.[17] Research escalates, and public awareness surges.
* 1987. *DSM-III-R* changes the category ADD to Attention-Deficit/ Hyperactivity Disorder (ADHD), eliminating the subtypes (i.e., With or Without Hyperactivity). CHADD (Children and Adults with Attention Deficit Disorder)—a national advocacy group for ADHD—is founded.[18]
* 1988. The Church of Scientology pickets major professional meetings regarding the overdiagnosis and overmedication of children with ADHD. Popular talk shows decry the use of ADHD medications. The negative media attention leads to a plummeting of medication rates, as much as 30% within 2 years.[19]
* 1990–1991. Congress reauthorizes the federal special education law as the Individuals with Disabilities Education Act (IDEA; PL 99-357). After strong resistance from key advocacy groups (including the National Association for the Advancement of Colored People), public opinion turns. The U.S. Department of Education subsequently issues a Policy Clarification Memorandum directing schools to include ADHD as one of several "other health impaired conditions" covered by IDEA. Also, a U.S. Supreme Court ruling dictates that Supplemental Security Income (SSI) payments must include, among covered low-income individuals, those with ADHD, with impairment criteria loosened.[20]

TABLE 1-1 (Continued)

* 1992–1993. Congress expands Medicaid coverage to include a far greater number of children, allowing public reimbursement for treatment of ADHD. Medicaid funding for psychotropic medications goes up 10-fold across the decade.
* 1994. *DSM-IV* is published, retaining the diagnostic category of ADHD but adding three subtypes: Predominantly Inattentive, Predominantly Hyperactive-Impulsive, and Combined.[21]
* 1995. The United Nations International Narcotics Control Board explicitly criticizes CHADD for accepting portions of its operating budget from medication manufacturers, calling into question the impartiality of this national advocacy group.
* 1997. The FDA Modernization Act becomes law, providing incentives for the pharmaceutical industry to develop and test drugs for children by extending patent exclusivity. Randomized controlled trials of stimulant medication expand. The American Academy of Child and Adolescent Psychiatry releases Practice Parameters related to ADHD, calling for thorough assessments, well-monitored medications, and the use of non-medication treatments. Also, the FDA issues new and relaxed guidelines related to direct-to-consumer (DTC) advertisements for medications.[22]
* Late 1990s. Across the decade, there is an at least three-fold rise in stimulant prescriptions in the United States, primarily to treat children with ADHD. Structural and functional brain imaging studies document specific neural abnormalities in individuals with ADHD.[23]
* 1999. The Multimodal Treatment Study of Children with ADHD (MTA Study), the largest clinical trial for children with behavioral or emotional disorders ever performed, supported by the National Institute of Mental Health and the Department of Education, publishes its initial results. The key finding is that well-monitored, three-dose-daily stimulant medication is optimal for reducing ADHD symptoms. Importantly, additional reports reveal the superiority of combined medication plus behavioral intervention for addressing comorbidities and building academic, social, and family skills.[24]
* 2000. Concerta—an evidence-based, long-acting formulation of Ritalin developed to mimic the three-dose-daily regimen of the MTA—is approved by FDA. It and other long-acting formulations (e.g., Adderall XR) soon gain a large market share. Several years later, atomoxetine (Strattera), a non-stimulant, gains FDA approval for use with ADHD.

*(continued)*

TABLE 1-1 (Continued)

* 2001. Utah, Minnesota, and Connecticut enact laws that prohibit school personnel from (a) recommending that a child take a psychotropic drug for a mental disorder, (b) requiring that such medication be taken as a prerequisite for enrollment, or (c) stipulating that a family's refusal to give such medication be considered child neglect. Since that time, 13 additional states have enacted similar laws. Also in 2001, the American Academy of Pediatrics releases Clinical Practice Guidelines for the assessment and treatment of ADHD.[25]

* 1993–2003. During this 10-year period the use of ADHD medications expands (diffuses) to 55 nations, with worldwide medication use tripling and worldwide expenditures increasing nine-fold.[26] ADHD and medication treatment become a truly global phenomenon.

* 2004. FDA issues "black box" warnings regarding selective serotonin reuptake inhibitor (SSRI) antidepressants in children and adolescents, related to the potential for increasing suicidal ideation. Concern over psychotropic medication of youth in general rises. As a result, rates of SSRI prescriptions for youth decline.[27]

* 2005–2006. Health Canada suspends sales of Adderall following 12 sudden deaths of U.S. youth receiving the medication but soon rescinds the ban. In the United States, the FDA initially votes to provide warnings on package inserts for stimulants related to cardiovascular risk but ultimately rejects a "black box" warning.[28]

* 2007. Prescriptions for adolescent and adult ADHD are growing at a faster rate than for children with ADHD. The American Academy of Child and Adolescent Psychiatry releases new Practice Parameters for the assessment and treatment of ADHD.[29]

* 2008. Experts recommend that it may be advisable to include an electrocardiogram as part of the initial evaluation for individuals considering treatment with ADHD medications. After considerable debate, this recommendation is not enforced. Additional stimulant and non-formulations of ADHD medications proliferate; these patented medications are much more costly than generic short-acting stimulants.[30]

TABLE 1-1  (Continued)

* 2009. Volkow and colleagues publish a landmark research article documenting clear neural differences—at the level of dopamine neurotransmitter receptors and transporters—in brains of never-medicated adults with ADHD. Along with attention and inhibitory control, low intrinsic motivation is revived as a core mechanism underlying ADHD. Around this time, discussion of neuroenhancement and reports of widespread diversion of ADHD medications for college student academic "boosts" become prevalent.[31]

* 2010. The National Survey of Children's Health reveals that, as of 2007, 9.5% of American youth aged 4–17 have received a diagnosis of ADHD, with two-thirds of the currently diagnosed group receiving medication. The youngest kindergarteners in the United States, aged late 4 or early 5, are found to be 60% more likely to receive an ADHD diagnosis than older kindergarteners.[32]

* 2011–2012. The FDA decides not to include more specific warnings about ADHD's potential for heart-related problems on prescription labels, given recent research findings. Discussions of neuroenhancement intensify, as rates of college and even high school stimulant use continue to rise. Shortages of ADHD medications are reported in many drugstores around the United States, as the supply falls short of ever-increasing demand. The American Academy of Pediatrics releases new Practice Guidelines for ADHD, emphasizing the importance of assessment and treatment as early as age 4. Throughout 2012, *The New York Times* publishes opinion pieces that severely criticize the use of stimulants for individuals with ADHD.[33]

* 2013. Fatal consequences of ADHD medication in a young adult, following lax diagnosis, become front-page news. The data from the 2011 National Survey of Children's Health (NSCH) are released, revealing an unprecedented rate of being "ever diagnosed with ADHD" for 4- to 17-year-olds (11%). *DSM-5* is published, keeping the same symptoms as those in *DSM-IV* but relaxing the requirement for the age of onset, from under 7 years of age to under 12 years, as well as the requirement for adult diagnosis from at least six to at least five symptoms per domain.[34]

Bradley documented the benefits of Benzedrine—an amphet-amine used as a bronchodilator for lung conditions—for youth with learning and behavioral problems.[35] But without a definitive name for the condition, the medicine didn't catch on for two more decades.

(4) After methylphenidate (trade name Ritalin) was approved for prescription in 1961, there was widespread drug use and abuse in the general culture during the ensuing decade. In fact, numerous accounts of overuse of stimulants appeared. In the early 1970s the International Narcotics Control Board was established, to monitor worldwide supplies of addictive medications.[36] Overall, it is hard to think of a more explosive issue in the realm of children's health than that raised by the prospect of medicating (or "drugging") immature brains for the purposes of behavior control.

(5) Once ADD (1980) and then ADHD (1987) became official diagnoses, the diagnostic criteria for ADHD continued to become more lenient over time, serving as one reason for increasing rates of diagnosis.[37]

(6) Educational and medical policies have also fueled the recent rise in ADHD diagnoses. Table 1–1 portrays the sudden changes in federal special education statutes, Medicaid regula-tions, and Supplemental Security Income (SSI) requirements in the early 1990s. For example, during that time period the percentage of youth in the United States eligible for Medicaid rose from under one-fifth to nearly one-third. Increased rates of ADHD soon followed suit.[38]

(7) The large-scale Multimodal Treatment Study of Children with ADHD (MTA) study revealed major success for well-monitored medication in reducing ADHD symptoms. Still, the combination of medication and home and school behavior therapy proved superior in terms of academic, social, and parenting skills as well as reducing associated problem behaviors.[39] Thus, the old maxim that pills alone do not yield skills is apt with respect to ADHD.

(8) Viable ADHD medications with effects spanning an entire school day hit the market in 2000. These new, patented pills were far more expensive than the generic, shorter-acting vari-ants; their widespread use has driven up costs at a far higher

rate (nine-fold) than sales (three-fold) during the past decade. At the same time, medication rates for adolescents and adults grew faster than those for children during the past decade. Moreover, the market for ADHD medication is expanding rapidly around the world.[40]

(9) As ADHD diagnoses and medication rates have continued to climb over the past years, diversion of stimulants from their prescribed indications—including use in college dorms as performance enhancers—has risen precipitously.[41]

(10) Like most psychiatric conditions, ADHD emanates from important genetic vulnerabilities and other biological forces (see Chapter 2). It's a far different world from half a century ago, when environmental and cultural theories were in ascendancy. But the undeniable role of biology cannot blind us to the fact that genetic tendencies unfold through interactions with a host of micro (families; schools) and macro (policy; health care) processes. Viewing ADHD as entirely biological is as misleading as it is to claim that ADHD is simply a social construction or the result of overly lax parenting.

## Money: The Costs of ADHD

Health economists use several ways of calculating expenditures for a given condition. These include immediate treatment costs as well as longer, "indirect" costs related to the condition's consequences, such as failing to recognize it and treat it. As the lens expands from individual and family expenses to the long-term societal costs, the economic impact of ADHD becomes staggering.

We start at the level of a given family, with the overall cost of childrearing for a youth without mental health, behavioral, or learning issues. *CNN Money* reported that in 2010, for a two-parent, middle-income family in the United States, the cost of raising a child from birth to age 18 was $226,920, representing a 40% increase from 2000.[42] Over the same time period, however, the median household income declined more than 7%, revealing just how financially difficult childrearing has become for increasing numbers of families. Of course, this figure is an average: families in different regions of the country, those at different income levels, or those with children in public and not private schools might well diverge from this overall figure. Still, the costs of raising children are going up substantially.

In terms of ADHD-related costs to providers and insurers, a 2006 study at Kaiser Permanente, the largest health maintenance organization (HMO) in Northern California, revealed an intriguing pattern. The "excess" costs related to a child with ADHD—over and above expenditures for a typically developing child—were almost $500 in the 12-month period 2 years *before* the diagnosis and nearly $700 in the year immediately preceding the diagnosis. (In current dollars, those published amounts would be 50% higher.) In other words, high health care costs predated formal diagnosis, probably related to accidents, frequent medical checkups, and higher use of ancillary services. But in the 2 years *after* diagnosis, excess costs grew even higher, at levels of over $1000 annually. These costs indicate larger-than-usual rates of pediatric and psychiatric services, including medication. By 2013, generalizing to the entire United States, they totaled over $20 billion.[43]

Our team analyzed numbers from a national database to see whether these kinds of excess costs were related specifically to ADHD or to the many other problems and disorders that often get linked to ADHD (known as "comorbid" conditions, including physical illnesses, high levels of aggressive behavior, other emotional disorders, and—by adolescence—substance abuse). Even when such comorbidities are factored out, along with any racial and income-related differences between ADHD and non-ADHD youth, the specific excess costs remained. In other words, it is the ADHD rather than any associated conditions or demographic factors that drives the treatment-related expenditures. Similar to the Kaiser data, we found that excess health care costs totaled about $1000 per year for youth with ADHD and over $2000 per year for adults with ADHD.[44]

Regarding school-related costs, adolescents with ADHD are much more likely to drop out of high school than their peers, to be retained at least once, or to receive suspensions or expulsions while still in school.[45] Since 1991, youth with ADHD have been eligible to receive accommodations under the Individuals with Disabilities Educational Act (IDEA), with complex formulas from federal, state, and local districts related to the financing of such additional services. The overall educational cost impact for a given youth with ADHD, between childhood and adolescence, was estimated to be $5000 per year, involving expenses linked to special education placements, grade retention, disciplinary incidents, and formal testing and evaluation. The comparable figure for youth without ADHD was just over $300 per year. This cost increment, multiplied by the number of youth with ADHD in the United States, equals $30 billion or higher annually.[46]

Cutting across multiple types of expenses, a conservative estimate of the yearly costs for a child with ADHD was, back in 2005, nearly $15,000. A small proportion of this amount was linked to health care costs, a third to educational expenses, and nearly half to crime and delinquency-related outcomes in adolescence. Extrapolating from this figure, assuming that 11% of all children and adolescents have received a diagnosis, and adjusting to 2013 dollars, the annual total is now over $100 billion per year, a truly mammoth cost level. Most of this amount relates to long-term indirect expenses, rather than the costs of immediate treatment. Because ADHD is linked with the development of both depression and substance abuse by adolescence, which were not factored into the equation, the actual long-term and indirect costs linked to ADHD may be far higher.[47]

Once we proceed to adulthood, it's noteworthy that a history of childhood ADHD predicts (1) a 10–14% reduction in the likelihood of being employed; (2) an average earnings reduction of 33%, and (3) a 15% increase in the chances of receiving some form of social assistance. Workplace problems are clearly legion.[48] Averaging across all relevant studies from the past 20 years, the figures are mind-boggling: long-term economic consequences of adult ADHD approach $200 billion annually. Most of this amount can be attributed to lack of full-time employment, absenteeism (people with ADHD tend to miss a lot of work), substandard performance while on the job, disability payments, and worker's compensation payments (like children with ADHD, adults have more accidents than the norm). Yet even this enormous figure is probably low, as it does not take into account the costs of traffic accidents or substance abuse.[49]

In addition, there is a huge but immeasurable *psychological* toll on individuals and families, who must contend with blame and consequent shame related to their own or their children's seemingly inexplicable failures. Although this burden does not carry a dollar figure, it can be crushing.[50] Once one considers the tremendous ADHD-related indirect costs to individuals, families, and taxpayers in general, the condition changes from being an overused, hyped, trendy label—a "term to avoid in 1994"—to a deadly serious problem with major-league economic consequences.

We turn to the science of ADHD in Chapter 2. Here, we find that the "immaturity" linked to ADHD is present even at the level of basic brain development. We also find that the mounting problems associated with this diagnosis are likely to last well beyond childhood.

# The Nature and Causes of ADHD: Where Biology Meets Culture

## Becky: "Lost Opportunities"

*Becky was an exuberant toddler with boundless energy. Always a handful, by first and second grade she still couldn't settle down. Although her IQ was above average, she paid little attention to directions from adults. Except for a caring teacher in second grade who gave Becky structure and got the best out of her, the rest of her teachers described her as messy, disorganized, and constantly interrupting others. Still, none of them ever thought that girls could have ADHD the way boys did.*

*Her classmates teased her for being "weird" and "crazy." On one memorable occasion at a classmate's ninth birthday party, she opened the presents intended for the birthday girl, ripping open the paper and ribbons as the other girls looked on, aghast. Soon, invitations stopped arriving.*

*Her older brother and younger sister cowered in her presence, because she would suddenly lash out if she thought they were getting favors. Each school year her parents—a salesman and day-care teacher—held on for dear life, trying to avert nightly tears and arguments over homework and household rules. She could be so sweet when she was in charge, but if things didn't go exactly her way, look out.*

*The hardest blows began in middle school. She found it impossible to follow the instructions of multiple teachers each day or to keep up with the increasingly difficult homework load, losing papers and then arguing that she'd actually done the work, though her parents suspected she hadn't. A seventh-grade evaluation revealed that her "executive functions" were well behind grade level, based on a large battery of tests her parents never quite understood. What they did comprehend was that she did not plan well, recognize mistakes, or correct herself. On a given report card, she received A's through D's and F's. A school psychologist raised the issue of possible ADHD. Yet Becky's pediatrician was more concerned with her fluctuating weight and occasionally "sneaky" behavior, including small thefts.*

*By high school, Becky had essentially given up. She gravitated toward a fast crowd, the only group that accepted her. As they took up smoking, alcohol, and drugs, she joined in. Becky's parents sadly watched the transformation of their enthusiastic, if erratic, little girl into an antisocial and depressed teenager. Increasingly alienated from her, they didn't know how to reach out to her or set realistic limits.*

*At 16 she wrecked two cars, one belonging to her family and the other to a friend. Her parents suspected that she was being treated at a community clinic for sexually transmitted diseases. She began carving her wrists and forearms with a knife, trying to cover the marks with long sleeves. She dropped out of school in 11th grade.*

*Now 19, Becky has few skills and is on a perpetual "drift." She tells her few friends that she's not sure life is worth living. How did Becky get to this point in life, with so few options?*

*Representative of the more than two million girls with ADHD in the United States, Becky and her story illustrate a tragic but all-too-common phenomenon: that of a child and then adolescent who has never received adequate evaluation or treatment.*

Our journey into the science of ADHD takes us from the micro-world of genes and brain chemicals, through variations in attention spans and behavioral patterns, and on into families and schools as well as social policies and cultural values. The journey also stretches across the lifespan, from the earliest years into adulthood. Think of, over time, Becky's increasing depression, pervasive sense of hopelessness, school failure, and lack of job skills, gradually resulting in a vicious cycle of despair.

Once one gets to know and work with youth like Jose and Becky, it becomes impossible to believe that ADHD is a made-up phenomenon, a label for children who are simply nonconforming, bothersome, or off-beat. In the toughest cases, the troublesome behavior patterns emerge early and persist for decades. There is no good evidence that ADHD results from lax or overly harsh parenting, even though the parenting styles that often emerge *in response to* the child's problematic behaviors do shape outcome. On the contrary, there is simply too much evidence that ADHD has an underlying biological reality to succumb to the thinking that it is solely a social and cultural phenomenon.

At the same time, stating that aberrant brain functioning is the only force behind ADHD ignores the social and cultural contexts in which this condition develops and persists. As noted in Chapter 1, ADHD emerged in the context of mandatory schooling, and rates have soared in recent decades with our ever-increasing push for performance. The challenge is to appreciate how brains and minds, intersecting with families, schools, and values related to education and productivity, collide to produce ADHD.

Given the huge volume of research flooding scientific journals as well as the popular press, our effort to present key findings in a brief chapter is like condensing the contents of a metropolitan telephone book down to an index card. Far too many details will get lost in the process. Even so, we aim for our index card to be topical, current, and accurate.

## A Continuum, Not a Category?

Just like inches of height, points of blood pressure, or the cardinal features of depression, the constituent behaviors related to ADHD exist on a continuum. Think of your family members, your kids and their friends, or your colleagues at work: some are incredibly focused and self-regulated, whereas others are so disorganized, distracted, and captured by any stray stimulus that they can hardly make it through the day. Importantly, there is no magic place on this bell curve where the normal range stops and the atypical part of the spectrum begins. This is clearly the case for blood pressure, too. In fact, a decade ago rates of hypertension "rose" dramatically in the United States simply because the official cutoff was lowered to encourage early treatment.[1]

Where to draw the line regarding a formal diagnosis of ADHD is based partly on convention, partly on research revealing how much various numbers of symptoms predict life impairment, and partly on political considerations. As with autism, clinicians once thought that a person either "had" or "didn't have" this condition, but it is now well known that autistic symptoms (just like those of ADHD) are arrayed on a continuum. This "spectrum" notion raises the provocative idea that a large number of people without diagnosable ADHD may benefit from ADHD-linked treatments, like medication. This contention is the source of major controversy in light of the major diversion of stimulants to those without a diagnosis (see Chapter 4).[2] It also means that many people have "a bit" of ADHD (or, for that matter, of depression or autism), a truth that, when it becomes better known, could have implications for reducing stigma.

Crucially, for ADHD—as well as for all other mental disorders—the underlying problems are not hard-and-fast values from a sphygmomanometer (blood-pressure cuff), measuring the pressure of blood on arterial walls. Nor are they objective readings from blood tests or pictures from brain scans. Instead, they comprise reports of problems at home, school, or the workplace made by a parent, teacher, coworker, or oneself (see Chapter 3). Because there is still no objective biological measure that can unequivocally rule in or out any psychiatric diagnosis, behavioral and emotional disorders are viewed with great suspicion. In fact, branding patterns of behavior as disordered will always have a cultural, value-laden component. How one acts in the world is inherently different from the functioning of the lungs, pancreas, or heart.[3]

Overall, drawing the line between normality and pathology is a contentious issue for medical *and* mental health–related problems. Yet the controversy is far greater in mental health, given the lack of objective "lab" markers, the common belief that people's actions are under volitional control, the high rates of stigma that still exist, and, in the case of ADHD, important issues concerning whether medications should be used to regulate problems in attention, focus, and impulse control.

## Symptoms, Problems, and Impairments: What *Is* ADHD?

The behaviors underlying ADHD constitute two partially distinct clusters of problems: (a) inattention/disorganization and (b) hyperactivity/impulsivity. Some clinicians and scientists contend that other features—such as emotional lability and explosiveness, or poor social skills—should be part of the official criteria, but for now the consensus is that such impairments are important but secondary.[4]

The official list from the 5th (and most recent) edition of the *Diagnostic and Statistical Manual of Mental Disorders* includes nine symptoms of inattention (e.g., "often fails to give close attention to details or makes careless mistakes in schoolwork, at work, or other activities; often has difficulty organizing tasks and activities; is often easily distracted by extraneous stimuli") and nine of hyperactivity/impulsivity (e.g., "is often 'on the go,' acting as if 'driven by a motor'; often interrupts or intrudes on others; often talks excessively; often runs about or climbs excessively in situations in which it is inappropriate [NOTE: in adolescents or adults, may be limited to feeling restless]").[5] One thing that pops out from a glance at these behaviors is that a lot of them indicate the behavior patterns of a very young child. In fact, if you have ever cared for a toddler or preschooler—particularly a boy—you will have experienced many of these issues at annoyingly frequent rates. Why would the diagnosis of a psychiatric condition be based on the symptoms of acting too young: isn't this a clear instance of pathologizing normal-range behaviors? Don't all children have at least a bit of ADHD?

There's a great deal of evidence, however, that when ADHD-style behaviors persist beyond toddlerhood, at levels that are extreme given the person's age, they reflect genetically transmitted vulnerability, they signal problems in brain development, and they are linked to major life problems. As a different example, think of the symptoms of depression (e.g., sad mood, poor concentration, loss of interest in daily activities, impaired sleep and appetite). These are clearly part of normal reactions to loss or grief. Yet when they persist for long periods of time, they predict demoralization, the fragmenting of relationships, physical health problems, and high risk for suicide, with a genetic vulnerability for the most severe cases.

Another essential point is that ADHD symptoms ebb and flow across days, weeks, and months, showing changes when schoolwork gets harder or easier, when tasks are routine or novel, and when an individual is stressed or relaxed. If people with legitimate ADHD are engaged in self-directed, highly rewarding activities—such as video games, which provide clear and immediate reinforcement directly linked to recent performance—it is often hard to see any attention deficit at all. Such individuals may actually become hyperfocused at these times. But don't be fooled: kids and adults with ADHD actually do not perform as well as their peers when playing such games. Moreover, in situations where someone else is in charge of the task, the activities are rote, or the work is challenging and requires restraint and self-control, things get really bad in a hurry. In other words, ADHD rears its head most when others are calling the shots and when sustained effort is required.[6]

Today's classrooms may not be as factory-like as those of a hundred years ago, but students must still defer to the teacher and group–based teaching methods in most schools. Stringent classroom demands and the press for achievement and performance throw a harsh light on individuals with underlying problems in attention and self-regulation. Indeed, serious attention problems are a major reason for failure to graduate from high school.[7] Home settings may well reveal ADHD-related behaviors, too, especially when sustained effort is at a premium—for example, doing chores or performing homework.

To qualify for a diagnosis, those children and adolescents with at least six of the nine listed inattentive symptoms (but fewer than six hyperactive/impulsive symptoms) are placed into the Inattentive subcategory, similar to the label of ADD Without Hyperactivity three decades ago. Those with the reverse pattern are placed into the Hyperactive/Impulsive group. This subgroup is rare except in preschoolers, who have not yet had a chance to display inattention in school settings. In the real world, most school-aged youth who get referred for help score high (at least six symptoms) on both dimensions, leading to diagnosis of the Combined presentation.[8]

Compared to girls, boys are nearly three times more likely to experience high rates of the behaviors linked to ADHD.[9] Yet this isn't the case just for ADHD: boys have higher rates of just about every developmental condition that appears during the early years of life, such as autism, Tourette's disorder, serious aggression, and some learning disorders. When girls have ADHD, they are more likely than boys to display its purely inattentive form, even though rambunctious, highly impulsive girls can and do exist. Crucially, when girls meet criteria for a diagnosis, they show continuing problems later in life that, if anything, are comparable to or even worse than those of boys (see Chapter 9).[10] Recall Becky, whose behavioral and emotional issues escalated and morphed over time, emerging into the devastating problems of self-injury and suicidal despair.

Finally, many of the *DSM-5* descriptions include qualifications to make the symptoms relevant for adults (e.g., mental rather than physical restlessness). Moreover, only five (rather than six) of the symptoms in either domain are required for adult diagnosis, because the symptoms tend to fade with time.

## ADHD Across the Years

### *Infancy and Toddlerhood*

In the child's first few months of life, patterns of *temperament* become apparent. These styles of behavior and emotion are undoubtedly biologically driven. Such temperamental traits include activity level, emotional intensity, the ability to be soothed, and the regularity (versus irregularity) of patterns of alertness and rest.[11] At the end of the first year of life, another temperamental dimension comes online: the potential for focusing attention on events in the environment and shifting focus when needed. By 2 to 3 years of age, this feature, called "effortful control," predicts long-term abilities to regulate behavior and emotions.[12] ADHD is thus not a simple condition of being overly active; it involves complex patterns of focus, sustaining effort, impulse control, and self-regulation.

## Preschool

It is virtually impossible to separate ADHD from the high end of the normal range at ages 2 and 3. But by age 4, extremely careful assessments can begin to discern those children in the clinical range of ADHD-related behaviors (see Chapter 9). When preschoolers are accurately diagnosed and followed for many years, the two strongest predictors of whether they continue to show diagnosable ADHD are (1) the severity of the early behavior patterns (not surprisingly, as the most extreme temperaments tend to persist), and (2) the negativity of the parent–child interchange during the preschool years.[13] This latter finding is crucial to dissect. The parent's negative, hostile, sarcastic patterns of interaction did not, in all likelihood, cause such behaviors in infancy (rather, the child's difficult temperament may have elicited such negative parenting). Yet parental responses to difficult behavior patterns may well promote a continuation of such patterns. In other words, genes and biology play a huge role in predicting temperament and early indicators of ADHD, but parental reactions to such behavior patterns are pivotal in forging their continuation and escalation. Calm, responsive, and firm parenting will yield better child outcomes than fighting fire with fire. The bottom line is that biology and context propel each other in a continuing cycle.[14]

## Childhood and Adolescence

The typical time for referral of children suspected of having ADHD is during the elementary grades, once formal schooling has begun and patterns of academic problems and misbehavior become entrenched. Another peak time is middle school, when the preadolescent is now expected to navigate multiple teachers per day and display greatly increased independence. Many youth with the inattentive form of ADHD do not get referred until such demands emerge in sixth grade and after.

For most of the 20th century it was believed that children essentially grew out of hyperactivity or hyperkinesis by puberty. Although it is true that the 8-year-old jumping on tables in the classroom may well become the 18-year-old who can sit still for relatively long periods, underlying problems in mental restlessness, impulse control, and self-regulation are highly likely to persist. ADHD in adolescence incurs major risk for delayed independence, problems in navigating the demands of a high school curriculum, substance abuse, accidents, and problems with the law. Even though it may change form, ADHD doesn't often vanish during the teen years.[15]

## Adulthood

The best estimates are that around half of children and adolescents with ADHD continue to meet criteria for diagnosis as adults.[16] Major problems in the workplace, relationships, and driving are salient for adults with ADHD, with astronomical costs to society. In fact, the evaluation and diagnosis of adult ADHD is now a cottage industry, with increasing amounts of scientific research each year devoted to patterns of symptoms and outcomes that linger well beyond childhood and adolescence (see Chapter 9).

## Impairments

Contrary to claims that ADHD is merely a label for nonconforming youth or an instance of overmedicalizing normal-range behavior, a large body of research indicates the serious impairments pertaining to ADHD.

(1) *Underachievement, school failure, employment.* Youth with ADHD have lower achievement test scores and are less likely to complete secondary school than their peers. Even for extremely intelligent individuals with ADHD, like those in gifted programs, ADHD symptoms get in the way of their achievement and performance rather than serving as a magical source of divergent thinking and creative potential.[17] As we have emphasized, adults with ADHD are extremely likely to show problems in the workplace.

(2) *Social relationships.* Children with ADHD prototypically blow out the candles at birthday parties, even when it's not their own birthday! Recall Becky, who ripped open her friend's ninth birthday party presents. Even Jose from

Chapter 1 was a mystery to his preschool age-mates because of his erratic, apparently selfish behavior. Individuals with ADHD often have key problems in attending to and "reading" others' facial cues and in modulating their responses to the situation at hand. As a result, they receive high levels of peer rejection, fueling a vicious cycle of lost opportunities for gaining needed social skills. Problems in close relationships are legion for adults with ADHD.[18]

(3) *Family interactions.* When contending with the challenging behaviors displayed by a child with high levels of ADHD symptoms, parents typically head toward anger and sarcasm ("how many times have I told you to do your homework?"), conflict and idle threats ("any more fights with your brother or calls from the principal and you're grounded for a year!"), and futility ("I give up—just play your video games all night; see if I care if you waste your life!"). Divorce is higher than the norm in such families, as are rates of child maltreatment.[19] A scientific lesson worth repeating is that the initial causes of a condition or disorder may not be the same as the forces that maintain or perpetuate it. In other words, discordant family interactions often magnify problems originally linked to biological factors. A major clinical goal is to remove the *blame* from parents for the child's symptoms but not their *responsibility* for changing the home climate and obtaining treatment.[20]

(4) *Accidents and physical health.* Risk for accidental injury is high, from falls or burns in preschool, driving accidents later on, or the results of risk-taking behavior across the lifespan. Given its potential to trigger injury, ADHD is a public health problem as well as a mental health issue. In some cases, head injuries experienced by individuals with ADHD may exacerbate the very symptoms and problems that generated the risk-taking behavior. This arena is a key argument against those who contend that ADHD is just a social construction or a product of overmedicalization. Try telling that to the family of the child in the emergency department or the individual with ADHD who has become critically injured—or has injured someone else—in a car crash. By adulthood, ADHD symptoms are associated with a range of indicators of

poor physical health (e.g., higher than average lipid profiles; being overweight). The underlying impulse-control problems and lack of planning often predict negative long-term health consequences.[21]

(5) *Comorbidities, including substance abuse.* Only rarely does a youth display ADHD in isolation from other conditions. Becky developed substance abuse, serious depression, cutting behavior, and suicidal ideation by her teen years. Jose was aggressive and defiant from an early age. Indeed, oppositional behavior, anxieties, learning disorders, and depression, along with movement disorders like Tourette's, accompany ADHD far more than would be expected by chance.[22] Such co-occurring disorders (formally called comorbidities) may well require additional treatments. Underlying reading problems, for example, do not respond to medications, and anxiety disorders may require specific cognitive-behavior therapies or SSRI medications (those used to treat depression and anxiety), beyond any treatments geared specifically toward ADHD.

Systematic research reveals that only a minority of youth with ADHD end up displaying adaptive behavior patterns and good school performance by their teen years.[23] Sadly—but all too understandably—the consequences of school failure, peer rejection, accidental injuries, and poor inhibitory control can be devastating. Leaving the structure of schooling in late adolescence allows some individuals to adjust and thrive, but only if they have developed an adequate skill base and only if there are real supports in the new settings. Those clinicians in affluent areas who follow just a few individuals with ADHD into adulthood and claim that things inevitably get better with time are undoubtedly cherry-picking from nonrepresentative samples and overlooking the majority of individuals whose problems continue and escalate.[24] Real success stories exist, but they are in the minority.

Overall, resilience is certainly possible, but it often takes the delivery of systematic, well-monitored, long-term treatments to foster it. Despite role models of people with ADHD who harness their energy, inquisitiveness, and restlessness to propel themselves to successful lives and noteworthy accomplishments, we still don't know enough about the factors that predict such successes.

## Models and Causes

If the symptoms of ADHD are not simply the result of poor parenting, crowded schools, inflated expectations for achievement, or intolerant adults, what *is* involved? High-quality research takes us beyond simplistic notions of "all culture" or "all biology."

### Models

Early models of the condition focused on extremes of activity, but several decades ago things shifted to the idea that ADHD reflects a core inability to pay attention (hence, the change in name to ADD in 1980). Yet this notion is overly simplistic. In fact, Canadian psychologist Virginia Douglas, whose research is often cited as being responsible for the emphasis on attention that led to the name change, discussed not only attention but also problems in impulse control and self-regulation.[25] Furthermore, there is not one form of attention but several. Regarding sustained attention or vigilance, one fights drowsiness or boredom to stay alert. In selective attention, one decides where to focus—for instance, on this page or anticipation of one's next meal. Attention span refers to how much information a person can hold onto at a time, which will be challenged in our readers if we continue to introduce more models and facts into this chapter. Distinct brain regions underlie different types of attentional processing.[26]

Research reveals that a core deficit in any one of these types of attention is not the hallmark of ADHD. Importantly, considerable *fluctuations* in attention often appear in people with the diagnosis, triggering erratic and inconsistent performance. Such inconsistency may in fact be a core reason for the belief that people with ADHD simply are not trying hard enough. The underlying problems appear to relate to inhibition, motivation, or the intrusion of "off-task" brain signals into one's performance.[27]

Important cognitive processes called executive functions (EF) are relevant. EF are the skills we invoke to keep ourselves focused, organized, and motivated to perform the complex tasks needed for academic, job-related, and interpersonal survival. They involve holding new information in mind until it consolidates (working memory), planning an approach to a task, monitoring our performance, maintaining focus, and correcting errors when required. In other words, it's not what one knows—most people with ADHD have at least normal intelligence—but whether one can use such knowledge, via self-regulation.[28]

In the view of ADHD expert Russell Barkley, individuals with ADHD are victims of their own impulses and habitual behaviors, so they never really get a chance to use the EF they possess. From this perspective, ADHD involves a deficit in *inhibitory control*, the ability to withhold a previously rewarded response (and thus to be able to consider alternative ways of acting). Without inhibitory skills, people are at the mercy of whatever was rewarded in the past. They suffer from a lack of freedom to try out new, more thoughtful strategies.[29]

Still another theory is that the underlying problem isn't so much attention, EF, or inhibition but rather motivation—especially if the task is long, dull, and directed by others. In other words, individuals with ADHD may not generate enough inner reward or intrinsic motivation. Recent brain imaging research using positron emission tomography (PET) has provided clear evidence along these lines. In brief, adults with ADHD who had never taken any medication— which might alter brain chemistry over time—showed a markedly reduced number of receptors for the neurotransmitter dopamine in precisely the regions of the brain that register and process reward, as well as other areas related to control of motor behavior. A number of cases of ADHD may therefore result from an inborn lack of reward-generating capacities. Little wonder that medications enhancing dopamine, plus behavioral treatments providing systematic incentives, are the two best-established treatments for ADHD (see Chapter 3).[30]

## Causes

Across the past two decades, twin and adoption studies have shown that genes play the major role in explaining differences between people regarding levels of ADHD-related behaviors. In formal terms, ADHD is quite heritable, at a rate of around 75%, which is higher than the comparable figure for depression or schizophrenia. What this means is that most of the reason for the high levels of focus and self-regulation of some people (and the lack of such abilities in others) is found in genes rather than child-rearing practices or environments.

Even so, there is no single gene responsible for ADHD. Many genes, acting together—and potentially "switched on" by inner chemicals or outer environments—produce vulnerability. (Think of height, which is over 90% heritable, though there's clearly no single gene for height.) Recent research indicates that several core genes related to brain development may underlie some of the risk for schizophrenia, bipolar disorder, autism, *and* ADHD. What is therefore crucial is how genes unfold and become activated over time, in combination with environments that either foster or hinder self-regulation.[31]

The lesson here is that even if a trait or condition shows strong heritability, environments still matter. Americans, on average, are several inches taller than a century ago, not because the many genes that contribute to height have quickly mutated over the past 100 years but because diet and nutrition have converged to lift levels of height across the entire population (quite possibly though activating relevant genes). In parallel, it is conceivable that other forces in the environment—like achievement pressures, ever-present media, or the push toward multitasking—make it more difficult for *everyone* to focus attention and self-regulate these days, even though *individual differences* in these traits are strongly linked to genetic influences.[32]

Two crucial points are that (a) the initial trigger for ADHD in the 19th and early 20th centuries was compulsory education, and (b) the recent press for academic and job-related performance has propelled rates of ADHD to new heights. The huge variation across people in terms of attention span, inhibitory control, and reward sensitivity is strongly related to genes, yet such differences were not terribly salient or impairing until society decided that all children needed to sit still in classrooms. Of course, extremes of inattention, poor focus, and impulsivity may well have been problematic during earlier times in human history. If a hunter-gatherer wasted too many arrows on "false alarms" of prey, the tribe might go hungry. Still, a restless, exploratory style may have been a more valued trait in some people when food was scarce than it is today, in our world of pressured academic performance and the need to sit still for long periods of time.

There is a parallel with learning disabilities. Genes are strongly implicated in difficulties with decoding symbols and linking them to sounds, but such biologically based differences were not terribly noticeable until the advent of compulsory education. With

ADHD, changes in cultural practices and expectations today place genetically mediated differences in attention, inhibitory control, and self-regulation into sharp relief.[33]

Other causes of ADHD symptoms are biological in nature but not specifically genetic. One is being born at low birthweight, which is defined as under 5 1/2 pounds. The immature brain is susceptible to problems with later self-regulation and attentional control. Maternal alcohol use is also a culprit. Extreme drinking (or binge drinking) during pregnancy can produce fetal alcohol syndrome, with facial abnormalities and mental retardation, while lesser amounts of pre-natal alcohol can produce "fetal alcohol spectrum disorder," featuring symptoms of inattention, impulsivity, and overactivity. Maternal smoking during pregnancy (or even exposure to secondhand smoke in the home) has also been tied to the risk for developing ADHD, although it is not a certain cause. Iron deficiencies, levels of lead in the bloodstream, and protein malnutrition during the early years may also be involved in selected cases. Sleep-related problems may not only accompany ADHD but also lead to ADHD symptoms. Like most physical and mental disorders—for example, heart disease, dia-betes, and depression—ADHD does not have a single cause.[34]

Some people contend that the main cause of ADHD is food addi-tives and dyes or excessive sugar in the diet. First, sugar is *not* the cause of hyperactivity or ADHD, even though many kids with this condition may gravitate toward sugar-rich foods. Second, food addi-tives, although not the primary cause either, have recently been shown to contribute to small amounts of hyperactive behavior in at least some youth, rekindling debates that started with the Feingold diet of 40 years ago.[35] In addition, early exposure to pesticides or flame-retardant chemicals may increase risk for both ADHD and autism-spectrum disorders.[36] Complicating matters is that genetic vulnerability to ADHD may be triggered by such toxic exposures. In other words, certain individuals are potentially more susceptible than others to toxic factors in the environment.[37]

Even though early parenting practices are not the primary cause of ADHD, negative parenting and insecure attachment bonds with caregivers early in life may spur aggressive behavior, which often accompanies ADHD.[38] Extreme deprivation—as found in the hor-rific orphanages in Eastern Europe from several decades ago, char-acterized by slatted cribs with minimal human contact—can yield extremes of inattention and overactivity. Here, affected children also display indiscriminate friendliness and other signs of highly disrupted attachment.[39] The core point is that different causes may converge on the outcome of ADHD-like behavior. Many roads lead to Rome.

Is there something unique about "ADHD brains?" High-resolution brain scans (via structural magnetic resonance imaging, or MRI) and moving images of brain physiology and blood flow (via functional MRI, or fMRI) are now the gold standard for research. One important finding is that the overall brain volume of individuals with ADHD is somewhat smaller than that of non-ADHD individuals. Size differences in specific brain structures are not as consistently found.[40]

The fascinating research of Philip Shaw and colleagues at the National Institutes of Health focuses on the brain's outer layer, the cortex, where much of the action occurs related to self-regulation and executive control, particularly in the frontal lobes. The thin cortex, which is densely packed with neurons and with neural connections (called synapses), undergoes periods of thickening and thinning during a child's development. Thinning, related to "pruning" of neurons that don't form viable connections with other neurons, occurs during the early years of life, but the cortex thickens again during the elementary school years. From research involving repeated MRI scans, youth with ADHD were shown to be 3+ years delayed in the time at which their frontal cortex shows its maximum thickness (closer to age 11 than age 8). Thus, the old name for ADHD symptoms—"immaturity"—may actually be quite apt, as developmental immaturity at the level of brain growth may be a hallmark of ADHD.[41]

Studies using fMRI (along with those that trace the brain's intricate pathways linking different brain regions) show that the frontal lobes, and their intricate connections with structures in the middle of the brain linked to regulation and attention, work inefficiently in people with ADHD. Recent investigations, in fact, reveal that ADHD-related problems are widespread throughout the brain.[42]

Even so, these important findings do not allow diagnosis of ADHD via brain scans. The variation across individuals is simply too great. In addition, the brain is unfathomably complex, and the field's knowledge of its workings is still rudimentary. Perhaps some forms of ADHD will one day be known to have a particular brain "signature," but for now diagnosis must be based on observations of behavior patterns and thorough clinical judgment (see Chapter 3).[43]

Finally, the brains of most people with ADHD are not actually sped up, as the term *hyperactivity* might imply, but instead are underaroused, linked to low levels of dopamine-related brain action. The high activity levels and impulsive traits characteristic of many people with ADHD may actually constitute an attempt to keep alert or maintain an inner sense of stimulation or reward.[44]

## Putting It All Together

In the end, is ADHD a biological reality or a reaction to environmental and contextual forces? We have taken pains to argue that it is not either/or but both/and. The strong heritability of ADHD, plus objective brain-imaging evidence for structural and chemical differences in the brains of many individuals with ADHD, might one day convince a skeptical public of the condition's reality. But the brain contains over 100 billion neurons, massively interconnected via over 100 trillion synapses. During prenatal development, literally thousands of new neurons are produced every *second*. The earliest years of life are marked by massive shaping of the developing brain, with language stimulation, responsive caregiving, and the culture's expectations for learning and behavior all playing key roles in forging brain development.[45] Biology and experience cannot be separated.

The more we push young children to become fast learners in school at ever-earlier ages—and the more that adults are valued for their performance and productivity in a ruthlessly competitive global workplace—the more that individual differences in attention, inhibitory control, and self-regulation will stand out. The next time you read a headline touting "the" newly found cause of ADHD, an op-ed author contending that it's just a label for creative kids or insensitive parenting, or a blog stating that it simply represents faulty brain chemistry at work, think instead about how our biological heritage plus our current values and contexts related to achievement and performance create a veritable test tube for the ADHD explosion.

# Diagnosing and Treating ADHD: Do It Right or Pay the Price

W E NOW GET TO THE IMPORTANT BUSINESS OF HOW ADHD should be evaluated and treated. Our central concern is the gap between existing standards for accurate diagnosis and responsive treatment and what too often happens in clinical practice. In fact, this gap is frequently an abyss. Far better outcomes would occur if we could hold clinicians to current professional standards and if society were willing to reimburse the kinds of high-quality assessments and treatments that are needed. Yet every day, hidden costs related to cursory evaluations and poorly supervised treatments emerge and multiply: wrongful diagnoses, missed opportunities for changing lives, and the potential for stimulant abuse when medications are not monitored carefully.

This following case study reveals how easy it can be to brand a traumatized, multi-problem child as having ADHD. Without adequate time and effort spent on diagnosis, misguided treatment may well compound the original problems.

# Tommy: "Problems Everywhere"

*Tommy was the product of a 17-year-old drug-abusing mother and a 28-year-old father who never met his son, both from a poor white neighborhood. Tommy's mother received no prenatal care and continued to use alcohol and pot and injected drugs while pregnant. Once her baby was born, she couldn't handle his constant tears or his many nearly sleepless nights. She claimed to love him but was hardly able to care for his needs in their spartan, publicly funded apartment.*

*The state intervened when neighbors complained of men coming to the apartment at all hours and of the baby's screams after episodes of slapping and yelling. After several investigations, Tommy was removed from his mother's custody and placed in a foster home before he was 2. But he didn't last long there, wearing out his new caretakers with his unruly behavior. He went to four additional foster homes before getting placed with a dedicated family, who doted on him despite his language delays, defiance, and persistent bedwetting. After a long legal battle, they adopted him when he was 6.*

*His adoptive home in Arkansas (a high-diagnosis state) is filled with toys, books, and love. Even so, first, second, and third grades were a nightmare. He failed most tests, was disruptive in class, and earned a reputation as an aggressive "enforcer" if he felt that he had been wronged. Testing revealed that he had a sub-average IQ, with poor planning ability and poor motor skills.*

*At the end of second grade, the School Study Team, composed of the teacher, principal, and school psychologist, concluded that Tommy had ADHD. He was prescribed stimulants at the local pediatric practice. However, none of the four different formulations he tried made much of a difference in his behavior. Not even a highly structured home environment could help him markedly improve his focus or reduce his feeling that he was always behind the eight ball, trapped in a threatening world.*

*An experienced child and adolescent psychiatrist tried to clarify the diagnostic picture. Was there neurological damage from his mother's alcohol and substance abuse during pregnancy? Did he have a serious behavioral condition, like aggressive conduct disorder, or was this actually a case of post-traumatic stress disorder (PTSD), given his early trauma? Or even bipolar disorder, a speculation based on his biological parents' severe mood swings? By the end of fourth grade, with Tommy's aggressive behavior escalating, the doctor put him on some heavy-duty second-generation antipsychotic medications. He gained weight and became sluggish, and he didn't lash out as much against others. The doctor stopped the medications, wondering whether Tommy might become diabetic.*

*Can Tommy ever finish high school and ever gain independence? Hard numbers are difficult to come by, but tens if not hundreds of thousands of kids like Tommy exist. Accurate diagnosis and preventive strategies are their main hopes.*

## Performing the Evaluation

Despite the major scientific discoveries in recent years regarding the brain-based underpinnings of ADHD (see Chapter 2), evaluating this condition is still a relatively low-tech affair. It involves the search for detailed information about everyday behavior patterns, particularly when organization, planning, and high levels of effort are required. Despite recent hype, it is simply not true that the latest computerized attention test or most vivid brain scan can provide an objective, definitive diagnosis of ADHD.

Diagnosis depends on two types of information: (1) a thorough developmental history and (2) data on life at home, in the person's peer group, and at school (or work for adults). Evaluators must leave their offices, figuratively if not literally, to get information from families, teachers, employers, and age-mates, if possible. Office-based measures of attention span and activity levels—for example, those in which an individual sits in front of a computer and attempts long, repetitive tasks—may supplement this information. But such tests do not always match up with everyday behavior patterns. There is no such thing as "the objective test" or "the brain measure" for diagnosing ADHD.[1]

### *What Must an Evaluator Consider?*

Not only are the core symptoms of ADHD often characteristic of very young children, but inattentive behavior, deficient impulse control, and poorly regulated motor behavior can result from a huge range of triggering factors.[2] Abused children may show such patterns, as may individuals who are depressed (poor concentration is a key aspect of major depressive disorder). Individuals with certain kinds of seizures, youth reacting to family distress (such as intense arguments at home, or separation or divorce), people with high levels of anxiety, and those with head injuries may also display ADHD-like symptoms. Assessing sleep patterns is important as well. Unless the evaluator systematically rules out the many psychological, family-related, and medical issues that can mimic ADHD, *overdiagnosis* is highly likely.[3]

Although some of Tommy's behavior patterns resemble core symptoms of ADHD, his prenatal drug exposure, the chaotic living situation of his infancy, his poor relationship with his mother, the abuse he suffered, and the sheer explosiveness of his behavior patterns signal that ADHD is a small (if any) part of the full story. There is no substitute for obtaining a thorough history of the individual's life experiences and development.

In addition, assessors who are sure that their expert observational skills in the playroom or clinic can be used to detect ADHD are likely to be fooling themselves. Many individuals with florid ADHD can be extremely attentive during an initial office visit, particularly if the doctor is wearing a white coat. In other words, *underdiagnosis* can result from an exclusive focus on in-clinic behavior, exemplifying what is termed the "doctor's office effect."[4] ADHD reveals itself when tasks are routine rather than novel, when competing contingencies abound, when work gets difficult, and when self-regulation is at a premium. In short, a brief office visit just isn't up to the job, leading to far too many cases of false positives (overdiagnosis) or false negatives (underdiagnosis).

To be accurately diagnosed, the individual must show high levels of ADHD symptoms in more than one setting. When a child is angelic at home but devilishly disorganized and disruptive in the classroom, or vice versa, issues in the problematic environment come to the fore. But if the symptoms occur more consistently, the evaluator can consider the presence of an inherent problem within the child, adolescent, or adult in question, even though behavior patterns may fluctuate during any given day.

Clinicians must be aware of stigma, particularly the shame that often accompanies disclosure of these kinds of problems. Countless families delay seeking help for months or even years because of a lack of knowledge and the fear of negative effects from the label of ADHD. For decades, families were explicitly blamed by mental health professionals for producing their offspring's ADHD (as well as nearly all other mental conditions). Considerable resistance must be overcome for a family to even show up at the clinic.[5]

We note, too, that a valid diagnosis of ADHD (or any other condition) does not reveal *everything* about the individual in question. Evaluators should probe for strengths and supports, as these may play a major role in forging a treatment plan.

## Beginning an Assessment

The starting point in assessing for ADHD is usually checklists, questionnaires, or rating scales. On such forms, parents or teachers rate each of the constituent behaviors of ADHD on a 3-, 4-, or 5-point scale. For example, the adult might rate the item *doesn't seem to listen* at the level of "not at all" (0), "just a little" (1), "pretty much" (2), or "very much" (3). Total scores for the Inattentive and Hyperactive/Impulsive symptom lists are then calculated.

Some checklists contain only the specific symptoms of ADHD. These brief scales, requiring only a minute or two to complete, are especially handy for monitoring the progress of medication or behavioral treatments, as they can be repeated on a daily or weekly basis. But for an initial diagnosis, longer scales are useful, as they include items related to a range of other behavioral or emotional conditions, such as aggressive behavior, anxiety, or depression. These scales often contain 100 or more items, assisting with appraisal of such related diagnoses.[6]

Most rating scales have parallel versions for parents and teachers. This is essential, as ADHD in youth should not be diagnosed unless problems are present at both home and school. If possible, the clinician should obtain rating scales from a past teacher or two, in order to get a sense of problems over time. Although more expensive to schedule, a school visit can be quite revealing: there's a world of difference between seeing scores on a checklist and observing actual behavior. Is the teacher overwhelmed or is the classroom overcrowded? At what periods during the day do problems emerge? Are peers imitating, ignoring, or rejecting the child in question?

Compared to a teacher untrained in dealing with problem behavior, a particularly warm and responsive teacher may rate the child as far less problematic. In second grade, Becky (Chapter 2) had a nurturing and firm teacher, who maintained high expectations. Her ratings of Becky's behavior were far more benign than those from her other grade school teachers. Similarly, parents themselves may vary in their perceptions of the child's behavior depending on their levels of stress, exhaustion, or skill in behavior management.[7] Jose's parents (Chapter 1) became more demoralized each year. Until treatment began, they could hardly think of a redeeming feature in their son.

Crucially, rating scales must have a "bank" of scores for large groups of children at each age level. Through the use of such norms, any particular youth's scores can be directly compared to those of age-mates. For a preschooler to qualify for a diagnosis, nearly every symptom on the rating scale would need to be endorsed at the top of the scale, because so many young children show these behaviors to some degree. A 12-year-old girl, by contrast, would require fewer symptoms, because older girls, on average, display less inattention and overactivity than younger girls or than boys.[8]

## What Else Is Necessary? What Else Really Helps?

Performing an in-depth interview about the person's developmental history is essential. What was she like as an infant and toddler? When did he reach his milestones of walking, talking, and learning social skills? Was the living situation stable; did trauma occur? For Tommy, his teenage, substance-abusing mother, along with the maltreatment he suffered, played a major role in his tragic developmental course. A complete history also reveals what has and has not worked in the past, crucial for forming a treatment plan.

Is a medical or neurological examination necessary? The short answer is no, if the goal is to "rule in" a diagnosis. No current medical test or brain scan can prove that an individual has ADHD. But the answer is yes if the clinician is trying to understand medical or neurological conditions that might mimic ADHD. Certain seizures, for instance, may look at lot like some forms of ADHD. Thyroid problems might also be relevant in rare cases; as we have noted, sleep problems should be examined as well.[9]

Evaluations of academic achievement or IQ testing cannot rule in or rule out ADHD. Yet they may be beneficial for understanding the individual's overall learning capacities and levels of academic functioning. They are also necessary to rule in the presence of a reading or math disorder. A large number of specialized cognitive assessments exist, such as computerized attentional measures, visual or auditory processing tests, or neuropsychological evaluations. These appraisals of attention span, learning abilities, and executive functioning can pinpoint areas of strength and weakness, but they cannot substitute for understanding the individual's everyday behavior.

ADHD does not usually exist on its own (see Chapter 2). In fact, comorbidity is the rule in all of mental health.[10] The evaluator must probe for depression, anxiety, aggression, and involuntary movements and noises (called tics, perhaps signaling the beginning of Tourette's disorder). For adolescents and adults, discovering patterns of substance use or abuse (e.g., tobacco or alcohol, or any one of a number of illicit substances) is vitally important. Such conditions require additional intervention.

Ideally, the clinician should observe parent–child interaction in the office, especially one in which the child performs schoolwork and is then asked to clean up the room. These interactions yield extremely valuable information about parental warmth and limit-setting, the child's oppositionality, and how the family supports or subverts the child. Even though negative and ineffective parenting styles are not the primary cause of ADHD, they are highly likely to maintain or fuel the relevant problems.[11] For Jose, an initial parent–child interaction revealed how much the parents cared for and tried to help him but just how ineffective their constant scolding actually was.

## The Ideal and the Real

Scoring and interpreting the rating scales, interviewing the family in depth, performing a medical exam, talking with the teacher (or observing the class), and appraising parent–child interactions can all take at least several hours. A helpful strategy is to send out rating scales to parents and teachers prior to the interviews so that the clinician has an idea of where to focus. Adding in a computerized attention measure could add half an hour; individual tests of achievement or executive functioning could add considerably more time. Overall, a typical 10- to 15-minute office visit is woefully inadequate. Major professional organizations, such as the American Academy of Pediatrics (AAP) and the American Academy of Child and Adolescent Psychiatry (AACAP), have produced evidence-based guidelines for the evaluation of ADHD, which emphasize many of the points we have just made.

The reality, however, is that most assessment of ADHD is done by general pediatricians (or adult family practice doctors), and not specially trained developmental/behavioral pediatricians or psychiatrists.[12] Enforcement of professional guidelines is not really possible, and many older clinicians have little or no training in current assessment strategies. Moreover, insurance plans rarely cover intensive evaluation: thorough developmental histories, testing, school observations, and parent–child interactions. Rating scales aren't often used. The bottom line is that far too many youth are being diagnosed with ADHD on the basis of extremely cursory evaluations. A large percentage of children receiving stimulant medication do not, in fact, even have a viable diagnosis of ADHD.[13] In sum, many people who deserve a diagnosis never get one because of inadequate evaluations; and too many others receive this label without justification. Improved professional training, team-based practice, and reimbursement of viable assessment strategies could prevent both overdiagnosis and underdiagnosis.

## Treatments for ADHD and Evidence for Their Effects

Over the years, many forms of intervention have been tried for ADHD. Some are popular (play therapy), some are controversial (special diets), some are growing in evidence but not yet proven (neurofeedback), and some are just plain weird (blue-green algae). Only two forms of treatment have a consistently strong evidence base: (1) medications, particularly stimulants; and (2) behavioral interventions, which aim to provide regular rewards and incentives to motivate improved performance and decrease disruptive behavior. The ultimate goal of each is to promote self-regulation. Yet this is an elusive target for ADHD, as no form of treatment provides the kinds of long-term, generalized gains so desperately needed.

## Less-Established Treatments

For years, the most common form of non-medication treatment for youth with ADHD—as for nearly all child disorders—was individual therapy, often in the form of play therapy. The idea is that adults can talk about their issues to gain insight and understanding, but children—inherently less reflective—express problems symbolically through play. Via careful observation, the therapist learns of conflicts and defenses, providing insight to the child. The major catch is that no evidence exists that such insight-based therapies are helpful for the core symptoms of ADHD. For some older youth and adults, discussing and receiving support to work through the *consequences* of ADHD can be important, but such treatment does not tackle the main symptoms.

For both youth and adults with ADHD, there has been a press toward use of complementary and alternative medicine (CAM), including meditation, acupuncture, dietary supplements, and the like. Despite the appeal of such interventions for many families, particularly given fears about medicating young children, the majority of CAM treatments for ADHD are not evidence based (even though some forms may be beneficial for some individuals).[14]

Forty years ago, dietary interventions for ADHD became popular, such as the Feingold diet, which eliminates dyes, colorings, additives, and salicylates. However, the initial research lacked control groups, and it often took massive structuring of the home to enforce such a restricted diet. Controlled research revealed that only a small fraction of youth with ADHD respond to dietary interventions. Still, recent data have rekindled the idea that, especially for young children, additives may trigger some degree of hyperactive behavior. A recent review has also shown that free fatty acid supplementation may yield modest effects on hyperactive behavior.[15]

An intervention that has moved from questionable to promising is neurofeedback, an alternate name for electroencephalography (EEG) biofeedback. Here, with electrodes placed on the person's scalp, he or she is connected to a machine that records electrical activity in the brain. Looking at a computer screen reflecting the recorded brainwaves, the person receives feedback (e.g., the screen changes from red to green) when neural activity reveals attention and focus. Thus, the person gradually learns to alter brain activity toward a more adaptive style, essentially learning self-control. However, this treatment is quite expensive. Also, despite better research in recent years, the ultimate control group—one in which the individual is hooked up to the brain-monitoring device but receives false feedback on the monitor—is only now receiving investigation. Without such a controlled study, it is impossible to know whether benefits are linked to the neural feedback per se or to increased hope and expectation related to the sophisticated machinery. Finally, even if well-controlled trials reveal benefit, the key question is whether the gains will generalize from the clinic to school, home, or social activities. Throughout the history of ADHD, *no* one-on-one intervention has crossed this bar.[16]

Another treatment is specific cognitive training, particularly to improve "working memory"—the ability to hold several bits of information in one's mind at one time. Many people with ADHD have relatively poor working memories. Without strength in this area, it is really hard to remember multipart directions or do well in challenging school or job settings. In training procedures, the individual experiences repeated trials on a computer to help build short-term memory capacities. Although individuals with ADHD can improve their working memory through such training, recent reviews display the same concern just discussed: a lack of carryover to the real world.[17]

The large number of fringe treatments for ADHD (e.g., spinal adjustments, various herbs) is daunting and depressing. As with autism, desperate parents may be willing to try almost anything. Neglecting treatments with proven track records can waste human potential and can even be dangerous.

## Medication

Stimulant medications have been used to treat attention problems and self-regulation deficits for 75 years (see Table 1–1). They surged in popularity with the approval of methylphenidate (trade name Ritalin) for hyperactivity over half a century ago. After periods of growth and retrenchment, use of these pills expanded rapidly during the 1990s, propelled even further during the first decade of the current century by viable long-acting formulations, enabling one dose to cover an entire day.[18]

But why on earth would a stimulant be helpful for someone who is already "hyper?" For many years it was believed that stimulants had paradoxical effects on individuals with ADHD, whose brains were somehow calmed by the same pills that activated the brains of everyone else. We now know that nearly everyone who takes a low stimulant dosage stays alert and fidgets less.[19] People with ADHD are no different; they show particularly large gains because of their large pre-existing problems and because their brains may actually be underaroused (see Chapter 2).

How effective are stimulants? Hundreds of controlled studies for individuals with ADHD reveal that, compared to placebo, outcomes include greater concentration, reductions in impulsivity, decreased activity levels, and higher levels of self-control. In fact, success rates from stimulant treatment are estimated to be in the neighborhood of 80%, with placebo clocking in at dramatically lower rates. There is no medication for any mental health condition that approaches this differential. Sometimes the effects of stimulants are night-and-day; more often, benefits are noticeable yet short of magic.[20]

Recent reports have suggested far-reaching impacts of use of ADHD medications. Take the example of Sweden, a nation with nationalized records of medical diagnoses, receipt of medications, and criminal records, thus a country with reliable data for assessment. According to a highly publicized 2012 report from the *New England Journal of Medicine*, during the periods when late adolescents and young adults in Sweden took medication for ADHD, rates of criminal behavior were reduced by 32% in men and 41% in women.[21] We caution that this study did not involve a random-assignment trial of medications, so cause and effect is hard to determine. Yet the findings are provocative.

Several points may help us cut through the vast scientific literature in this area. First, it is important to find not only which particular medicine works but also which dosage is optimal. There is no way to predict this ahead of time: a careful trial of several different dosage levels (and, in some cases, different stimulants) is needed, with feedback from parents and teachers being essential. Because stimulants are in and out of the bloodstream within a day, doing such a trial is easy, with informants completing brief rating scales on a daily or weekly basis to help determine which dose works best.

Second, stimulants can produce side effects, usually mild (appetite suppression, sleep problems), but sometimes they are more troublesome. When use of stimulants is unsupervised, real problems can ensue. In Chapter 4 we discuss these issues in more detail.[22]

Third, stimulants improve focus and reduce disruptive behavior, but a major question is whether they can actually enhance needed skills. Such medications improve short-term memory, the number of schoolwork or homework problems attempted and completed, and even complex problem-solving. In other words, they do far more than simply make the individual compliant for performing rote tasks.[23] But the real question is whether stimulants promote gains in reading and math performance, a central question addressed in Chapter 4.

Having ADHD creates risk for substance abuse in adolescence or adulthood (see Chapter 2). A vigorously debated question is whether stimulants foster or reduce this likelihood. To answer this question definitively, we would need to randomly assign a large group of youth with ADHD to either active medication or placebo for many years, from childhood through adolescence. Such research would be unethical and impractical. Existing studies strongly suggest that taking these medications during childhood neither increases nor reduces the risk for substance abuse. It may be that protective benefits in some cases (e.g., reduced impulsivity, better friendships) are counterbalanced in others by raising abuse potential (i.e., those for whom prescription medications might be "gateway" drugs).[24]

A major issue is whether medications are harmful to the developing brain or potentially protective. Once again, this question is impossible to answer carefully without long-term, random-assignment trials. Yet one team of researchers provided evidence that youth with ADHD who had received stimulants had *less* reduction in brain volume over time than did nonmedicated youth.[25] Conceivably, stimulants are neuroprotective.

To be sure, stimulants are not the only medical recourse for ADHD. Over the past 15 years a nonstimulant agent, atomoxetine (trade name Strattera), has proven successful. Rather than target dopamine, it boosts levels of norepinephrine. After a decided bump in sales a decade ago, this medication has been falling into relative disfavor. Other medications that affect norepinephrine in different ways may have benefits for ADHD. Thus, at least two neurotransmitter systems in the brain underlie impulse control and self-regulation, one related to dopamine and one to norepinephrine.[26]

Unfortunately, little evidence exists that medication-related gains are maintained after the last dose wears off. As a result, many clinicians now recommend that patients take medication as long as ADHD symptoms remain without it. Yet medication may lose its effectiveness over time, in part because (1) dosages are not monitored carefully, (2) the individual doesn't take the pills reliably, or (3) stimulants can alter brain receptors when taken long term, undermining long-term effectiveness. In other cases, people can learn to self-regulate or end up in settings that don't place a high premium on self-control, reducing the need for continued medication. Crucially, in the MTA Study, medication use was followed up long after the 14-month phase of randomly assigned treatment. Over the long haul, medications did not provide the same kind of long-range benefit that they had initially, when their use was carefully monitored. The debate is therefore intense: are medications a short-term palliative treatment, or can they work well over many years, in the context of high-quality medical follow-up? Careful long-term research is needed.[27]

Essential for medication use (indeed, for any treatment) is the need for regular, ongoing evaluation of its effects. Far too many clinicians lack the time or expertise to obtain regular feedback on the effectiveness of medicine. As a result, symptoms and related impairments may well re-emerge. Moreover, diversion of medications is far more likely with lax monitoring. If we were appointed treatment czars, we would insist that all treatments used for ADHD receive regular, careful monitoring and evaluation. Nurses or paraprofessionals linked to medical practices could assist with medication monitoring, adding to cost-effectiveness.

Many families resist giving medication to their children, especially when problems relate to behavior, attention, and discipline. They ask: *Shouldn't such behaviors be under volitional control? Why should my child need medicine when other kids don't? Isn't it unethical to give pills for behavioral regulation—especially to those whose brains are rapidly developing?* If inattentive/hyperactive behavior is thought to emanate exclusively from free will, medications would be considered coercive if not downright wrong. Yet even when stigma is overcome and medications are tried, a large percentage of families stop after one or two prescriptions.[28] Current medication practices simply are not doing the job.

## Behavioral Interventions

The premise of behavior modification is that individuals with ADHD don't experience the same kinds of intrinsic motivation for task completion and academic performance as others do. In fact, findings of low levels of dopamine receptors in never-medicated adults with longstanding ADHD fuel such arguments (see Chapter 2).[29] Perhaps people with ADHD aren't "wired" for intrinsic motivation. Thus, regular, consistently delivered rewards (and punishments) are needed to motivate optimal performance.

One form of behavioral intervention for ADHD is called *direct contingency management*. Here, in special classrooms or summer programs, trained teachers or counselors deliver regular rewards for individually targeted behaviors. These programs can certainly be effective, but they are costly and there is no guarantee that the benefits carry over from the specialized setting to the child's regular environments. More common are the strategies of *clinical behavior therapy*, whereby professionals work, individually or in groups, with parents and teachers, teaching them behavioral principles. The clinician first provides psychoeducation (teaching basic facts about ADHD and its management) and then trains parents and teachers to measure target behaviors with precision, provide prompts and cues for desired behaviors and learning goals, dispense regular rewards for progress, and apply timeout or "response cost" (i.e., removal of previously earned rewards) procedures for misbehavior. Vital is the integration of home and school components, so that expectations and rewards are consistently applied.[30]

Another kind of treatment includes *social skills groups*, in which important social competencies (e.g., cooperation, teamwork, sportsmanship) are modeled, practiced, and rewarded, at first in small-group situations and later in more everyday settings. The idea here is that children with ADHD need to learn—indeed, overlearn—such essential skills and practice them under realistic conditions. One of the potential downsides to this treatment is that unless the group leaders take firm control, these groups can breed aggressive and antisocial behavior when the kids in the group reward one another for misbehavior.[31]

For adults, *cognitive-behavior therapy* has real benefits. Here, the individual learns to problem solve and to self-monitor and self-reward his or her own performance. For youth, however, gains are elusive with such procedures; more direct rewards are usually needed.[32]

In sum, direct contingency management can readily improve behavior, but it is not clear that the gains will carry over to the child's regular environments, as noted earlier. Parent management training and teacher consultation can also produce important benefits. On average, medication yields stronger effects for reducing ADHD symptoms, and it takes considerable effort on the part of families and schools to put the behavioral programs into practice.

## Combination Treatment

If medications alter neurotransmitter levels (decreasing impulsivity and enhancing motivation), and if behavioral treatments promote important skills, combining the two strategies should produce optimal benefits. But the actual picture is more complex. In the MTA Study (see Chapter 2), in which systematic interventions were delivered in a controlled experiment to nearly 600 children, extremely well-monitored medication was just as effective as combination treatment—medication plus intensive behavior therapy—in reducing symptoms of ADHD. Thus, if the goal is to lower ADHD-related behaviors, stimulant medication works quickly and well in the majority of cases (but only if prescribed and monitored with care).

When the outcomes were broadened, however, to include (1) comorbid symptoms of aggression and anxiety/depression plus (2) academic achievement, improved parenting, and better social skills, the combination treatment came out on top. In other words, it took active family and school intervention *plus* medication to make a difference for key impairments, comorbidities, and skill-building.[33] Furthermore, combination treatments are likely to bring problem behavior into the normal range of functioning. Crucially, the pairing of medication and behavioral treatment provides optimal benefits when parents make major changes in their discipline at home, moving from a negative and inconsistent parenting style to a more positive and regulated style.[34] At the same time, combined (multimodal) intervention takes coordination across physicians, psychologists, parents, and teachers, involving a level of effort, teamwork, and cost that is not often attainable in practice.

How do children and adolescents with ADHD experience the treatment they receive? We point to a remarkable study of 9- to 14-year-olds in the United States and United Kingdom, called VOICES (Voices on Identity, Childhood, Ethics and Stimulants). Most of the interviewed youth believed that medications actually helped their decision-making and "moral agency," even though a small proportion felt that side effects were costly. That is, the children and early adolescents who were studied believed that medication did not remove personal choice but instead facilitated their making of better decisions. In addition, when youth with ADHD receive medication, they tend to attribute their improved behavior to their own effort rather than to the pills themselves. Such findings reduce fears that medication treatment undermines personal control.[35]

## Real versus Ideal: The Large Gap

Just as was the case for assessment and diagnosis, the kinds of practices necessary for effective treatment are far too often not used in practice. In terms of medication, protocols of finding the right dosage and monitoring benefits carefully are seldom performed. In addition, the vast majority of physicians do not have expertise in behavior therapy procedures, nor do they engage with psychologists or other mental health providers who could provide multimodal intervention.[36] In short, the professional guidelines for optimal treatment emanating from the American Academy of Pediatrics and the American Academy of Child and Adolescent Psychiatry appear to be gathering dust on shelves.[37]

Far more education in evidence-based practices is required, and reimbursement for viable treatments is needed. The unfortunate state of affairs is that too few individuals with ADHD ever get treatment at all—and even those who do usually fail to receive optimal, evidence-based help. It is little wonder that ADHD has such detrimental long-term outcomes. If ADHD is a condition related to fundamental immaturity, it is arguable that we as a society are not yet sufficiently mature ourselves in terms of recognizing the essential truths about its nature, diagnosis, and treatment. As a result, we all pay the price. The antidote is careful evaluation and diagnosis, responsive treatment, use of multimodal interventions, and adequate monitoring of treatments. We owe it to patients, family members, and society at large to provide such optimal assessment and care.

# The Upward Spiral of ADHD Medications: Enhanced Performance or Potential for Abuse?

## Ralph: "Miracle Cure"

*Ralph, age 9, has been struggling in school. The puzzling thing to his parents is that most other aspects of his life don't seem so bad, except for remembering to do chores or finishing homework, which requires several reminders. He likes people, he's always had a close friend, and he tries to do the right thing. He seems happy much of the time, especially when he's away from school.*

*Still, Ralph can't stop fidgeting or talking in class. He asks his teachers to repeat instructions, over and over. Because he's so intelligent, it's a mystery as to why he can't stay focused. Whatever comes into his mind grabs his attention, and he constantly loses track of what he is supposed to be doing. His test scores are plummeting, and he's falling behind grade level in a number of subjects. His teacher claims that she spends half her time on Ralph, leaving too little time for the other kids.*

*Finally, after reading an article in the newspaper—one that talked about ADHD in realistic rather than sensationalistic terms—his parents began to talk with the family doctor about their son's behavior. She examined Ralph and collected parent and teacher rating scales as well as a lengthy family history, confirming that he was showing high levels of the classic signs of ADHD compared to other kids his age. She then prescribed a stimulant, Concerta.*

*The very first morning after taking the stimulant, Ralph's parents noticed how much calmer Ralph was on the way to school. The teacher nearly fell out of her chair: Ralph was a positive force for learning, rather than a disruption. Over the next several months his grades picked up, and at the end of the year his achievement test scores showed clear improvement over those from the year before. Although he has little appetite for lunch, he makes up for it at dinner and with a bedtime snack.*

*Ralph's dad remembers how he himself struggled to pay attention in class as a boy, although he was never diagnosed. As one of the 4.5 million youth in the United States receiving medication for ADHD, Ralph is part of a trend that has witnessed nonstop growth for several decades.*

With a clear case of ADHD, uncomplicated by other conditions, Ralph is one of those kids for whom stimulant medication produces dramatic results. But it is not always this simple. In fact, we ask you directly: as a parent, would you have your child take a pill to perform better in school, become less disruptive, and make your own life easier? You might have to cope with derogatory comments from neighbors and relatives who are convinced that ADHD is just a modern-day excuse for poor behavior, and with opinion pieces in *The New York Times* claiming that ADHD is actually caused by bad parenting and that giving your children medication is like roping children's hands in bed so they can't masturbate.[1]

Alternatively, as an adult athlete with ADHD, suppose you could take a pill—banned across the major leagues as an illicit performance enhancer—that might help you become a starting player and help your team win the World Series or the Super Bowl. Are stimulants for athletes fair to those who cannot take the medication to increase their focus and peformance?[2]

Beyond ADHD, the use of stimulants for boosting academic outcomes has become a major concern, linked to the major question of how much performance enhancement our society should allow. Because millions of individuals without any kind of diagnosis now take these pills during crunch time for writing papers and taking exams, the medications are sometimes called "steroids of the mind" or "smart pills." Think of modern-day parallels: pills for Alzheimer's disease (to stave off mental decline in normative aging); SSRIs (to help with neurotic, self-defeating tendencies even in the absence of major depression); statins (to reduce borderline-level cholesterol); and, of course, Viagra or Cialis (to enhance normal-range but suboptimal sexual performance in men). A core difference, however, is that stimulant use in the general population appears to result in clear risk for stimulant abuse or dependence, whereas instances of such stimulant abuse are far rarer among youth with ADHD under close medical supervision. The tragic story of Richard Fee, described in the Introduction, shows just how devastating the outcomes can be when stimulant-aided performance enhancement goes awry, without viable diagnosis and without careful monitoring of prescriptions.[3]

In this chapter we discuss the major increases in the use of ADHD medications over recent decades. We also provide details on how these medicines affect the brain and discuss their side effects. We address the crucial issue of whether pharmacological treatment for ADHD actually enhances school performance and academic achievement, beyond improving classroom behavior or laboratory measures of cognition. Finally, we tackle the major diversion of stimulants in recent years, a trend that has accompanied growing pressures for academic and vocational success.[4] In short, the societal and ethical implications are enormous.

## Skyrocketing ADHD Medications

Since methylphenidate (trade name Ritalin) was approved, over a half century ago, for treating children with hyperactivity (Table 1–1), private insurance companies and eventually public insurance programs such as Medicaid have paid for most of the cost of ADHD medications. Stimulant prescriptions tripled between 1990 and 2000.[5] As the new millennium began, viable time-release formulations of stimulants became available, so that children no longer had to visit the school nurse to be medicated, which reduced stigma and saved professional time. These patented formulations, priced four to five times as much as generic, shorter-acting medications, boosted costs at a much higher rate than medication volume per se.[6]

Presently, nearly 70% of children and adolescents with a current diagnosis of ADHD are prescribed medication for their condition.[7] As discussed in Chapter 3, however, this does not mean that relevant prescriptions always (or even usually) follow a careful evaluation or that physicians monitor the individual's progress with diligence. One of our core contentions is that the cursory manner in which ADHD gets evaluated and diagnosed fuels the high rates of stimulant use (both prescriptions and diversion) we now see (discussed in Chapter 3).

## Stimulants and the Brain: Main Effects and Side Effects

Although a thorough discussion of how stimulants affect the brain could fill many chapters of a psychopharmacology text, we offer here a brief summation, beginning with the neurotransmitter called dopamine. Like other neurotransmitters, dopamine shoots across brain synapses, forging communication from neuron to neuron. It is found in a few specific brain regions and pathways, one of which is involved in the sense of pleasure and reward, located deep in the brain's limbic regions. Another pathway is centrally involved in coordinating and organizing behavior, traversing the brain's frontal lobes to several areas involved in motor control and behavioral regulation. Recall the study cited in Chapter 2, in which National Institute of Drug Abuse (NIDA) director Nora Volkow and colleagues showed convincingly that never-medicated adults with ADHD have substantially fewer receptors for dopamine in precisely those two regions of the brain. Little wonder that problems in motivation, effort, and self-regulation are linked strongly to this condition.[8]

At the tail end of most neurons, right at the spot where neu-rotransmitters are released into the synaptic gap, molecules called transporters are found. These transporters "scoop up" the neu-rotransmitter that has just entered the gap and usher it back into the initial (presynaptic) nerve terminal. Through this process of reup-take, as it is called, the dopamine can no longer communicate with the next neuron in the chain (i.e., the postsynaptic neuron). If there is lots of transporter activity, not enough dopamine remains in place to cause the next neuron in the chain to fire.

Here is where the medications come in: stimulants block the action of transporter molecules. In other words, they temporarily stop reuptake and allow more dopamine to stay in the synapse, promot-ing communication with the next neuron. Through this enhanced action of dopamine, the individual is more likely to inhibit impulsive responses, focus attention, and register a strong sense of reward for completed tasks.[9] Traditional stimulants perform this action for 3 to 4 hours; the longer-acting formulations extend it to 8 to 12 hours.

Hundreds of carefully controlled studies, contrasting medication with placebos, reveal that for individuals with ADHD, stimulants reduce fidgeting and other excess motor behavior, deter impulsiv-ity ("Ah, that's right, it's not my birthday after all—I'll let the host blow out those candles!"), and enhance attention to repetitive tasks or long bouts of homework. It takes careful supervision, through an educated trial-and-error process, to find the optimal medication and the right dosage level (see Chapter 3).[10]

Like all medicines, stimulants produce side effects. Excess dopa-mine action causes alertness and wakefulness, a desired goal when you need to study for hours on end but a problem if you need to sleep. Stimulants also suppress appetite, which is why they used to be commonly prescribed as diet pills. For ADHD, this effect can usu-ally be minimized by adjusting the timing or dose of the medication. The medications also affect the peripheral nervous system, slightly speeding up one's heart rate and lifting one's blood pressure by a few points. For growing children who take the pills over longer time periods, ADHD medications may reduce their ultimate height by an inch or so, probably because excess dopamine activity slows down release of growth hormone. For many families, a centimeter or two of reduced height may be a small price to pay for improved behavior and enhanced performance.[11]

When adolescents or adults use stimulants casually, a feeling of euphoria (a "high") may occur, so that substance abuse and substance dependence (a more formal name for addiction) can result. Such serious effects as psychotic behavior (paranoia, hallucinations, and delusions) may take place. It is crucial to note that dependence rarely occurs for children with legitimate ADHD under close medical supervision. For them, the medications may serve a kind of normalizing function in the brain, probably related to the inherently low levels of dopamine receptors in many people with ADHD. (Such individuals don't experience any "high" at all.) Yet the risk is appreciable when stimulants are used sporadically by adults seeking performance enhancement, without any medical monitoring. As many as 13% of casual stimulant users may become medication dependent. The risk is highest when stimulants are injected or snorted—a risk virtually eliminated by the newer, longer-acting medications, which are nearly impossible to crush or inject.[12]

Stimulants are therefore considered "Schedule II" medicines—illegal and unsafe except for specific medical reasons and under careful supervision. Indeed, the buying and selling of Schedule II medications for nonmedical use is a felony. In many states, prescriptions are written in triplicate so that state agencies can track them. Even so, with the large increases in prescriptions these days, especially for young adults, supplies are available in many college environments. It is also possible to receive mail-order stimulants from unscrupulous merchants on the Internet, fueling the growing diversion of these medications for the general public.[13]

## Reducing Problems or Enhancing Skills?

A major question is whether ADHD medicines work mainly to squelch annoying and disruptive behavior patterns—to keep kids calmer and more docile in classrooms, or adults more content with their mind-numbing jobs—or whether these pills aid in the learning of important social or academic skills.[14]

We begin with social skills and social competence. Poignantly, children and adolescents with ADHD are often strongly disliked by their peers. Recall Becky from Chapter 2: her impulsive behavior made other kids think she was weird, and her social relationships declined as she gravitated toward a rough, drug-abusing crowd and, ultimately, self-injury. Recall, too, Jose from Chapter 1, rejected by his preschool peer group before the age of 5. His story reveals just how early a negative spiral of peer interactions can begin. Tommy (Chapter 3) wreaked social havoc wherever he went, although his problems clearly transcended ADHD. By contrast, Ralph, in this chapter, is one of the few youths with ADHD whose problems are mainly academic.

How long does it take kids with ADHD to develop a negative peer reputation? Two decades ago, Hinshaw's research team found a depressing answer. At a summer program for boys with ADHD (all of whom spent the first week unmedicated) and a comparison group without ADHD, the staff made careful behavior observations in the classrooms and on the playground, right from the opening bell of the first day. The team also performed confidential interviews with each boy that first afternoon, requesting information about which camp-mates he most liked or disliked. After just a few hours of interaction, the boys with ADHD were far more likely to be disliked and rejected by their peers than the boys without a diagnosis. Furthermore, their explosive, retaliatory, and impulsive behavior patterns were the main reason for the quick formation of such dismal peer perceptions.[15] Kids with ADHD get behind the eight ball with their peers distress-ingly quickly.

By reducing impulsive and disruptive behaviors that age-mates so often dislike, ADHD medications might be expected to alleviate social rejection. Yet even though negative social *behaviors* are reduced by stimulants—sometimes dramatically—one's *standing* in the peer group isn't so easily reversed.[16] For one thing, initial reputations are hard to overcome, even with a shift in behavior. Additionally, although the medicines can help reduce troublesome behaviors, they cannot, in and of themselves, teach social skills.

Regarding academic achievement, the crucial question is whether medication-related boosts in attention, along with reductions in impulsive and disruptive behavior, translate into better cogni-tive performance. On average, use of ADHD medications leads to improvements in cognitive skills, measured by laboratory tests of effort, sustained attention, and memory. When children with ADHD complete academic worksheets composed of problems right at their skill level, the number of problems attempted and correctly completed goes up on medication days versus placebo days. Medication does more than reduce problem behavior; it can enhance academic productivity.[17]

Still, the question remains regarding actual test scores in reading and math. Until relatively recently, there was no evidence that stimulants could boost such gold-standard measures of academic performance. Think about it: most medication trials are only a few weeks long, whereas standardized reading and math tests require considerable learning over many months to yield measureable gains. Furthermore, for ethical reasons it is not possible to randomly assign large groups of youth with ADHD to medication versus placebo for years at a time and track effects on achievement.[18]

Yet several important findings are highly suggestive. In the MTA Study (Chapter 3), the combination of (1) well-delivered and carefully monitored medication plus (2) intensive home and school behavioral treatment led to significant improvements in reading during the 14-month controlled trial, especially compared to reading scores of those receiving the community standard treatment of periodic, brief appointments with a pediatrician.[19] Next, in a follow-up of 370 youth with ADHD through high school, the average daily dose of medication each youth received was significantly associated with reading achievement. Not surprisingly, taking medication was also linked to less absenteeism and lower risk of failing a grade.[20]

Several years ago, Scheffler's research team analyzed data from a representative, national sample of 10,000 kindergarten children. About 7% of the children had received a diagnosis of ADHD over the 6-year period of the study, with somewhat over half of the diagnosed group having begun medication. Comprehensive math and reading tests were administered to the children throughout grade school. The crucial question dealt with the effect of starting medication on the next round of reading and math scores.

Through careful statistical analyses, we found that by the first and second tests after medication had begun, gains in reading (about a third of a school year) and math (about a fifth of a school year) were evident, compared to abilities of those children with ADHD who had *not* begun medication during that interval. In short, medication was linked to a boost in actual reading and math scores, not just tests of memory or attention in a laboratory or brief daily worksheets.[21]

There are at least three important qualifications. First, these gains were not large enough to normalize these achievement levels. In other words, the medicated youths' scores still lagged, on average, behind those of the large sample of grade school children without ADHD. Not surprisingly, medication alone wasn't the whole answer. Second, it was impossible to determine how many of the children with ADHD (either those with or without medication) received supplemental academic programs over and above their standard, elementary school curricula. With receipt of such programs, medication-related gains may well have been stronger. Third, this was not a random-assignment, experimental study. Instead, it was a "naturalistic" study of children who—for any number of reasons—started or did not start medications. In such studies, it is impossible to know whether it's the treatment itself (in this case, medication) or the motivation or resources of the treated group that contributed to any improvement. (On the other hand, maybe it was those youth with the largest academic problems who started medication, thus any treatment-related gains would be doubly impressive.) Even so, the results reveal real achievement gains once medication starts.

In Iceland, systematic national records track diagnoses of ADHD, all medications received, and regular achievement test scores. A recent study there showed that for youth with ADHD in fourth to seventh grades, the earlier a child began medication, the less his or her achievement test scores declined. Medication, therefore, helped to "hold the line" with respect to actual academic performance, which usually gets worse in children and adolescents with ADHD over time.[22]

These results are potentially groundbreaking. Yet not all relevant studies have shown such findings. Moreover, medications always work in concert with a viable curriculum, as they cannot in and of themselves supply the teaching. Any consideration of whether medications facilitate achievement and performance is actually a question of how the medicines are paired with responsive teachers, a challenging yet tailored curriculum, and needed learning supports. In sum, the tantalizing possibility is that medication can produce better report cards, higher standardized test scores, and maybe even improved college entrance exam performance, whether through enhanced motivation and attention or direct effects on learning new material. In Chapter 5 we revisit this issue, asking whether stimulant-related enhancement of academic performance might actually boost economic productivity.

## Diversion and Neuroenhancement: Stimulants for Everyone?

Our focus now turns to whether stimulant medications can act as equal-opportunity drugs, providing benefits in learning and achievement for anyone who takes them. If so, many people in society might be eager to use them for a boost in performance. In fact, a whole lot of people already have, as neuroenhancement has moved ever closer to the mainstream.

Let's take a step back. Even though Viagra and Cialis are approved medications for "erectile dysfunction," it is obvious that such pills are used to enhance male sexual performance more generally, and prescribed far beyond those with a diagnosed condition. Perhaps we might become a more productive, mentally sharper society by making stimulants universally available. One might ask whether they should be placed in the water supply, like fluoride to prevent tooth decay. After all, coffee drinking is rampant, used to fend off tiredness and boost performance at school or work. Yet the whole topic is fraught with huge ethical and medical implications. So we need to evaluate carefully whether ADHD medications work for everyone in the population and consider the medical, social, and ethical costs of making stimulants universally available.

### Stimulant Effects Beyond ADHD

Countering the longstanding assumption that stimulant effects on ADHD are unusual and paradoxical, the eminent child psychiatrist Judith Rapoport performed a trial during the late 1970s in which normally functioning boys took dextroamphetamine (trade name Dexedrine) for a week. In this placebo-controlled study, these preadolescent boys displayed better attention and showed less motor movement while receiving the active medication. There was no paradoxical effect at all: a low stimulant dosage provided benefit (albeit small) for children in the normal range. Other investigators have shown parallel findings.[23]

In 2011 a major review paper—featuring the provocative title "Are Stimulants 'Smart Pills'?"—summarized all scientific studies on cognitive benefits of stimulants in normal-range individuals. The conclusions are intriguing. First, these medications help normal-range individuals, including adults, to retain material they have just learned. Second, however, in terms of recalling strings of information (working memory) or executive functions like planning, the effects are hugely inconsistent. In other words, some people show real gains, but for many others, the pills don't seem to help.[24] In short, the stimulants are far from a panacea in terms of producing "smartness." As one sifts through the findings, what stands out is the specific tests used to measure cognitive gains, the medication dosages tried, and the initial attentional skills of the individuals who participated in the studies.

Specifically, for those with initially poor attention or cognitive performance—which at its extreme includes people with diagnoses of ADHD—cognitive boosts were often noteworthy. Yet medication-related enhancement was usually weaker for those in the middle of the bell curve and potentially *negative* for those with highly developed prior skills. Thus, although people with ADHD show widespread and substantial gains from stimulants, across the general population it is not clear that these medications act as universal "smart pills," on the basis of objective evidence.[25]

Even for those who did show gains, it is difficult to know whether the stimulants enhanced core aspects of memory and learning or instead increased alertness, focus, motivation, and perseverance, giving the appearance of "smartness" but without enhancing actual cognitive performance. For many, the medications might work primarily to make repetitive, dull material more interesting, with minimal benefit for creative, synthetic thought. Still, being able to stay up late with better focus could be a real advantage when, for example, cramming for tests.

Surveys reveal that the clear majority of individuals who use stimulants as study aids *believe* that the pills provide benefit, even though the objective evidence is not uniformly supportive. We reiterate that current estimates of the percentage of college students *without* diagnosed ADHD using these medications (i.e., rates of diversion) range from 5% to as high as 30% or more. The major increases in prescriptions for adolescents and young adults with ADHD in recent years signify that there are usually medication supplies on a given dorm floor at any time. Adding to the controversy, a number of professors and scientists admit to stimulant use to boost their productivity, as indicated in prestigious scientific journals like *Nature*.[26] In short, the temptation is great—and so are the dangers.

## Motivations and Costs

It would be important to gain clarity regarding people's motivations for the rapidly increasing nonmedical use of stimulants. As discussed aptly by Smith and Farah, who wrote the major review on stimulant effects in the general population, the relative percentages of those who use these agents as "smart pills" or as "awake pills," "party pills," "diet pills," or some combination is not fully known.[27]

If much of the current motivation is, in fact, for neuroenhancement, and if a cognitive, motivational, or alertness-related boost exists for at least some individuals, the potential downsides must also be addressed. Here is where the issue of drug abuse and dependence rears its head. As noted earlier, when children with ADHD are treated with stimulants under close supervision, no more than a tiny fraction (probably under 1%) go on to develop dependence or otherwise abuse these pills. But with nonmedical or recreational use for older individuals, the risk is substantially higher, as much as 13%.[28]

Why are problems of abuse or dependence so much higher with recreational use or performance enhancement than with prescription treatment for well-diagnosed cases? Starting medications in childhood (the usual time for medical use), at the instigation of adults, is clearly a different motivation than beginning to take the pills on one's own during adolescence or beyond. Moreover, regular dosing on a daily basis may protect the brain against the "reward surges" incurred by sporadic use, especially if the latter involves injection or snorting, which causes an ultra-fast flooding of brain receptors with dopamine.[29] Also, the brains of individuals with ADHD—many of whom appear to have inborn dopamine receptor deficiencies—could be protective against prescription abuse, although this is not known for certain.

Social history is cyclic rather than linear. Nonmedical use and abuse of stimulants was rampant during the 1960s and 1970s, for diet control and recreational purposes. International organizations were subsequently created, with the goal of regulating worldwide supply.[30] Rates of production were subsequently slowed, and abuse became less frequent. In recent decades, however, the quotas have increased again, as a function of the steady rise in ADHD diagnoses and medical demand for stimulants, as well as increasing pressure for academic and vocational performance. Not surprisingly, rates of diversion have increased at the same time. The bottom line is that we are now at a crossroads with respect to supply versus demand for ADHD medications (see Chapter 10 for predictions of future trends).[31]

## Ethics and Values

Should athletes be able to use protein powder or other dietary supplements to boost power and speed? Bumping it up several notches, what about steroids, now banned but commonly used in the NFL and major league baseball for many years? Alex Rodriguez, plus a number of other former Most Valuable Players in MLB, have served major suspensions. Or use of human growth hormone (HGH), or blood-thickening agents among professional cyclists, long a scourge in that sport, revealed most dramatically with the confessions of Lance Armstrong in early 2013? Stimulants are banned in sports because they can enhance reaction time, endurance, and coordination. However, players with a documented diagnosis of ADHD can get an exemption, as was the case for Andres Torres, who helped lead the San Francisco Giants to an unexpected 2010 World Series title.[32]

Our focus is not on athletic enhancement but on neuroenhancement—the intentional tweaking of one's brain to produce higher productivity (or, as it was put in the title of a 2009 *Scientific American* feature, "turbocharging" the brain).[33] The ethical issues in this area are both murky and profound. As the authors of the "smart pills" review put it:

> Personal and societal values will dictate whether success through sheer effort is as good as success with pharmacological help, whether the freedom to alter one's own brain chemistry is more important than the right to compete on a level playing field at school and work, and how much risk of dependence is too much risk.[34]

It is essential to keep in mind the ultra-competitive cultural backdrop these days. The admissions rates at Harvard, UC Berkeley, and other elite colleges are at all-time lows, with more and more applicants for a generally frozen level of prized admissions slots. At the same time, outsourced jobs are omnipresent. More and more college graduates are returning to their parents' homes after graduation, unable to find work. With such fierce competition in a culture obsessed with success, the debate over maximizing performance is intense.

Affluent, well-connected individuals already have many means of "neuroenhancing" their offspring (or themselves), via private schools, tutors, enriching after-school activities, personal assistants, and the like. The playing field is certainly *not* level. As tempting as it is to believe that pharmaceutical neuroenhancers could be a panacea in terms of increased productivity, the dangers are grave. Until we know far more about the long-term neural effects of providing stimulants across a wide range of the population, far beyond the documented, safe benefits for individuals with ADHD who are carefully monitored, our position is necessarily conservative.

In March of 2013, American College of Neurology (ACN) issued a clear statement to the effect that stimulants should *not* be prescribed to individuals without diagnosable ADHD to enhance test performance. This esteemed group pointed out that the potential for adverse effects is high, emphasizing that medications should be reserved for diagnosed individuals. Unlike the publicized calls for neuroenhancement a few years before, there is a growing a backlash against illegal stimulant use, regarding the addiction potential it unleashes and the ethical concerns it raises.[35] Medicines may be the rage for sexual enhancement or body building, but with respect to ADHD, we follow the lead of the ACN in urging high levels of scrutiny regarding clinical evaluations as well as the prescribing of stimulants only to those with documented diagnoses.

In many respects, the correct analogy is not medications to enhance sexual performance or body building but opioid pain medicines, like Oxycontin. On the one hand, the current professional view is that medical practice has for too long ignored the need to treat chronic pain humanely—and that a range of medications, including opioids, are essential to prevent needless suffering, from pain due to back injuries all the way to severe ramifications from cancer. On the other hand, the long-term use of opioids, which can lead to abuse, dependence, and widespread diversion, is a medical and societal problem of huge proportions. Antidotes to opioid abuse are the consideration of nonpharmacological means of treatment of pain whenever possible, attention to the careful diagnosis of chronic pain, and rigorous monitoring of prescriptions when they are in fact given.[36] Likewise, when it comes to stimulant treatment of ADHD, we completely concur.

# What a Difference a State Makes: How Educational Policy Determines Diagnosis and Treatment

## Jessie: "A New Home"

*Relocated from Los Angeles to the Research Triangle of North Carolina because of high-tech job offers for both mom and dad, the Jones family was stunned. Their 12-year-old son Jessie had not been exactly a straight-A student out West but had held it together each school year. Now, a couple of months into seventh grade, they read a report by a school psychologist in Raleigh, essentially diagnosing him with ADHD. "With the demands of multiple classes each day, he can't maintain adequate focus," the report stated. "Further testing is needed to determine the presence of underlying processing deficits. The behavioral profile and a class observation reveal evidence for an attention deficit."*

*The parents reflected on their experiences at the beginning of the school year, when they began to suspect that nearly every other boy in middle school had received an ADHD diagnosis—with most of these kids taking (or at least prescribed) stimulants. Whether Caucasian or, like Jessie, African American, it didn't seem to matter: The diagnosis was widespread. What kind of a world had they entered?*

*Had Jessie—kind, athletic, and yes, maybe a little scattered—changed after the cross-country move? Or was the family witnessing a regional phenomenon, where any kid (especially a boy) who doesn't perform up to ultra-high academic and behavioral standards must have some kind of diagnosis related to attention or learning problems?*

*Before pursuing further evaluation at the school, they talked with family members and a local counselor. How thorough had the school's evaluation been? What were the standards for diagnosis? Most important, should they just go along with the report, or fight it?*

We have highlighted throughout these pages that ADHD ignites high levels of passion and conflict. The diagnosis is often viewed as a modern-day excuse for social problems, a reflection of society's intolerance of children's natural spontaneity, or the product of poor parenting, inferior schools, or both. Medication raises core issues about the dangers of pills for young minds, parental values related to behavioral control, and the utter importance of education and achievement in our society. Especially in light of the increasing diversion of medications for individuals without a diagnosis, it is little wonder that the area remains wrapped in name-calling, conspiracy theories, and arguments about human rights.

The vast geographic differences across the United States in rates of ADHD diagnosis and rates of medication treatment, first highlighted in the Introduction, create a real puzzle. In the 2007 National Survey of Children's Health (NSCH), the overall rate of ADHD for children and adolescents aged 4 to 17 was 9.5% (for a diagnosis made at any point in the youth's life), a clear increase from just 4 years earlier. Figure 5–1 shows the state-by-state rates of ADHD diagnoses from the 2007 survey, revealing that Southern states (and a few in the near Midwest) had the highest rates, especially compared to the Far West.[1]

Medication rates were also highly discrepant. The NSCH asked parents whether their currently diagnosed child was taking medication

**Diagnostic Prevalence:**

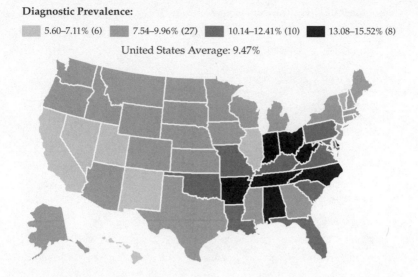

Source: 2007 NSCH, Children Aged 4-17

FIGURE 5–1  Rates of ADHD Diagnoses (Ever Diagnosed) for Youth Aged 4–17 in 2007, by State.

for ADHD. Across the nation, two in three children diagnosed with ADHD were taking medication, signaling a large increase from previous decades (this overall rate climbed slightly by 2011–2012 to just under 70%). Figure 5–2 shows that the South again had the highest rates of medication use, but now joined by states in the Midwest and Plains regions, as well as New England. In contrast, the West again had low or very low rates, revealing considerable regional differences.[2]

Comprehending this major variation within the United States may help us understand the broad forces at play related to this disorder. It should provide insights as to why America continues to lead the world in the diagnosis and treatment of ADHD, and how geography, culture, and school policy are linked in determining who gets diagnosed and medicated.

## A Tale of Two States

To provide a point of contrast, we focus on two states at the extremes of the geographic and numerical spectrum: North Carolina and

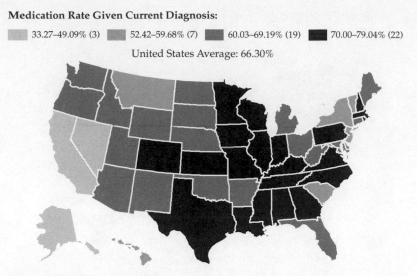

**Medication Rate Given Current Diagnosis:**

  33.27–49.09% (3)    52.42–59.68% (7)    60.03–69.19% (19)    70.00–79.04% (22)

United States Average: 66.30%

Source: 2007 NSCH, Children Aged 4-17

FIGURE 5–2  Rates of ADHD Medication for Currently Diagnosed Youth
Aged 4–17 in 2007, by State.

California. This isn't the only contrast we might have made; we could
have chosen Arkansas (with even higher rates than North Carolina's
by 2011–2012) and Nevada. A comparison of these two states allows
us to drill down and try to understand mechanisms underlying
such extremes. In the 2007 NSCH, for youth aged 4 to 17, North
Carolina had a rate of ADHD diagnosis that was 15.5%; California's
rate was just over 6%. Furthermore, North Carolina had a medication rate (for those with a current diagnosis) of 74.4%, in contrast to
California's rate of 49%.

Think about it for a moment. By living in North Carolina instead
of California, the chances that a child would be diagnosed with
ADHD were two and a half times higher. For boys in North Carolina
aged 9 and over, the probability of an ADHD diagnosis in 2007 was
between 25 and 30%—a startling rate of one in four to one in three.
Furthermore, the probability of receiving medication was 50%
higher in North Carolina than in California.

Substantial variation in the rates of diagnosis (and especially
treatment) of many diseases is not new. Indeed, "small-area variation" is a hot topic in medicine and public health, having spawned
a cottage industry of detective work of figuring out the underlying

reasons. The health policy guru John Wennberg spurred this area of inquiry several decades ago by showing that rates of many medical procedures vary enormously across and within states and nations. Such variations were unaccounted for by accumulated scientific evidence regarding their medical necessity or outcomes of the treatments. Instead, local medical "culture" and payment policies were often highly relevant.[3]

For example, within a single New England state, rates of hysterectomies for women ranged from 20 to 70%, linked largely to local physician practices or health care services. Regarding children's tonsillectomies, rates varied from under 8% to nearly 75%, often in districts or regions right next to each other. Such dramatic variation, which also exists in countries besides the United States, does *not* reflect different degrees of scientific or medical knowledge, or key differences in the makeup of patient populations in different regions. Rather, it appears to be a function of what Wennberg terms "practice style" factors, including physician beliefs and preferences as well as profitability of the treatment. Local medical culture, regional differences by which treatments are authorized, and the supply of providers are all likely to play roles.[4]

It is important to recall that ADHD in children and adolescents is, in many respects, a functional impairment linked to academic performance and classroom behavior. Children tend to be diagnosed after they have entered the school setting, with low school grades or test scores a major trigger for referral. ADHD often results from a lack of "fit" between the school setting and expectations on the one hand, and behavior and learning styles on the other.[5] Beyond medical practice-style effects, school-related influences will be a key consideration in our own sleuthing into the varying rates of ADHD diagnosis and treatment.

Overall, there are four major contenders as potential explanatory factors:

(1) Different states may have different mixtures of kids (e.g., boys versus girls; different racial and ethnic compositions) or different family income levels. In our examination, we must therefore consider racial, ethnic, socioeconomic, and gender differences between North Carolina and California to see if

they are responsible for the discrepant rates of diagnosis and treatment.

(2) Differences may be related more to patterns of health care policies and providers, including the training of doctors, health care reimbursements, or other practice-style effects.

(3) An essential factor could be cultural values, including standards for behavior linked to a region's historical ways of understanding how youth should comport themselves or achieve academically.

(4) Differences between school settings and school practices across states—for example, regarding test scores or special education—could also be relevant. In fact, over the past 30 years, school-wide and district-wide testing has become a huge issue, as state legislatures have made it their business to keep a close eye on test scores. A growing number of states have also passed laws regulating whether school personnel can even talk with families about ADHD and medication, as part of a backlash against ever-growing rates of diagnosis and treatment.

We take up each candidate factor in turn.

## Demographics: Who Lives in a Particular State?

Table 5–1 shows the demographics of California and North Carolina and how they differ on key factors beyond rates of ADHD diagnosis and medication. First, in 2007, girls received ADHD diagnoses a little over 1.5 times as frequently in North Carolina than in California, but boys were over three times more likely to be diagnosed in North Carolina. Yet boys and girls were nearly evenly distributed in each state, so the reason for the higher rates in North Carolina was *not* simply that North Carolina had a higher share of boys.

In terms of diversity, California was (and still is) the more ethnically diverse state: the 2007 child and adolescent population there was under 30% Caucasian compared to almost 60% Caucasian in North Carolina. North Carolina had almost four times the rate of African Americans, but California had five times the rate of Hispanics. We know that rates of ADHD diagnosis among Hispanics have

TABLE 5–1 Comparisons of North Carolina and California, 2007

| Statistic | North Carolina | California |
|---|---|---|
| **ADHD** | | |
| Diagnostic prevalence | 16% | 6% |
| Medication rate, given current diagnosis | 74% | 49% |
| **Racial/Ethnic Demographics** | | |
| White | 59% | 29% |
| African American | 26% | 7% |
| Hispanic | 9% | 49% |
| Other | 6% | 15% |
| | 100% | 100% |
| **Health Care Providers** | | |
| Pediatricians per 10,000 children | 7.0 | 7.6 |
| Family and general practitioners per 10,000 persons | 3.1 | 2.9 |
| Child psychiatrists per 10,000 children | 1.0 | 0.9 |

traditionally been well below those in other ethnic groups.[6] Thus, the statewide diagnostic and treatment differences could relate primarily to ethnicity.

In data analyses performed explicitly for this book, our team used methods from epidemiology to calculate an "adjusted" rate of diagnosis in each state, effectively equalizing (and thus neutralizing) demographic differences across the states in terms of age, gender, race, ethnicity, family structure, number of children, and household income. When we made this adjustment, the large difference between North Carolina and California in terms of ADHD diagnosis was reduced somewhat, from a ratio of 2.5 to 1 to a bit under 2 to 1. That is, some part of the divergence was explained—largely because of California's greater Hispanic population—but North Carolina's rate was still substantially higher.[7] We note that rates of ADHD diagnosis (and treatment) are rising rapidly among Hispanics. Thus, it is not surprising that rates of ADHD diagnosis between 2007 and 2011–2012 rose from 6.1 to 7.3% in California.[8] Still, there has to be something beyond demographics and ethnicity at work here.

## Health Care Factors

Health care variables, such as insurance coverage or physician practice style, are the factors that appear to drive much of the small-area variation in other aspects of medicine, such as rates of hysterectomies or tonsillectomies. We know that certain doctors can be hugely influential regarding ADHD diagnosis and treatment. For example, back in the 1990s in the state of Michigan, a handful of doctors with ADHD specialties diagnosed and medicated vast numbers of children.[9] In other words, a few doctors may have determined much in the way of treatment practices. We know, too, that the concentration of medical providers within a given *county* is linked to rates of ADHD medication use. National studies have shown that medication rates are positively associated with the number of physicians per capita in a county.[10]

Yet the number of medical professionals per county was similar in North Carolina and California in 2007 (see Table 5–1), ruling this out as a relevant factor. Still, *the way* in which doctors perform evaluations and dispense treatment may make a difference. In other words, Wennberg's "practice style" factors could be relevant. Our team statistically examined the rates of diagnosis and medication for those children with private insurance versus those with Medicaid coverage (i.e., children whose families are below or near the poverty line). Several decades ago, ADHD was diagnosed and treated mainly in middle-class or upper-middle-class children. But by 2007 rates of ADHD diagnosis and medication treatment were essentially equal between youth with private insurance and those with public insurance. In our analysis of rates of ADHD diagnosis in North Carolina and California, the insurance status of youth in North Carolina and California—that is, rates of uninsured versus private insurance versus public insurance—was not greatly different.[11]

Still, a publicly insured youth in North Carolina had an almost four-fold higher chance of being diagnosed with ADHD compared to a publicly insured counterpart in California. The practice styles of physicians who see low-income, publicly insured youth might well differ between the states. Yet we could uncover no "smoking gun" when we questioned health care leaders in the two states about the types of assessment tools and scales used, the types of training provided, or other potential differences in assessment or treatment procedures. For example, each state has major departments of pediatrics and psychiatry in top medical centers in which evidence-based assessment and treatment procedures are taught (though not, we believe, often followed in routine practice).

In addition, the data in Table 5–1 reveal few differences between California and North Carolina in terms of numbers of pediatricians, family doctors, general practitioners, or psychiatrists. Thus, medical practices appear not to be the key issue, and we must continue our search for relevant influences.

## Cultural Values

It is not hard to come up with depictions of different cultural values across states and regions in the United States. For example, the South is still noted for a "culture of honor," whereas the West may still hold to "rugged individualism."[12] Yet such values may be more stereotypic than real at this point in history, given the huge mobility of populations in recent decades and the increasing homogenization of cultural values in postmodern America. Statewide differences do exist: California is a prototypic "blue state" while North Carolina is "red" (despite the closeness of the Presidential vote in North Carolina in 2008 and 2012). At the same time, urban areas in both states are far more liberal than rural areas, and it may be such local cultures that are salient. In other words, the culture of the Research Triangle in North Carolina is probably similar in many respects to that of California's Silicon Valley, and small towns may be more similar than different across the states. In sum, communities and subcultures with clearly distinct values and cultural practices may matter for small-area variation, but we could not specify potential *statewide* differences in culture that made a difference in rates of ADHD diagnosis or medication.

In addition, if culture *does* play a role across states, we would assume that relevant cultural values would persist, at least over the period of a single decade. But the NSCH surveys reveal that between 2003 and 2007, rates of ADHD diagnosis rose in North Carolina by 63%—versus only 16% in California.[13] It is hard to imagine that statewide cultures could shift radically enough within a 4-year time interval to predict such major differences in rates of ADHD diagnoses.

We hasten to point out that cultural values and norms are clearly important for understanding people's beliefs about the nature of mental disorders, their responses to receiving a psychiatric diagnosis, and their acceptance of (and willingness to stay involved in) treatment. Clinicians must be aware of underlying beliefs in their clientele. Indeed, certain subcultures may question whether Western conceptions of a medical model are good explanations of personal pain, behavioral disturbance, or both.[14] Yet it is hard to imagine that such cultural beliefs and practices could explain the major state differences we have been discussing here.

Our fourth factor that may explain these differences pertains to schools and statewide policies surrounding education. Here, we get somewhere fast. Although complex, the information presented next is quite revealing, pointing to the importance of education, educational philosophies, and educational policies related to ADHD. The material merits a new section.

## Schools and School Policies Matter

How have schools responded to increasing pressures for producing higher achieving students? In the 1980s and earlier, school reform was largely "input focused." That is, the belief was that schools would do better if their budgets were increased, if student–teacher ratios were lowered, if more science was integrated into the curriculum, or even if the school day or school year was lengthened. The huge literature on this topic is contentious, with arguments both for and against the ultimate effects of such policies.

More recently, the educational focus has moved to measuring and incentivizing output. Graduation rates and test scores are the performance measures, and incentives to schools to lift such measures directly have become a national priority.[15] Recent presidents have brought output-based educational reform to center stage. Notably, President George W. Bush signed the No Child Left Behind Act of 2001, which provided incentives to encourage schools and teachers to improve educational quality. President Barack Obama's "Race to the Top" has continued this trend but with a different emphasis, including major incentives for states showing innovation in producing positive academic outcomes.[16]

But certain states began the process even earlier. Nearly three decades ago the United States entered the era of school accountability, meaning that explicit standards and assessment measures for performance became a priority. Such accountability measures have included public ratings of schools and teachers, financial rewards for enhanced performance, and sanctions for lack of gains. Under such legislation, schools have been increasingly made to compete with one another for funding.[17]

Regarding this trend, we wondered specifically whether states' adoption of such consequential accountability statutes, or the mandating of high school exit exams—which place a premium on mastery of certain content prior to graduation—would be linked to rates of diagnosing ADHD. Our reasoning was as follows: it is well known that kids with ADHD perform poorly in school, and their behavior can markedly affect the classroom (see Chapter 2). Students with ADHD pose a real problem for teachers in classroom climate, the potential for disruptive behavior, the compromised learning of classmates, and the entire class's test scores. Indeed, our research team demonstrated that the "clustering" of children with ADHD in a single school is associated with the school's lowered reading performance, providing an example of "school composition effects."[18]

Recall that a comprehensive federal special-education law was first passed in 1975. When it was reauthorized in 1991 as the Individuals with Disabilities Education Act (IDEA), ADHD was included for the first time as a specific category of disability that could allow special educational accommodations or services. Because rates of diagnosis of ADHD rose dramatically across the United States throughout that decade, it certainly appears that educational policy matters. In other words, labels that produce mandated services tend to get used. At the same time, battles between families and school districts over accommodations can be fierce. Box 5–1 provides an example.

More generally—and well beyond ADHD and special education—a number of states began to push public schools to improve their performance in the 1980s and 1990s. Texas and North Carolina were among the first states to implement school accountability laws, whereby schools were sanctioned for not meeting achievement-related targets and were rewarded for exceeding them. By 2001, 30 states had implemented some version of these statutes, which are named (somewhat awkwardly) "consequential accountability" laws, because of the

BOX 5–1  **The Battle over Accommodations**

Those who know of families of children or adolescents engaged in battles with school districts over accommodations for special needs have a sense of how contentious such battles can be. A Tennessee case made headlines in 2009, revealing how high the stakes can get.

Specifically, Charles Kildgore, who had been diagnosed with ADHD prior to seventh grade, was denied IDEA-related special services in the Williamson County school district. A plan was implemented under another federal statute, Section 504 of the Rehabilitation Act of 1973, in which he received extra time on assignments as well as organizational assistance.

Still, the family pressed for stronger accommodations and things subsequently got complicated. Kildgore was implicated in a fight on school grounds. The county district issued punitive sanctions against him, claiming that his ADHD-related disability was unrelated to this aggression. In turn, his family sued, claiming his ADHD was, in fact, to blame for the fight.

Ultimately, the courts decided that Kildgore was eligible for IDEA-related services related to his attention deficits and that the fight in question must be expunged from his disciplinary record. Moreover, the district was held liable to cover nearly $137,000 of the family's legal fees in the lengthy court battles that had ensued. Along with its own fees, the overall legal costs to the district—already strapped for cash—totaled over a quarter of a million dollars.[19]

consequences to districts if scores do not improve. By 2002–2003, the federal No Child Left Behind Act made the movement national.

Furthermore, other states had implemented high school exit-exam statutes, whereby graduating seniors had to have a certain level of academic proficiency to obtain a diploma. We examine both types of laws next.

What are the implications for youth with ADHD? The intriguing answer is that such laws provide a real incentive to have children diagnosed and treated. Accountability encourages schools to place children with ADHD in special education classes for two reasons: (1) such children are afforded more services, which might raise their test scores; and (2) in at least some areas, they do not have to be "counted" in the district's overall test score average. That is, an ADHD diagnosis and resultant special education placement might exempt a low-achieving youth from lowering the district's overall achievement ranking. At the same time, high school exit exams place a premium on adequate test scores for all graduating seniors.[20]

In extensive data analysis of these patterns, our team recorded, for each state, precisely when a consequential accountability law or exit exam law was passed. For states without such laws, the implementation of No Child Left Behind (NCLB) in 2002–2003 placed all states in the era of consequential accountability. We then calculated the number of years these state laws had been in effect. Adjusting for all other relevant state-by-state differences, we found the following.

The focus was 2003 to 2007, the interval for the first two waves of the NSCH. Children aged 8 to 13, living in low-income homes and in states without previous consequential accountability laws, went from a 10.0% to a 15.3% rate of ADHD diagnosis once NCLB started. This is a huge rise of 53%. Children from those states living in middle-class or upper-class homes, however, went from 8.1% to 8.4%, a negligible rise of 4%. We did not find such a difference, by income, in those states with prior consequential accountability laws. Although the result dissipated by 2011, once NCLB had been replaced by the Race to the Top, this dramatic finding occurred, we believe, because NCLB and its sanctions targeted low-income public schools, particularly those receiving Title I funds.[21]

Intriguingly, the geographic pattern of consequential accountability laws and high-school exit-exam laws is that they cluster in the South (see Table 5-2). Indeed, 15 of the 17 states in the South had consequential accountability laws in place prior to NCLB, a far higher rate than for any other region. Exit-exam laws also predominate in the South, but we did not find a linkage between their passage and increased rates of ADHD diagnosis.[22]

We did not, of course, randomly assign states to consequential accountability laws or NCLB. Still, the federal adoption of NCLB in 2003, which made consequential accountability the law of the land, was associated with a dramatic increase in ADHD diagnoses for low-income youth in states that had not previously passed such

TABLE 5–2 ADHD-Related Laws, by Region

| Region | Number of States | Consequential Accountability before NCLB* | High School Exit Exam | Psychotropic Medication Law |
|---|---|---|---|---|
| Northeast | 9 | 5 | 4 | 2 |
| Midwest | 12 | 5 | 3 | 2 |
| South | 17 | 15 | 13 | 5 |
| West | 13 | 5 | 8 | 5 |
| United States | 51 | 30 | 28 | 14 |

*NCLB = No Child Left Behind. 51 states are listed because of the inclusion of Washington, DC.

legislation. Because a strong relation exists between school-policy legislation and state-by-state differences, we believe that, in relation to ADHD, the push for performance matters.

## Other Laws Regarding Schools and ADHD

Increasing medication rates for youth with ADHD in the 1990s were met by an outcry from certain parents and antimedication advocates. Sheila Matthews, a mother in Connecticut in 2001, refused to medicate her first-grade son, even though the school psychologist diagnosed him with ADHD and suggested Ritalin. She thought the school was at fault for her son's behavior, claiming that he was bright and a little overactive. After intensive lobbying, her voice and the voice of other parents carried the day. Connecticut subsequently passed a law that prohibited schools from even suggesting that parents medicate their children. Other states soon followed. Fourteen states have now passed laws that limit the school's role in suggesting ADHD or that strengthen parental rights in regard to refusing to medicate their child.

The resulting "psychotropic medication laws" can be grouped into three categories: some laws specifically prohibit schools from recommending medication, some prohibit the requirement that children take psychotropic drugs as a condition of enrollment, and still others stipulate that parents' refusal to medicate their children cannot be considered neglect in and of itself. Some states have laws dealing with one of these guidelines, some with two, and some with all three.

The impact of such legislation on the diagnosis and treatment of ADHD is a difficult question to address, as it is hard to tell whether high rates of ADHD diagnosis preceded passage of these kinds of laws, or whether the laws had subsequent impact on ADHD diagnosis or treatment. Yet our team examined the period between 2003 and 2011. In states that had enacted psychotropic medication laws, the rate of increase of ADHD diagnosis, for 6 to 9 year olds, was between one-half and one percentage point lower, per year the law had been in place, than it was in states without such legislation. In terms of the geographic distribution of such legislation, there is no clustering in the South, as there was for consequential accountability and high school exit exam laws. Of the four states in the South with such legislation, North Carolina is not among them.[23]

Overall, consequential accountability legislation had an unintended effect: it was associated with increases in the diagnostic prevalence of ADHD. On the other hand, psychotropic medication laws were linked with a measurable impact, namely a decrease in ADHD's rise in diagnosis, subsequent to their passage. Policy matters, and the main venue for ADHD-related policy is schools, where the push for performance is ever stronger.

# The Cost of ADHD: It's the Economy, Stupid

## Frank: "Will It Always Be This Way?"

*At 37, Frank wonders where he's headed. On his fourth job of the past decade, from IT to advertising, consulting, and blogging, he's finding it hard to make ends meet. "You're super smart," his employers have said, "but you can't cut other people off the way you do." Frank is perennially late for meetings. Once a business session starts, ideas spill into his mind so quickly that clients wonder whether Frank is listening.*

*Back in grade school, Frank moved faster than everyone else. Teachers branded him a mild troublemaker because of his sarcastic tone and penchant for disrupting class. His test scores were inconsistent.*

*Frank was diagnosed with ADHD in fifth grade. Yet his parents—heading through life at the same erratic pace as Frank—never bothered to refill his first prescription for Ritalin, even though his grades picked up dramatically during the few months he took it. They wondered whether the medicine would stifle his creativity.*

*Frank was reasonably popular in high school but never fit in with any particular crowd. He was pressured, always talking about how he would do things. He'd do almost anything on a dare, driving all night just to meet someone new or returning a bunch of clothes he had bought because someone said they didn't look perfect on him. In college, Frank could work at his own pace but always ended up with a jumble of course syllabi, study guides, and half-read books strewn across his desk. He graduated after 6 1/2 years, with several changes of his major.*

*Frank has had a number of relationships and was married during his late 20s for under a year. His partners find him initially charming, but his temper flares when anyone asks why he never seems to be living up to his potential. Frank has been in several car accidents, forgetting to signal before lane changes or to figure out his destination ahead of time. He is carrying just under the limit of "points" for speeding and reckless operation. He likes alcohol and how it makes him feel—finally relaxed for a few minutes—but has trouble stopping after two or three drinks. At his last job he worked 65 hours per week to get things done but remained unproductive and unfocused.*

*He has always thought that if only the world could keep pace with him, or his ex-wife had appreciated his "spark," he'd be okay. He recently ran into a former workmate he liked and respected. Hoping that Frank wouldn't get upset, the guy noted that his son had been diagnosed with ADHD and that the symptom list reminded him of Frank.*

*Initially dismissive, Frank later checked out some Web sites and decided that he'd been protesting too much when he wrote off ADHD as a label for losers. At a self-help meeting, he learned that many people were in the same boat: smart and energetic but spinning in circles. Could he make up for lost time with treatment?*

Frank is one of the nine million American adults who are estimated to have ADHD, with only a minority of such adults having actually been diagnosed or treated. A few decades ago, the established view was that ADHD vanishes by puberty. This perspective has changed radically, however, as adults are now the fastest growing segment of the population in terms of medication treatment. Although the most visible symptoms of ADHD (i.e., floridly hyperactive behaviors) may fade by late adolescence, inattention and impulse-control problems typically persist into adulthood, portending negative consequences of major proportions.[1]

Long-term costs to society with respect to ADHD are astronomical. As highlighted at the end of Chapter 1, for children and adolescents these annual "indirect" costs approximate $100 billion, over and above the immediate costs of treatment per se. Most of this amount is related to educational consequences, such as school-related special services, along with the burden of delinquency and substance abuse as children become adolescents. For adults, the parallel price tag of indirect costs is even higher, up to $200 billion annually. These costs are linked chiefly to unemployment, underemployment, and lost productivity in the workplace.[2] If the criminal outcomes that pertain to some individuals with ADHD were included, this total would certainly be higher.

Controlled studies of stimulants for adults have shown that they yield increased attention, reduced impulsivity, decreased risk for accidents, and improved workplace and relationship performance. Intriguingly, crime rates are reduced while adults with ADHD are actively medicated.[3] Moreover, cognitive-behavior therapy, in which adults learn to cope with triggers of ADHD-related behaviors and manage their emotions and impulses, has shown real success in clinical trials.[4]

We now take on the crucial issue of whether these evidence-based treatments, delivered with quality by professionals and school personnel, could improve personal and family outcomes for youth with ADHD *and* the overall performance of our workforce. That is, viable treatment might yield greater lifetime incomes by keeping youth invested in school and preventing eventual work-related impairments. It might reduce the nation's economic burden of ADHD and lift the overall economy.

We begin with information on the skyrocketing costs of treating ADHD. We focus on medication, the costs of which are measurable in multiple billions of dollars. Once we have established these costs, separately for youth and adults, we can examine whether such treatments might at least partially offset the major downstream, indirect costs linked to ADHD. In this chapter, it's all about the economy.

## Ever-Increasing Cost Escalation

The most precise estimates of treatment costs involve contrasting expenditures related to people with ADHD to those without the condition—in other words, "incremental costs." Information from the most recent survey of national medical expenses is extremely helpful in this regard, whereby the medical costs for people with an ADHD diagnosis are contrasted to costs for people without it. The figures below are conservative, because they assume costs only for youth or adults who have actually been *diagnosed* with ADHD (there may be less visible medical costs for individuals with the symptoms who have not yet received a diagnosis). We begin with youth and then move to adults; the calculations behind these statements are found in the notes.

## Children and Adolescents

In 2008, the cost of treating children aged 4 to 17 with ADHD was $12.6 billion, with a third of that figure being for medication. The annual rate of increase for such expenses from 2000 through 2008, adjusting for inflation, was 9.8% (see Table 6–1). During that time period the nation's overall health spending increased 4.3% annually, adjusted for inflation, so it is clear that ADHD-related treatment expenditures went up at a rate more than double the national average.[5] In short, ADHD treatment costs are escalating. Applying this annual rate of increase of 9.8%, treatment spending for ADHD would amount to $20 billion by 2013.[6]

It is important to note that for the poorest children in the nation (not shown in Table 6–2), treatment costs were 3.4 times higher for ADHD than for non-ADHD youth, with spending on medication being 8.6 times higher. Expansion of Medicaid coverage for children at or near the poverty level during the early 1990s (and beyond) has enabled them to be treated at similar rates to those of children whose families have greater resources. Impoverished children often have other medical conditions as well, yielding greater treatment expenses.

Thus, two main forces are driving the rates of increase of child and adolescent treatment: (1) the sheer numbers of youth receiving services, which are rising; and (2) the per-child costs of providing ADHD-related treatment, which are increasing as well.[7]

TABLE 6–1  ADHD Use Prevalence and Expenditures for Youth Aged 4–17, 2000–2008*

| Variable | Annualized Change 2000–2008 | 2000 | 2001 | 2002 | 2003 | 2004 | 2005 | 2006 | 2007 | 2008 |
|---|---|---|---|---|---|---|---|---|---|---|
| Number of users of ADHD treatments (millions) | 6.0% | 2.4 | 2.6 | 2.4 | 2.6 | 2.7 | 2.7 | 2.7 | 3.1 | 3.9 |
| Use prevalence† | 6.0% | 4.2% | 4.5% | 4.1% | 4.5% | 4.7% | 4.6% | 4.7% | 5.4% | 6.7% |
| Expenditures (millions in 2008 dollars) | 9.8% | $5,953 | $5,123 | $5,594 | $7,095 | $6,444 | $7,869 | $8,441 | $9,461 | $12,578 |
| Medication expenditures (millions in 2008 dollars) | 14.0% | $1,492 | $1,881 | $1,889 | $2,883 | $2,873 | $3,059 | $3,446 | $3,507 | $4,252 |

*Source: Medical Expenditure Panel Survey.
†"Use prevalence" in row 2 refers to the number of treated youth with ADHD divided by the total number of youth in the United States.

TABLE 6–2 ADHD Use Prevalence and Expenditures for Adults Aged 18+, 2000–2008*

| Variable | Annualized Change 2000–2008 | 2000–2002 | 2003–2005 | 2006–2008 |
|---|---|---|---|---|
| Number of users of ADHD treatments (millions) | 13.1% | 0.6 | 1.3 | 1.7 |
| Use prevalence† | 12.0% | 0.3% | 0.6% | 0.7% |
| Expenditures (millions in 2008 dollars) | 15.7% | $3,109 | $7,431 | $9,954 |
| Medication expenditures (millions in 2008 dollars) | 19.7% | $818 | $2,528 | $3,456 |

*Source: Medical Expenditure Panel Survey.
†"Use prevalence" in row 2 refers to the number of treated adults with ADHD divided by the total number of adults in the United States.

## Adults

Relevant information on adult treatment costs related to ADHD is presented in Table 6–2. Because of the smaller numbers of adults with ADHD included in these data, we have grouped the columns into annual figures within 3-year periods rather than 1-year periods. First, only one in six adults with ADHD is actually getting treatment, a far lower rate than the nearly 70% rate for youth. Second, for the period from 2006 to 2008, treatment costs were just under $10 billion annually for adults. But the rate of increase for adult treatment costs is a remarkable 15.7% per year, meaning that costs would amount to over $20 billion annually by 2013.[8]

We also note an intriguing pattern related to sex differences for adults. Most treatments for children and adolescents go to boys, who are diagnosed two to three times more often than girls. Yet in adulthood there are now *more* medication prescriptions for women with ADHD than for men. Women appear to be accounting for the bulk of the increases in rates of adult treatment.[9]

Just as for children and adolescents, more and more adults are being treated each year, even though the vast majority of adults with ADHD are still not receiving treatment. The rate of increase of treatment costs for adults is rising quite rapidly. For adults as well as for youth, the ADHD treatment-cost spiral is considerable, indeed.

## Benefits of the Spending

The question now moves to whether this treatment-related spending is worth it. In human terms, we can certainly justify treating people with ADHD as a means of helping not only the individuals in question but also their families, colleagues, and friends. Yet because the economy is essential to our collective well-being, we take an economic perspective. Specifically, we ask whether accurate diagnosis of ADHD and appropriate treatment of those diagnosed could boost our nation's productivity and thereby reduce the huge indirect costs of ADHD: $100 billion annually for youth and $200 billion for adults (see Chapter 1).

We highlight immediately that treatment costs for ADHD would go up appreciably if two conditions were met. First, not everyone is receiving treatment. For children and adolescents, about 30% appear to be unmedicated; but for adults, over 80% appear to be receiving no treatment.[10] Thus, if a comparable proportion of adults received medication, their treatment costs would increase dramatically. Second, a major theme we have emphasized throughout the book is that treatments in the community are far from ideal. Both medications and behavioral (or for adults, cognitive-behavioral) treatments can provide real benefits, but in much clinical practice, interventions are delivered suboptimally (see Chapter 3).[11] To provide responsive, intensive, evidence-based treatment, major investments in training professionals, enforcing practice guidelines, and implementing reimbursements for gold-standard care will be required. Quality services are bound to be far more expensive than current levels of care.

Second, it's a stretch to argue that providing even the best, evidence-based treatment will eliminate all of the major, long-term negative social and economic outcomes that are linked to ADHD. Neither behavioral treatments nor medications provide a cure even when performed optimally. In an intriguing cost-effectiveness analysis of the MTA Study's treatments, for uncomplicated kids with ADHD—that is, those with no comorbid conditions—well-delivered medications were beneficial and extremely cost-effective. For more complex cases with additional psychiatric issues (e.g., depression, aggressive behavior), far more costly behavioral and combined treatments showed the potential for providing long-term benefit that might justify their cost (i.e., preventing juvenile justice interventions and thereby reducing eventual indirect costs).[12]

Effective treatment of ADHD is a desirable state of affairs in and of itself. In other words, even if enhanced treatments did not offset, dollar-for-dollar, the long-term negative economic consequences of ADHD, there is still an obligation to reduce pain and suffering. Our nation spends huge sums of money on general health care to improve the lives of many individuals, even when, in some cases, actual health-related impacts on ultimate productivity may be low. It is well known that investments in enhanced health care for some populations (e.g., those with extremely severe mental illness) may not result in complete (or even partial) cost offset, even though there are important moral reasons to provide such investment.[13]

Still, regarding ADHD, the potential benefits of a renewed commitment to evidence-based treatments are enormous. If youth become engaged in school and obtain greater academic skills, lifting them from trajectories of delinquency or substance abuse, they may have greatly enhanced chances of employability. If adults are treated with optimal interventions, both jobs and relationships have a far stronger chance of staying intact. We contend that investing in viable, evidence-based treatments for ADHD is justified on clinical, moral, *and* economic grounds.

## Economics Matters

Those who analyze the success of the U.S. economy often come up with the same conclusion: our economic success depends on the quality of our labor force. Our nation has one of the best educated workforces in the world.[14] This is no accident: as a country, we believe in education and invest in it. At the same time, however, our academic test scores now lag behind those of many other nations. Thus, there is even more need to invest in our "human capital," a term used by Gary Becker in the book that helped earn him the Nobel Prize.[15] The human-capital concept is that investments in education and training can be thought of in the same way we value other forms of capital, such as investment in a machine. The machine's cost is balanced, across its lifetime, against the value of what it produces, addressing the question of whether the initial investment will ultimately pay off.

Investments in youth are largely educational in nature, which may ultimately be compensated by increases in their later earnings. In other words, the human-capital model posits that more learning equals more earning. Economic analyses show us how to quantify the investment returns in relation to the resources that societies allocate to education and training.[16] Specifically, going to college incurs costs: tuition, books, room and board, and the loss of potential wages while the individual is in school. Such costs must be weighed against the eventual increase in productivity engendered by education. The rate of return to education and training lies at the heart of the human-capital model. If the payoff is substantial, it is little wonder that families and students are willing to pay ever-steeper rates for higher education, with government-backed loans and subsidies for low-income families.

In terms of the economic benefits of education, Figure 6–1 presents information on average weekly earnings, across the past three

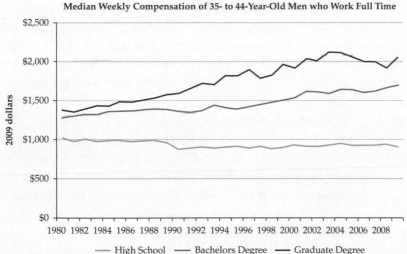

FIGURE 6–1 Economic Benefits of Different Levels of Education, 1980–2010.
Adapted from Levy, F., & Kochan, T. (2012). Addressing the problem of stagnant wages. *Comparative Economic Studies, 54*, 739–764, from *Comparative Economic Studies*, ISBN 08887233, with kind permission from Palgrave Macmillan.

decades, for individuals in the United States, grouped by their highest level of educational attainment. The graph clearly shows that back in 1980, people with a college degree earned about 30% more than those with a high school degree. Yet by 2010 this figure had risen steeply, to nearly 70% more. Note, too, that those with a graduate degree hardly earned more than those with a bachelor's degree at the start of the time period, but in the past decade, their earning differential had risen to about 40% more. (This "graduate school advantage" declined at the end of the last decade, coincident with the rapid economic downfall in 2008, but it has risen again recently.) In short, a college degree is worth a major amount in terms of earning potential, with a graduate degree providing further increments.[17]

Another slant on this issue was provided in an op-ed piece from September 2012 by Thomas Friedman in *The New York Times*. He noted that the unemployment rate in the United States for individuals with 4 years of college was 4.1%, with the comparable figures of 6.6% for those with 2 years of college, 8.8% for high school graduates, and 12.0% for high school dropouts. Clearly, greater employment rates and higher earnings are a function of higher levels of education.[18]

From this line of reasoning it seems clear that education improves productivity and wages. Yet the precise direction and magnitude of this association are sometimes difficult to assess. After all, more productive individuals are often the very ones who seek and obtain more education in the first place, a process known as "selection bias." In terms of ultimate benefits, we should therefore not attribute everything to schooling. Yet education at least indirectly influences labor outcomes, because it is used as a signal about an individual's productivity. When making a hiring decision, employers are not able to obtain all the information about a potential employee, yet the amount of education is often used as a proxy to predict subsequent productivity. In short, educational attainment has a clear, positive impact on labor-market outcomes.

All of these numbers and arguments confirm the increased emphasis on educational performance in recent years. At the federal level there was George Bush's No Child Left Behind, evidenced today by Barack Obama's emphasis on educational output via the Race to the Top program. We have already examined state laws intended to hold our educational system to performance standards such as test scores and graduation rates (Chapter 5). Also, the economic impact of improving the quality of teachers in grade schools is remarkable: improving teacher quality increases students' lifetime earnings. A high-quality teacher is associated with an increase in the lifetime income of a student by $400,000. Other estimates suggest that replacing a poor-quality teacher with an average teacher increases student earnings by over $250,000.[19]

In terms of evidence, math and reading scores on the National Assessment of Educational Progress (NAEP) were improved in states that introduced educational accountability systems, compared to states that did not.[20] A randomized experiment on class size in Tennessee showed that smaller class size was associated with improved test scores—an immediate gain of over a fifth of a standard deviation—which, in turn, were linked with higher lifetime earnings.[21]

Two rigorous studies of human capital and ADHD have been published. One used data from both Canada and the United States to obtain a large sample of 8,000 children. In this analysis, ADHD was clearly associated with lower math and reading scores and a higher probability of repeating a grade. Even small amounts of ADHD-related behaviors—below the threshold for an ADHD diagnosis yet still measurable—were linked with such academic consequences. Moreover, data from the United Kingdom have shown that ADHD (present at age 10) is associated with lower earnings at age 30, with stronger effects for females than for males.[22] The upshot is that viable treatment could yield major potential rewards for its eventual effects on income and productivity.

Along these lines, recall from the Introduction that children with ADHD are 10 to 14% less likely to be employed as adults than those without ADHD, their adult earnings are lowered by *one third*, and their likelihood of needing formal social assistance is upped by 15%. Such figures graphically reveal the major long-term economic consequences of ADHD, particularly in the workplace.[23]

Our arguments from Chapter 5 now come into play. The study of Scheffler's team showed that treatment with medication was associated with reading gains of a third of a school year, contrasted with unmediated peers. The comparable increase in mathematics scores was closer to a fifth of a school year. These are sizeable gains, on par with what might be found from reducing class size or improving teacher quality.[24] Other research (e.g., from Iceland) has produced parallel findings.[25] Not all studies show that ADHD medications are linked to improved scores; it takes time to translate treatment-related gains into sufficient progress to elevate reading and math performance. Moreover, intensive behavioral and educational treatments and responsive school curricula are essential for academic gains, particularly when combined with medication.[26]

The bottom line is that if academic gains are sustained (via combination treatments in particular) and if employability is thereby enhanced, a considerable amount of indirect costs can be offset. Yet a strict human-capital model may be incomplete. ADHD merits evidence-based intervention even if ultimate productivity is not always greatly enhanced, to reduce problem behavior, enhance the productivity of other students, and alleviate personal and family suffering. Society should bear the costs of identifying and treating ADHD to heal impaired relationships, reduce accidental injuries, and slow the development of crushing comorbidities (e.g., depression, self-harm, substance abuse), even without a direct benefit to the nation's overall economic prosperity. Economic arguments are nonetheless powerful adjuncts to such clinically based lines of reasoning.

## Education–Production Function

Let's return to our fundamental assumption, that learning actually does influence later earning. A landmark international investigation tested this crucial hypothesis, probing what is sometimes termed the "education–production function." Across 24 nations of the Organization of Economic Cooperation and Development (OECD), a positive association was found between mathematics, science, and reading achievement scores and the growth of the nation's economy, as indexed by gross domestic product (GDP). In sum, a better educated labor force was linked to the country's economic well-being.[27]

How much should society be willing to pay for ADHD-related intervention? "Getting it right" with viable ADHD treatments might prevent a lifetime of serious psychological and employment-related impairments. It will cost several times more than current expenditure levels to enact such systems of evidence-based care and reach previously untreated individuals, over and above the cost inflation now in place for the types of treatment we already provide. Yet the potential benefits for human capital are of major proportions with respect to productivity, wages, and reduced crime as well as reductions in pain and suffering.

## High School and College Accommodations

One index of the influence of ADHD on higher education—and the influence of higher education on ADHD—is the growing number of accommodations for students with a diagnosis. The 1991 reauthorization of the federal special education act (IDEA) led to ADHD's listing as an "other health impaired" diagnosis mandating special education services in public schools. Such accommodations and services range from low intensity (e.g., pull-outs for reading instruction a couple of times a week) to ultra-high intensity (e.g., separate school programs for highly disruptive youth).

In college, however, it is up to students to advocate for themselves. If the university, through its disability resource center, deems that a disability is present, then reasonable accommodations must be provided, even though students are still expected to learn from the same curriculum and master the same content. Common accommodations include priority registration; reduced course load; note takers and recording devices; extended time for testing (possibly including a small-group or individual room for exams) and extended deadlines for assignments; course substitutions; and tutoring, mentoring, or study skills training. Schools cannot charge extra fees for providing such accommodations.[28]

As shown in a major 2010 report highlighting the University of North Carolina, over a third of all accommodations on the campus were, by that year, related to ADHD or learning disabilities, double the number from 2002 and up eight-fold from the 1980s.[29] Whereas many applaud such accommodations, the report highlights lingering suspicion that the relevant requests come disproportionately from white, middle-class, male students—and that sympathetic clinicians will diagnose ADHD quickly to enable the student to obtain such accommodations. Another criticism pertains to the greatly discrepant standards across universities as to who may qualify, leading to unfairness.[30]

Students with disabilities can also appeal to the Educational Testing Service, which administers the Scholastic Aptitude Test (SAT) as well as professional-school entrance exams (e.g., Graduate Record Examination [GRE], Medical College Admission Test [MCAT], and Law School Admission Test [LSAT]). The benefit is extra time on these crucial placement tests. Requests for such accommodations are rising rapidly, with many such requests emanating from claims of ADHD. For these entrance-exam accommodations, a consistent national set of standards does exist, with clearly specified evaluations and tests needed to document the relevant disability.[31]

Under current interpretations of these statutes, schools or testing services cannot "flag" transcripts or test reports with information that the student has received an accommodation. Such notation would be tantamount to punishing, stigmatizing, or otherwise discounting the grades or scores. Yet many students just short of accommodation-level problems may well believe that *they* could have done better with extra time, too. A provocative, alternative view is that *any* student should be allowed reasonable accommodations, such as extra time, with the stipulation that all such events would receive explicit flagging on relevant transcripts.[32]

In short, with the increasing pressure for higher grades and higher test scores in the present-day climate, along with an ever-increasing ratio of applicants to admittees for college and graduate and professional schools, a serious run on accommodations is occurring. It is legitimate and legal for individuals with ADHD or a learning disorder to be granted extra test time, individual testing rooms, or other forms of aid. But the sharp rise in ADHD-related accommodations fuels suspicion that obtaining a quick ADHD diagnosis is a means of gaming the system. The entire phenomenon reveals the utter importance of achievement and productivity for the current era of increasing ADHD diagnoses.

We raise a more general question about our educational system. Perhaps students whose learning styles differ from the norm—including those with ADHD—might prosper in schools that did not place a premium on group learning in a classroom, listening to a lecture, or regurgitating material on standardized tests. Tailored learning objectives, individualized instruction, well-designed online learning, hands-on educational experiences, and other means of tailoring education to the needs of particular students could, from this perspective, reduce the impact of ADHD on academic performance. If this were the case, it is conceivable that medication, often used to aid learning success in rote environments, might be less needed. We return to these points in Chapter 10.[33]

Of course, such major educational reforms would incur substantial costs. Online education is currently spreading like wildfire at the postsecondary level.[34] Earlier in learners' lives, however, public school class sizes are going up, rather than down, in these economically stressed times. It is essential to consider the ways in which schooling could meet the needs of diverse students in the educational system, including those with ADHD.[35]

## Conclusion

If Jose's preschool ADHD (see Chapter 1) could be transformed into better behavioral control, enhanced learning, and improved peer relations, his life might take a different course. If Becky's symptoms and impairments (see Chapter 2) had been taken seriously when she was a girl, her huge impairments—including substance abuse, self-injury, and suicidal despair—might have been prevented. If Frank's ADHD (this chapter) had been recognized before his late 30s, his life might have been redirected and his round-robin employment history transformed. As professionals, scientists, clinicians, family members, and citizens, we must relinquish our own immature views about ADHD—plagued by myths and half-truths—if progress is to be made.

Multiplying these case vignettes by the multiple millions of individuals affected, the societal and economic savings are potentially staggering. Educating professionals in evidence-based treatment and enforcing the excellent standards that now exist are a major part of the equation. Such enhancement and reimbursement of quality intervention will, of necessity, increase treatment costs. Still, given the astronomical indirect expenses linked to ADHD across a lifetime, the ultimate savings to society and benefits to our economy could be of major proportion. Lost wages and low productivity will be less and less tolerated in our era of ever-increasing global competition. Investing in the evidence-based treatment of more than a tenth of our youth will provide clear benefit at personal, family-related, social, *and* economic levels. The potential gains in terms of both human capital and human potential clearly outweigh the costs.

# ADHD and the Media: What's Being Said and What's Being Sold?

ADHD IS WIDELY REPRESENTED IN THE MEDIA. Our first focus is on news coverage, which provides a baffling mix of informative reports and misleading information. A major part of our analysis is focused on articles and opinion pieces from America's most influential newspaper, which have sometimes played fast and loose with sound data and presented throwback views on ADHD that could hurt the cause of individuals and families with genuine diagnoses. Second, we examine pharmaceutical advertising, addressing how much of the continuing surge of ADHD diagnosis and medication use is driven by the promotion of pills. We probe whether direct-to-consumer advertising, which came of age in the late 1990s, is a good thing, reducing the stigma of mental disorders and allowing consumers to seek appropriate treatment, or if it is a far more nefarious means of creating unneeded markets.

## What Does the Public See and Hear?

To put it mildly, media coverage of ADHD is mixed. Many articles on the topic present one-shot research findings that are not replicated.[1] A sample from recent accounts in the media reveals how hard it is to understand the truth.

*The real cause of ADHD is...SpongeBob SquarePants!* In a 2011 investigation, young children were randomly assigned to watch 9 minutes of a SpongeBob episode, watch 9 minutes of a calm public television children's show, or spend 9 minutes drawing pictures. In the SpongeBob condition, the children's "executive functions"—those essential, high-level mental abilities involved in planning, regulating, and guiding behavior and learning—temporarily disappeared following the exposure to the media. The data are intriguing and important, but news coverage implicated fast-paced media and children's programming as the major cause of fragmented attention in everyone, particularly our youngest and most vulnerable children.[2] Readers could be forgiven for thinking the following: If only we could revert to an earlier time; if only everything weren't so frenzied; if only we could just shut down the overload of media confronting everyone these days—then perhaps what we now call ADHD would just vanish before our eyes.

*Hidden talent or hidden curse?* A decade ago, JetBlue CEO David Neeleman claimed that his long-standing ADHD was a gift spurring his far-ranging mind, which developed electronic ticketing and other innovations. Similarly, the founder of Kinko's, Paul Orfalea, contended that ADHD-fueled curiosity was central to his business acumen. Less well publicized, though, was Neeleman's termination in 2007 following a disastrous week of stranded planes and passengers. Relatedly, scientific articles—receiving little attention in the media—revealed that for highly gifted students, ADHD is not just a mislabel linked to boredom but a major impediment to academic success.[3] It is extremely difficult, in fact, to reconcile the publicized contention that ADHD is a "gift" with the findings that 25% or more of prison inmates have histories of ADHD, or that substance abuse, underemployment, and high rates of motor vehicle crashes are common outcomes.[4]

*Kindergarten at age 4?* "Nearly one million children in U.S. potentially misdiagnosed with ADHD," shouted the headlines in 2010. Kindergarten children who were the youngest for their grade—late 4 or early 5—had a 60% higher chance of receiving an ADHD diagnosis and medication than those entering in the middle of the age cluster. A 2012 report, based on a study of over 900,000 children in Canada, reached similar conclusions, with young kindergarteners being 39% more likely to be diagnosed with ADHD than classmates born just after the cutoff (for girls, the effect was even larger).[5] What went undiscussed, however, was the seriousness of true ADHD in young children—or the possibility that waiting a year to put boys in school might not alleviate their relative immaturity the following fall. The timing of the stories was intriguing, as the nation's leading group of pediatricians recommended in 2011 that diagnosing ADHD by age 4 is legitimate.[6] Readers of the kindergarten-diagnosis coverage might believe that there is no biological basis to ADHD whatsoever.

*Steroids of the mind, Viagra for the brain!* In June 2012, a provocative *New York Times* piece revealed rampant use of stimulants in exclusive high schools, as students described how easy it is to score pills for exam or term-paper preparations. In addition, professional athletes, banned from using steroids to enhance physical performance, could claim exemptions related to stimulant use—to help with concentration and focus—if they documented underlying ADHD.[7] Fewer pieces, however, have documented the clear successes of medication treatment for legitimate cases of ADHD. We would be the last to defend wanton abuse of stimulants, but most media coverage fails to present the benefits of accurate diagnosis and responsive treatment.[8]

*Medication and the heart.* On a searing day in Kentucky during the late summer of 2008, a 15-year-old sophomore collapsed during wind sprints as part of a rigorous, two-a-day high school football workout regimen. Exhausted, denied water, and with his temperature reaching 107 degrees, he died, causing a firestorm over the role of the team's training ideas and the long wait to call for medical attention. The boy, Max Gilpin, had been taking Adderall, a stimulant medication for ADHD. Major stories wondered out loud whether this drug accelerated his rise in body temperature, heart rate, and blood pressure, adding to his risk.[9] Only minor coverage discussed the fact that stimulant-related cardiovascular risks do not comprise a major health concern or that the U.S. Food and Drug Administration (FDA) decided once again not to issue related warnings on prescriptions.[10]

*Students faking ADHD symptoms to gain accommodation—or get high?* A 2011 study, with associated Internet coverage, reported that up to a quarter of college students completing ADHD questionnaires either exaggerated or outright faked their own symptoms in order to get academic accommodations or to get access to stimulant prescriptions.[11] The stories add doubt to the reality of adult ADHD, or to the perspective that many individuals are finally given a valid diagnosis that often persists well beyond childhood. Of course, if an abundance of students are gaming the system, the public needs to know. Yet the lingering impression is that adult ADHD is largely faked.

## Stigma and the Media

Before going any further, we need to pause to discuss the issue of media depictions of mental disorders in general. Most of the research on this topic pertains to television, newspaper, and magazine accounts of schizophrenia, depression, bipolar disorder, and obsessive-compulsive disorder. The main conclusion is that a huge proportion of media coverage related to such conditions—particularly disorders featuring irrational, psychotic behavior—is sensationalized, focused on portrayals of violence, incompetence, or both. Otto Wahl's 1995 book, *Media Madness* (a fine play on words), starkly reveals the stereotypic views of adult mental illness often conveyed in the popular media, including chilling newspaper headlines, graphic film portrayals of people with mental illness as violent killers, and rampant television depictions of foolishness or utter incompetence.[12] Even many children's programs and cartoons are laden with stereotypes: think of the classic Loony Tunes cartoons, with such characters as Daffy Duck. Despite some improvements, stereotype-laden media portrayals of mental illness have persisted in the United States and elsewhere for decades.[13] In tandem, whereas the American public clearly knows more about mental illness than ever before, levels of prejudice and stigma have not receded over the past half-century and may, in important respects, actually be *higher* now than in the 1950s (Chapter 9).[14]

## ADHD's Portrait to the Masses

Media controversy surrounding ADHD is far from new, as this condition has been newsworthy for a long time. Things heated up, for example, in the 1970s when the *Washington Post* reported that up to 10% of all schoolchildren in Omaha, Nebraska were being treated with Ritalin, fostering a public outcry regarding overmedication and prompting a Congressional inquiry. During the ensuing decade, antipsychiatry books targeting hyperactivity began to appear, including Schrag and Divoky's provocative *The Myth of the Hyperactive Child*.[15]

With respect to magazine coverage, by 1996 *Newsweek* had declared ADHD the nation's "No. 1 psychiatric disorder."[16] A 2009 analysis examined magazine portrayals of ADHD from 1985 through 2008. The main conclusion was that, in outlets ranging from *People*, *Newsweek*, and *Better Homes and Gardens* to *Psychology Today* and *The New York Times Magazine*, most stories were informative in tone rather than sensationalistic. Common themes included (1) the linkage of ADHD with school-related problems (no surprise there, given this book's overall theme) and (2) the potential for overdiagnosis of the condition. By the second half of the time span (1999–2008), a greater number of stories featuring brain-related aspects of ADHD and human interest portrayals (including sympathetic first-person accounts) were appearing. Medication-related stories often featured comparisons with taking insulin for diabetes or wearing glasses for impaired vision.[17]

Along with the spike in ADHD diagnoses and stimulant prescriptions in the 1990s, a focus on rampant overdiagnosis and overtreatment appeared on TV programs and in books with titles like *A Dubious Diagnosis, Running on Ritalin*, and *Ritalin Nation*.[18] Yet in a prescient *New Yorker* article from the late 1990s ("Running from Ritalin," a play on words related to ADHD critics), Malcolm Gladwell contended that ADHD is a real phenomenon, in terms of actual attentional and cognitive deficits, but one "revealed" by the complex demands of modern society.[19]

Newspapers tend to feature late-breaking, exciting stories of recent scientific findings. An intriguing analysis identified 47 scientific articles on ADHD from the 1990s and traced the subsequent "echoes" of these publications in 347 newspaper articles that were based on the findings. Among the top 10 most reported break-throughs, six were eventually refuted. The upshot is clear: the public is likely to see splashy newspaper articles on ADHD that turn out to be inaccurate, yet the subsequent non-replications are almost never written up in the news to set the record straight.[20]

As for the Internet, if one goes to the Web and Googles "ADHD," the top 10 hits (as of Spring 2013) include the follow-ing: (1) a lengthy and comprehensive (though not entirely accu-rate) Wikipedia article; (2) a WebMD "ADD & ADHD health center" site; (3) a comprehensive site from the Centers for Disease Control and Prevention, with a prominent link to the American Academy of Pediatrics guidelines stating that assessment and treatment can begin as early as age 4; (4) the National Institute of Mental Health's thorough and accurate site; (5) a link to KidHealth for teens; (6) a link to KidHealth for parents; (7) the homepage for CHADD, the national self-help and advocacy organization for ADHD; (8) a promotional site from the drug manufacturer Lilly; (9) a link to PsychCentral's ADHD Webpage; and (10) a health information site from the Mayo Clinic. None of these is fringe, radical, or anti-ADHD. In fact, most of them are laden with the kind of information presented in Chapters 2 and 3 of this book. Critics would undoubtedly contend, however, that only main-stream, biomedical views of ADHD are conveyed in these popular Google searches, with the influence of big pharma clearly repre-sented (e.g., the Lilly site in the eighth slot above; the history of support of CHADD by pharmaceutical firms).[21]

## ADHD Cardiovascular Risks and Medication Shortages

Regarding media coverage of relatively recent controversies related to ADHD, we first consider the contentious FDA debate in 2006 over the cardiovascular risks of ADHD medications, and the additional risk of hallucinations and delusions that might result from overuse of these pills. Recall from Table 1–1 that Canada had temporarily banned sales of Adderall in 2005 in the wake of the sudden death of 12 children receiving stimulants. In the United States, a panel of the FDA initially voted to issue "black box" warnings on stimulant pre-scriptions, but the decision was soon reversed.

An analysis of media responses to these events found that major newspaper articles and network television coverage were relatively balanced. This was in marked contrast to a related controversy just a few years before, when drug manufacturers had failed to report information on potential side effects (specifically, of increased suicidal thinking) among youth receiving SSRIs for depression. This SSRI controversy had sparked a spate of negative press coverage. Perhaps, the authors of the analysis stated, the strong evidence for the efficacy of ADHD medications (in contrast to the inconsistent evidence related to SSRI medications for youth) played a role.[22]

Regarding the 2011–2012 medication shortages related to stimulants (see Introduction), WebMD provided a brief and balanced account in early 2012, noting that insufficient Drug Enforcement Administration (DEA) quotas on production were the apparent culprit, but also commenting that quotas must be upheld to prevent diversion for illicit purposes. The article implied that the most salient shortages were for lower cost generic medications, not for those of more expensive trade-name medications, a contention that invokes profit motives as being a key factor in the shortages.[23] A *Consumer Reports* posting in April 2012 reported that the medication shortages were about to end, given the increases in quotas.[24] It took an alternative forum to produce the strongest story on the profit motive. During the depth of the shortages, Moe Tkackic's provocative article for the Web site "The Fix"—entitled the "The Great American Adderall Shortage"—implicated pharmaceutical company profit-mongering as the true villain. Tkackic explicitly stated that pharmaceutical companies were purposefully cutting back production of lower cost generics in order to promote their newer, far more expensive trade-name products.[25]

## The New York Times: Back To The Past?

At this point, we present a detailed probing of ADHD coverage appearing in a vital media source: *The New York Times*, arguably the most influential newspaper in the United States. During 2012, readers of the *Times* must have wondered about their calendars, as the content and tone of a number of influential opinion pieces and feature stories on ADHD and medications were clearly slanted against much of the science related to ADHD. It began in late January of that year, in the influential *Sunday Review* section, when psychologist Alan Sroufe blamed ADHD on maladaptive parenting—a view that does not hold up to scientific scrutiny (see Chapter 2)—and dismissed stimulants as a means of covering over the social roots of this condition. Three weeks later, in the same section, playwright Hanif Kureishi stated that medicating ADHD is tantamount to punishing young people for sexual exploration. Other opinions and op-ed pieces on ADHD followed throughout the rest of 2012 and continued into 2013.[26] Other, more accurate news stories on ADHD appeared as well, but the feature placement of the opinion pieces is noteworthy. They conveyed the distinct impression that ADHD is a sinister label—a medicalized excuse for problems in parenting, schools, and the culture at large—with medications being Band-Aids at best and politically charged poisons at worst.

The stereotypes, outdated information, and outright hostility to the reality of ADHD are alarming. In fact, addressing the misinformation expressed in such pieces is one of the prime motivations behind this book. What is particularly distressing is that, at precisely the same time, other *Times* pieces on mental health were masterpieces, including Nicholas Kristof's "War Wounds," an impassioned and accurate portrayal of traumatic brain injury, post-traumatic stress disorder (PTSD), and suicide risk among recent war veterans.[27]

A closer look at the ADHD coverage is revealing. Sroufe ("Ritalin Gone Wrong") claimed that (1) there's really no biological deficit in individuals with ADHD, (2) the real cause of ADHD is negative parenting early in life, and (3) in terms of medication, we are relying on an inappropriate treatment for a misguided label. The first two points were based on his own team's research on a low-income, inner-city sample, but the measures of biological vulnerability that they used were not state of the art. Crucially, without a genetically informative sample (i.e., one able to separate genetic from environmental similarities between parents and children), his ascription of ADHD's cause to negative parenting was overstated. Sroufe summarized his view regarding medications as follows: "Drugs get everyone—politicians, scientists, teachers and parents—off the hook. Everyone except the children, that is."[28]

Even more egregious was playwright and novelist Hanif Kureishi's "The Art of Distraction." Decrying the dehumanization of any psychiatric diagnoses, as well as the lack of creativity engendered by psychotropic medications, Kureishi wrote that "Ritalin and other forms of enforcement and psychological policing are the contemporary equivalent of the old practice of tying up children's hands in bed, so they won't touch their genitals. The parent stupefies the child for the parent's good."[29] What people need is downtime, Kureishi claimed; any medication limiting even a scintilla of unfettered creative spark is misguided. Yet the claim that medications "stupefy" youth with clear cases of ADHD is itself ignorant and misguided. In reply, we would ask Kureishi and other critics to consider the high rates of criminality, accidental injury, and self-injury and suicide attempts linked to so many cases of untreated or poorly treated ADHD.

Richard Friedman's opinion piece in May was admittedly speculative: he himself wrote that correlation cannot prove causation (and we note that his scientific accuracy in other articles is usually unassailable). His concern was that the increases in stimulant prescriptions for today's soldiers might be fueling ever-higher rates of PTSD, because these medications, which increase levels of norepinephrine (as well as dopamine), may keep traumatic memories permanently entrenched. Yet there was no mention of alternative hypotheses, including the key point that a major trigger for increased rates of PTSD is the devastating nature of current warfare, with far more shoot-to-kill orders and far more survivors of vicious head trauma than ever before.[30]

On July 5, 2012, David Brooks wrote an op-ed piece about the deplorable state of our schools for the optimal development of boys: "The education system has become culturally cohesive, rewarding and encouraging a certain sort of person: one who is nurturing, collaborative, disciplined, neat, studious, industrious and ambitious. People who don't fit this cultural ideal respond by disengaging and rebelling." Using the hypothetical example of the impetuous King Henry V, transposed to a contemporary school, Brooks wrote: "If schools want to re-engage Henry, they can't pretend they can turn him into a reflective Hamlet just by feeding him his meds and hoping he'll sit quietly at story time." A single word we would use for such gratuitous, decontextualized ridicule of ADHD medications is "appalling." It is hard to reconcile this kind of stigmatizing analysis with the astute points Brooks often makes regarding other social and psychological issues.[31]

Bronwyn Hruska's opinion piece ("Raising the Ritalin Generation") provided a detailed, if rather pedestrian, account of their family's horrified reactions to their inattentive son's 2-year course of receiving stimulants. The predominant messages were that he never really had ADHD, such a diagnosis is entirely subjective, medication side effects were denied by the doctors, and he thrived after getting off the pills in fifth grade. We note that teachers can certainly be overzealous in suggesting medication—witness the states that have enacted laws prohibiting such discussion (Chapter 5). Moreover, we have emphasized repeatedly that medication should never be the only treatment option and that evaluations must be both rigorous and sensitive. Yet we question why this piece was chosen for the *Sunday Review*, instead of the many related articles that might have given even a hint of a different side to the story.[32]

By contrast, a March 27, 2012, article by John O'Neil, heading the Tuesday *Science Times*, carefully weighed the evidence regarding the serious effects of ADHD on driving performance, offering practical strategies.[33] In May, K. J. Dell'Antonia reported the results of a *Parents* magazine survey, which showed that many if not most parents believe that ADHD is caused by poor parenting—which shouldn't have been surprising, had any of those parents read Sroufe's *Sunday Review* piece several months before. The message in Dell'Antonia's article was clear:

> The fact that professionals and parents alike still debate things like medication for A.D.H.D. or therapy styles is less of a problem than the fact that shame and stigma continue to surround mental health issues. As long as family failure is associated with any issues of mental health, families are going to fail to seek treatment, and children are going to fail to find the help they need.[34]

The high-impact June 9, 2012 *Times* article on high-schoolers flocking to stimulants for performance enhancement ("Risky Rise of the Good-Grade Pill" by Alan Schwarz) was provocative. Although somewhat sensationalized—including an opening scenario of a student snorting a stimulant before taking the SAT, but nearly all current ADHD medications are snort-proof—the piece raised important ethical issues related to performance enhancement. One teen quoted in the article discussed these pills as "academic steroids," but the kind that parents would actually help kids procure. Despite misconceptions (e.g., that stimulants "calm down" kids with ADHD but "speed up" the brain processes of normal-range youth, a myth that we overturned in Chapter 3), the warning served an important purpose.[35]

A few months later, in October, Schwarz wrote another provocative piece, on a doctor prescribing stimulants to youth who did not qualify for a diagnosis of ADHD. This piece raised the specter of neuroenhancement for youth from impoverished backgrounds or inadequate schools. Then in early 2013, Schwarz's bombshell front-page story ("Drowned in a Stream of Prescriptions") told the harrowing story of a young adult, Richard Fee, who became addicted to stimulants because of inadequate assessment and lax medication monitoring by doctors (see Introduction). Many readers may have left this emotion-laden piece with the sense that all ADHD medication is wrong-headed. By early spring of 2013, the 2011–2012 NCSH data were available and were presented by Schwarz and Cohen, emphasizing the new 11% rate of "ever diagnosed" with ADHD for American youth. Paralleling the *Times* coverage of the past year and a half, a related editorial emphasized overdiagnosis and medication side effects far more than legitimate diagnoses or the potential benefits of treatment. Moreover, in April of 2013, the lead article of the *Sunday Review* announced that ADHD is often a misdiagnosis for sleep disorders. Certainly, assessing for sleep problems should be part of any workup, but the title of the piece ("Diagnosing the Wrong Deficit") continued to dismiss the legitimacy of ADHD.[36]

In response to these accounts, the Sroufe article in particular generated much mail, both pro and con. We provide here an excerpt from a thoughtful blog by Ned Hallowell, MD:

> As is usually the case when the use of stimulant medications like Ritalin makes it into mainstream media, the [Sroufe] piece pushed emotional hot-buttons in a way that would scare the daylights out of uninformed readers and lead them to avoid ever using such medications or allowing their children to, thereby giving up on a class of medications with enormous potential benefits…. It is with his scare tactics and wrong-headed assumptions that I take issue…. [W]ho said there would be a single solution?…We offer it as one tool that can help, but always as part of a comprehensive treatment plan which

also includes other key elements like education of parent, child, and teacher; lifestyle modification…on how to better organize life; and ongoing follow-up to monitor progress and offer encouragement and various specific tips on managing life with ADHD.[37]

In sum, *The New York Times'* portrayal of ADHD and ADHD medications during 2012 and 2013—especially in high-impact slots such as the *Sunday Review*—makes us wonder about the underlying agenda at this venerable newspaper. Derogatory and stigmatizing, laden with stereotypes and promoting outdated myths, and often scientifically inaccurate, these pieces reached wide audiences. If history is a guide, such strongly slanted accounts could alter the national dialogue. In our final chapter, we make predictions regarding the future of ADHD on the basis of a number of recent trends, including those in the media.

## Advertisements and the Selling of ADHD Medications

We open our section on the promotion of ADHD medications through advertisements with several representative, large-circulation print ads. The first, from Johnson & Johnson (manufacturers of Concerta), shows a smiling mother and her beaming son, presumably while he is actively medicated with this long-acting ADHD medication (Figure 7–1). The message is clear: the right pill breeds family harmony, especially when the medicine's effects persist beyond the hours of the school day. Indeed, given the noteworthy effects on discipline styles engendered by raising a child with ADHD, this ad gets straight at a key motivator for medication use: restoring order to troubled families. We speculate, too, that the mother's pride may also reflect her pleasure over her son's assumed academic success on medication. The text ("I see Jason. Not his ADHD") gives the clear implication that medication allows the family to encounter the real child underneath the problematic behaviors engendered by the diagnosis. In other words, the ad's message is that medication can combat stigma.[38]

The second advertisement targets the fastest growing market for ADHD medications: adults (Figure 7–2). It explicitly points

FIGURE 7–1 Advertisement by ALZA.

out linkages between diagnoses of ADHD and higher than average divorce rates as well as the documented comorbidity between adult ADHD and major depression. Scientific articles attesting to such linkages are even cited in the fine print of the body of the ad. Family distress and psychiatric comorbidities are documented features of ADHD throughout the scientific and clinical literature, but the ad is noteworthy for its explicitness along these lines.[39]

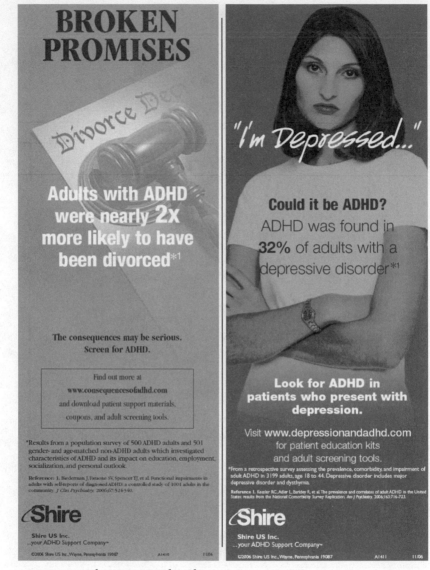

FIGURE 7–2  Advertisement by Shire.

The third, reprinted from a 2012 issue of *Newsweek*, shows a major league baseball player, Shane Victorino, discussing (in the YouTube video accompanying the ad) his lack of shame over admitting that his long-standing ADHD persists into adulthood, linked to his sports career (Figure 7–3). This ad does not represent any particular medicine; it is sponsored by two of the major national ADHD

FIGURE 7–3 Advertisement in *Newsweek* picturing Shane Victorino.

organizations, Attention Deficit Disorder Association of America (ADDA, a key adult ADHD group) and CHADD (the primary organization for children and adults with ADHD), along with the medication manufacturer Shire. Victorino, a handsome and successful player (with a World Championship ring to his credit), serves as a role model for "coming out of the closet" regarding his ADHD, testifying to the benefits of medication for adult success. The marketing of athletes and celebrities as role models for various forms of mental disorder is now a major strategy for brand promotion as well as stigma reduction.[40]

Messages from these ads are clear: ADHD often yields major life problems, but medication promotes academic success, produces improved parent–child relationships, helps alleviate problems of divorce and depression, and enhances the careers of professional athletes.

Yet why are such advertisements in the public eye? In the past, practically the only way to advertise psychoactive medications was through communication with doctors themselves, as witnessed by the now-curtailed courting of medical professionals at lavish retreats and the still-prevalent major page allocations in medical journals for medication ads. In a long and complex history, regulation of advertising information about medications has shifted across several different federal agencies over the years. Although direct ads to consumers were not explicitly prohibited by such agencies, tradition dictated that ads for pills be channeled through medical providers. The American Medical Association (AMA) strongly opposed such ads, threatening to take away medical licenses from violators. Furthermore, any consumer ads needed to include lengthy, fine-print disclaimers about the specific indications for the medicines along with side effects, making this an unattractive option for advertisers.[41]

Advertising in health care has always been controversial. Advertisers and many consumer advocates aim to increase competition by giving consumers more choice and the needed information to make well-informed decisions. Moreover, advocates of ads directed toward consumers contend that such direct advertising can improve patient knowledge, increase the quality of health care, and reduce costs through competition. The alternative view is that such advertising misleads consumers by providing biased, one-sided information and promoting unrealistic expectations. They may also distort the doctor–patient relationship (i.e., through "doctor shopping" for a physician who will prescribe the advertised medicine). In addition, the costs of such advertising might actually increase the price of what is purchased.[42]

The careful study of advertising in health care began in the 1970s. The Federal Trade Commission (FTC), which oversees market competition, successfully sued the AMA over its restrictive advertising policies. Their case was built on the results obtained by studies of optometric services: some states allowed such advertising while others didn't. This natural experiment showed that, in states allowing advertising, prices were lower with no decline in quality. The FTC generalized this finding to the entire health care system.[43]

Fast forward to 1997, when the FDA issued new guidelines related to direct-to-consumer (DTC) advertising. A key provision was that only major points related to potential benefits and side effects had to be included, rather than detailed lists of potential adverse effects (pricing information did not need to appear, either). These guidelines provided a clear incentive for manufacturers to produce ads intended for consumers. By 1999, the FDA further revised guidelines to permit DTC ads in the broadcast media: TV, radio, magazines, and even Web sites. The United States joined New Zealand as the only nation actively encouraging DTC advertising. European nations, as well as nearly all other countries, continue to strictly prohibit it.[44]

These altered regulations have changed the playing field. Spending on DTC ads for pharmaceuticals rose from $150 million in 1993 (when such ads were virtually prohibited) to a staggering $4.24 billion in 2005. Furthermore, addressing the debate over whether such ads lead to competition and lowered medication prices, a critical review stated that "broadcast advertising was responsible for 18% of the overall increase in prescription drug expenditures in the U.S. during the [1999–2005] period."[45] Yet data on improved health outcomes related to such ads are hard to find. Furthermore, information in DTC advertisements on the benefits of the medications occupied 85% of print in magazine ads and 67% of air time for television commercials. In parallel, explicit presentation of risks was given less than 15% of print space in magazine ads and under 18% of air time for television commercials.[46]

## Ads for ADHD Medications

Regarding ADHD-related medications, Figure 7–4 traces ADHD ad trends from 1998 to 2010 across five leading national magazines that target the market for parents. Advertising expenditures for ADHD medication averaged $88 million per year from 2000 to 2011. Two-thirds of expenses were for magazine ads and 30% were for television. Internet advertisements showed an increase of 200% during 2004 to 2008.[47]

Figure 7–4 shows that all magazines showed upward trends in ADHD advertisements until 2004, with four of the five magazines having at least one full-page ADHD advertisement in each issue. This pattern corresponds to the introduction of a new generation of long-acting formulations of ADHD medications, starting in 2000. But once the market was flooded with these patented, high-cost brands, ads quickly tapered. The South had the largest number of subscriptions. Whether the timing and regional placement of these ads—along with school policies (Chapter 5)—help to explain the

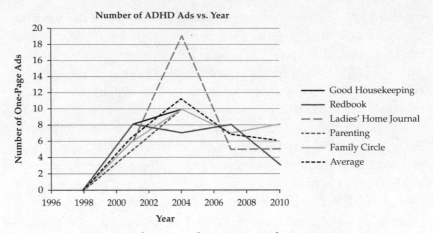

FIGURE 7–4  ADHD Medication Advertisements by Year, 1998–2010.

high ADHD diagnosis rates in the South is a provocative but unanswerable question.

Do such ads increase medication sales? Although no direct evidence is available for ADHD per se, the noted health economist Richard Frank suggests that for every 10% increase in spending for advertising for medications in general, sales of medications increase by 1%. In relation to the information just presented, the increase in spending on ADHD medication ads went from $97 million in 2003 to $128 million in 2004, a bit over a 30% increase. Using Frank's formula, this result suggests that a 3% increase in medication sales should be attributable to advertising during this time. In fact, however, ADHD medication sales in the United States increased from about $2.2 billion in 2003 to about $2.9 billion in 2004, more than a 30% increase. Other forces must certainly have been at play (including the higher cost of long-acting formulations).[48]

Pharmaceutical ads that undermine or oversell appropriate product use (e.g., by overzealous claims) can prompt the FDA to censure the firm in question. For example, the FDA found an advertisement for Strattera (a nonstimulant medication for ADHD) to be misleading in that it failed to communicate adequately the actual indication for the prescription. This advertisement also included quick scene changes, visual changes, and erratic camera movement to minimize the display of side effects. The tension between ads that promote products and provide misleading information is ever-present.[49]

A major question, however, is whether the pharmaceutical market actually represents a competitive economic endeavor. If not, a relevant question is whether it should receive regulatory protection. The background is that when a drug receives a patent at any point in the manufacturing or marketing process, the patent is protected for 20 years. However, "patent exclusivity" is a separate and far more important process. It is awarded only when the drug is approved by the FDA and lasts for 3 to 7 years. During that period the manufacturer has exclusive marketing rights for the drug; far-less-expensive generic medications are usually prohibited from entering the market. The goal of patent exclusivity is to provide incentive for manufacturers to undertake major expenditures needed to develop the medications in the first place.

Yet during this inherently noncompetitive time period of patent exclusivity, advertisements serve mainly to generate support for high-priced, patented formulations. Interestingly, when generic medications emerge several years later, ads tend to plummet because the profit margin is reduced, often dramatically. In short, advertising for medications during the early years of drug promotion is *not* the kind of free-market enterprise one might imagine.[50]

## Ultimate Effects

A rigorous research review was undertaken several years ago to assess the evidence in favor of DTC ads, in terms of potential benefits to consumers and their overall health. Among over 2,800 possible research articles reviewed, only *four* investigations with any rigorous data emerged. These studies included the conditions of migraine headaches, allergies, fungal infections, and cholesterol reduction.[51]

One of the relevant studies was intriguing. It compared the matched cities of Sacramento, California and Vancouver, British Columbia. Sacramento's location in the United States meant that consumers saw DTC ads, but Vancouver's location in Canada meant that most consumers did not. Overall, Sacramento patients believed that they needed medicines more than Vancouver patients did. They were also more likely to request DTC-advertised drugs, and they received far more new prescriptions from their physicians. These findings can be interpreted as supporting the conclusion that DTC ads produce artificial needs. Still, no information on overall health of the two cities was available for direct comparison. In short, DTC ad campaigns appear to increase diagnoses as well as prescription rates—but without evidence of corresponding enhancement of health outcomes.[52]

There is increasing pushback against DTC ads, largely because of the arguments that such ads may actually *increase* medication costs. Congress has been considering banning DTC ads during the first 2 years of a medication's existence, the time period when safety problems often emerge (and when patent exclusivity is in full swing). Recall that Europe—with its policies of government-funded medications—uniformly bans such advertising.[53]

As the debate continues, ADHD medications are in the middle of the controversy. In the future, when newer formulations enter the market, we fully expect that advertising runs will occur, with the intention of promoting sales for these formulations, which are protected by patent exclusivity. Whether this is a good thing or bad thing depends, we suspect, largely on one's core values about advertisements, competition, the liberal DTC regulations at present, the role of patent exclusivity, and the nature of mental illness and the stigma it still receives.

# ADHD Around the World

*A* SCENE AT THE CASH REGISTER OF THE CORNER DRUGSTORE, *the pharmacy closed for the evening. A customer heads over to the register and the checker scans his cart: distilled water, cough syrup, Band-Aids, condoms, a quart of milk…and Ritalin!*

*A real store? It very nearly could have been, at least in Israel. In early 2011 the Israeli Ethics Committee of the Medical Federation announced that the stimulant methylphenidate—trade name Ritalin—would now be available over the counter, without a prescription, just like aspirin or cold remedies.*

*Soon thereafter, a backlash forced a change in the policy. Ritalin is not currently displayed along with mouthwash and allergy medicines at drugstore counters; it requires a prescription. Yet doctors can prescribe it to improve memory and learning or help with schoolwork or job-related stress, without any need of an ADHD diagnosis. At least in Israel, neuroenhancement is teetering on official policy.*

*Countervailing forces have been at work. Israel's evolving policy is that every prescription provided must be reported to the Ministry (as in many states in the United States, where Schedule II medicines like stimulants must be written in triplicate, with the doctor, the pharmacy, and a state agency retaining the copies). Indeed, in reaction to the growing use of stimulants in Israel over the past 10 years, a movement is afoot that only psychiatrists, neurologists, and specially trained pediatricians are allowed to give the initial prescription following a diagnosis of ADHD, to be followed up by a general physician. Conflicting views and opposing policies are now the norm in Israel.*[1]

*In Brazil, the situation is radically different. The military dictatorship ruling the country until a few decades ago spurred widespread distrust of forced biological treatments in the service of political repression. In addition, the predominant theoretical perspective on mental health remains psychoanalytic. As a result, theories of biological causation of ADHD as well as medication treatment remain in major disfavor. Additionally, the Brazilian educational system has been under the influence of the doctrine of "constructivism," through which physical exercise and light physical punishment are among the preferred disciplinary measures. Teachers throughout the country have little belief in the viability of ADHD as a valid condition. In those cases where a child is suspected of having attention problems, usually in an urban, affluent area, referral to a neurologist is standard, with EEGs or neuroimaging evaluations often performed.*

*However, a recent spike of interest in ADHD medications is now apparent. Even so, while many medications are government subsidized (such as antiretrovirals for HIV), ADHD medications are not. Behavioral treatments are far behind psychoanalytic interventions in terms of popularity and use, and they, too, are available mainly for the well-to-do. In terms of diagnosing and treating ADHD, Brazil appears to be the diametric opposite of Israel.*[2]

On the face of it, the high value that Israel places on education, learning, and productivity might explain its recent policy shifts that nearly legalized neuroenhancement. Alternatively, the painful historical wounds in Brazil, along with its predominantly psychodynamic approach to mental health, appear responsible for its patterns of disavowal of ADHD. With the push for academic and vocational performance and productivity now a worldwide phenomenon, questions related to ADHD and medication treatment are clearly part of the mix. Will more and more nations come to embrace neuroenhancement, moving from universal coffee to universal psychostimulant medication, to promote alertness and focus? Or will more cautious stances emerge?

At this point in the book we address global trends regarding views of individuals with attention and inhibitory problems—and the types of policies and systems of care around the world to deal with ADHD. We highlight that this condition's borders have stretched considerably in recent years and that this diagnosis and attendant medication use are now a popular, albeit highly debated, topic worldwide. Although our book's overall focus is on patterns, practices, and policies within the United States, an international vantage point places American perspectives in sharp relief. In light of the increasing press for performance in nearly all nations that are above subsistence-level economies, we contend that ADHD diagnoses will continue to grow around the globe.

## International Recognition and Diagnosis

The stereotype remains that ADHD is an American phenomenon, the result of our nation's belief that higher education is attainable for everyone in society and our tendency to medicalize deviance by giving psychiatric diagnoses for what are essentially social and cultural problems.[3] Only in the United States, critics assume, does unfocused, disinhibited, fidgety classroom behavior signal a psychiatric condition worthy of diagnosis and medication.

Reviewing the evidence, however, reveals a far different reality. Over the past 30 years ADHD has been recognized, assessed, investigated, and treated around the world. An explosion of international research shows convincingly that (1) attention deficits and hyperactivity are omnipresent, at least in countries with minimal economic development and compulsory education; and (2) the major consequences of ADHD—educational failure, impaired social relationships, disrupted family life, accidental injury, and lowered economic productivity—are not limited to the United States or even other highly industrialized and postindustrial nations.[4] Wherever children are made to go to school, a subgroup is likely to show significant problems with focus, self-regulation, and behavioral control. (Extremes of such problems are likely to reveal themselves in any culture, but schooling makes these issues particularly salient.) At the same time, adolescent and adult forms of ADHD are increasingly recognized internationally as an important clinical concern, linked to major problems with employability, relationship stability, and risk for accidental injury.

But isn't it the case that different nations, societies, and cultures have vastly different expectations for behavior and self-regulation? Think of the Middle East, with many beliefs and practices that stifle individual expression, particularly that of girls and women. Or consider the continuing, massive surges in economic development in India and China, which together account for nearly a third of the world's population. According to our view, their ultra-rapid modernization should portend the adoption of American values and practices related to ADHD. On the other hand, in subsistence-level countries, performance enhancement would appear to be extremely low on the priority list, given the sheer struggle for economic survival and sufficient nutrition. In short, one might expect vast differences in rates of ADHD across different regions and countries, given their divergent economies, values, and belief systems, as well as their disparate views on the role of youth in society.

In 2007 this important hypothesis—namely, that that there would be major variation in the frequency of ADHD diagnoses around the world—was put to the test. Across nations throughout the world, official rates of ADHD among youth through age 18 were contrasted via sophisticated statistical analysis conducted by Guillherme Polanczyk and his colleagues. Overall, the international average for the rate of ADHD diagnosis was just over 5% of the population of children and adolescents. Thus, ADHD is certainly not a rare problem internationally. Yet except for generally higher rates in North America than in either Africa and the Middle East, none of the other regional comparisons yielded any meaningful difference.[5] In other words—and surprisingly—rates of ADHD diagnosis were more similar than different around the world.

This relative parity was the case even though clear regional differences *within* specific nations were often apparent, such as the North Carolina–California contrast within the United States (see Chapter 5). Similar differences occur throughout the states of Australia, between Jewish and Arab youth in Israel (with the latter receiving lower rates of diagnosis), throughout the United Kingdom, and in many other locations. Overall, local culture appears to matter considerably regarding assessment and diagnosis *within* nations, despite similar rates *across* nations.[6]

What does make a big difference internationally is the specific diagnostic system used by a given country, as well as the specific assessment practices that clinicians put into practice. A clear example is that the United States uses the *Diagnostic and Statistical Manual of Mental Disorders,* whereas many other nations use the *International Classification of Diseases (ICD),* now in its 10th edition.[7] The relevant category in the *ICD-10* is called "hyperkinetic disorder," rather than ADHD. It is more difficult to receive a diagnosis of hyperkinetic disorder in the *ICD* than it is a diagnosis of ADHD in the *DSM.* The main reason is that more symptoms are required for hyperkinetic disorder; there is also no equivalent in the *ICD* to the *DSM*'s Inattentive type. As a result, countries using the *ICD* have lower rates of diagnosis.

The clearest instance here involves the United Kingdom. For decades, hyperkinetic disorder was diagnosed there only when the child was floridly overactive just about all the time, usually part of a syndrome involving moderate to severe mental retardation. In other words, the U.K. had adopted a definition that was extremely stringent even by the standards of the *ICD.* Most children with impulsive and overactive behavior patterns, branded as hyperactivity, ADD, or ADHD in the United States, were instead judged to have "conduct problems" in the U.K.

Around 25 years ago, when an international team made diagnoses in both the United States and the United Kingdom with a standard, uniform diagnostic system, the cross-national rates were actually quite similar. Thus, rather than any real difference in occurrence of ADHD, the assessment and diagnostic standards in the United Kingdom appeared responsible for the lower diagnostic rates. The United Kingdom has recently adopted a more lenient set of criteria, closer to the standard *ICD* diagnosis for hyperkinetic disorder. As a result, rates of diagnosis have been increasing, along with rates of medication treatment. Still, they remain lower than in the United States, Canada, or Australia.[8]

In addition, some nations require that parents and teachers agree on the presence of a symptom in order for it to count. Some require that the child's problems must cause serious impairment before a diagnosis is made, while others simply count symptoms. It turns out that these kinds of diagnostic practices, rather than overall national beliefs, are the key factors that make rates of diagnosis higher or lower in a given country.[9]

Still, culture cannot be ignored. As just one example, we noted earlier that Hispanic youth in the United States still receive substantially lower rates of diagnosis than other racial and ethnic groups, despite recent (and rapid) increases for this ethnic group.[10] Although the reasons for this phenomenon are not entirely clear, strong family values, high levels of stigma regarding behavioral and emotional disturbance, and low access to responsive services have undoubtedly served to prevent recognition and help-seeking for this ethnic group. Importantly, there has been a pointed call for greater recognition and greater treatment of ADHD in Caribbean and Latin American nations, which have often failed to recognize the importance of ADHD.[11] Furthermore, it is difficult to know if the substantially lower rates of diagnosis in Africa and the Middle East relate to true differences in the occurrence of ADHD in those regions or (1) a lack of knowledge about its existence; (2) a dearth of responsive health care systems; (3) the low level of wealth of many countries there, relegating behavioral and educational differences to an extremely low priority; (4) different schooling patterns; or (5) other factors.

The case of China is noteworthy. In this huge nation of nearly 1.4 billion individuals, the era since the Cultural Revolution has placed strong emphasis on educational attainment, magnified by one-child-per-family policies and high levels of parental socialization pushing toward academic success and self-control (even self-denial). The Chinese gross domestic product (GDP) has been growing steadily for 10 years, despite current global economic woes.[12] Under the collectivist mode of thinking in China, children must conform to the prevailing group and classroom norms, which usually involve high levels of teacher control. Schools, teachers, and classes are highly unlikely to accommodate to the special needs of a given child. Instead, the child must bend to the teacher's authority and the classroom norms of long, passive learning sessions each day.

The result is an intriguing blend—even clash—of cultural values. On the one hand, there is increasing recognition of ADHD and increasing pressure to diagnose it, in order to foster optimal academic performance. On the other, there is little flexibility in terms of special education options involving tailored accommodations for the diagnosed child. Because medication can promote improved classroom behavior and learning without classroom-wide special services or adjustments, its use is growing. Still, heavy restrictions on the use of stimulant medications in at least some regions of China have limited their widespread adoption. Where China is heading with respect to ADHD is a complex question, but ADHD is now part of a national dialogue there.[13]

If the *actual* rates of ADHD around the world are relatively similar, this would bolster biological arguments about its origins. That is, if similar percentages of children and adolescents have trouble functioning in classrooms within any nation featuring mandatory schooling, this pattern suggests that underlying, genetically mediated (or other biologically based) processes may be the core influences on levels of ADHD symptoms.[14] However, regional differences within nations suggest strongly that culture and schooling clearly influence who gets brought to clinical attention.

Even if rates of ADHD are more similar internationally than one might think, treatment practices vary vastly around the world. Cultural beliefs and values, plus historical and economic circumstances, have much to do with the provision of services and with public attitudes toward people with a diagnosis. We now turn to a review of recent medication trends.

## Treatment and Services for ADHD Around the World

Our research team published an article in the journal *Health Affairs* in 2007, where we examined global trends in medication use and medication costs for ADHD medicines from 1993 to 2003. A major finding was that the dominance of the United States in the world market for such medicines diminished across that time span. Indeed, by 2003, fully 55 nations had crossed the threshold to being considered "ADHD medication users," up from 31 in 1993. Even more striking was that although overall global *use* of these pills tripled from 1993 to 2003, global *spending* went up by a factor of nine, even adjusting for inflation. The reason is that, in 2000 and beyond, the United States quickly adopted the newer, patented, and far more expensive long-acting forms of these pills. The rest of the world began to follow suit, with costs soaring higher than usage per se.[15]

Since that time, the global market has continued to expand. In 2000, for example, the United States accounted for 86% of the total international volume of ADHD medication, but by 2010 the percentage had dropped to 75%. Thus, over a quarter of all ADHD medications are now used outside the United States. From a different angle, between 2000 and 2010, the United States increased the volume of ADHD medicines it used by 32%, but the rest of the world increased their usage by 165%. ADHD medicine use is rising over five times faster around the world than here.[16]

In terms of costs, the United States increased its sales dollars of ADHD medications more than nine-fold from 2000 through 2010, but the rest of the world increased its spending 18-fold—double the American rate. From a somewhat different angle, the United States accounted for 93% of all dollars spent on ADHD medications in 2000, but that amount dropped to 88% by 2010. Certainly, the United States still dominates in terms of sales dollars—because of the high concentration of patented, long-acting formulations sold here, which cost far more than generics—but the rest of the world is catching up.[17]

Importantly, our research team also found that the wealth of a given country, as measured by its GDP, was a good predictor of how much ADHD medication it used. Not surprisingly, nations with more financial resources tend to use more medication for ADHD. Yet certain countries—namely, the United States, Canada, and Australia—use more medication than would be predicted by their national income. A number of European countries, by contrast, use lower amounts of medication than would be predicted by their GDP. We noted above the historical reasons for low rates of diagnosis and medication in the United Kingdom. As other examples, strict government regulations of prescriptions in France and Sweden might help explain the relatively low use of ADHD medications in those countries.[18]

In short, economic and regulatory policies clearly make a difference with respect to ADHD medication use around the globe. Other potential explanations include historical, political, and cultural values placed on academic achievement, as well as the beliefs and values of the education system. Our example of Israel versus Brazil provides a vivid illustration.

To get beyond the published literature on the topic, we held a highly interactive, 10-nation workshop in the spring of 2010. Our idea was to sample some countries known to be high users of medication and others known to be low users, with the objective of uncovering different patterns of service delivery for ADHD. Resource limitations precluded our inviting more than nine nations over and above the United States, so our conclusions are more impressionistic than might have been yielded from a full (yet inordinately expensive) United Nations–style survey. Even so, intriguing portraits emerged.

After obtaining agreement from clinical and research leaders of these nations to participate, we sent them a questionnaire addressing core diagnostic and treatment practices in their respective nations. Then, at the workshop we held lengthy discussions of the roles of culture, schools, insurance, and health policy in accounting for the patterns of prescribing medications and adopting psychosocial treatments in each country. We also promoted dialogue about recognition and treatment of adult forms of ADHD.[19]

Given how similar the rates of ADHD appear to be across the world, it is startling how discrepantly this condition is recognized, funded, and treated internationally. Treatments and services for ADHD have much to do with ideologies, with acceptance (or, in some cases, lack of acceptance) of ADHD on cultural grounds, and with organizations both within and outside the mental health profession that work to either promote or deny the existence of ADHD. In some countries, ADHD's existence is still being debated in the medical community. In others, it is the subject of intensive collaborative efforts to provide systematic interventions to those who need them. Overall, the use of medication and psychosocial treatments is socially and politically determined.

## Differences Across Cultures and Nations: A Bird's-Eye View

Proceeding alphabetically, we highlight the core themes raised by each nation represented at the workshop.[20]

### Australia

Like the United States, Australia has witnessed a major spike in the diagnosis of ADHD over the past 20 years. The current rate is estimated to be over 10% of the youth population, comparable to that in the United States. In a striking additional parallel, marked differences exist in the distribution of ADHD diagnoses across the states of Australia, just as they do across U.S. states.[21]

School personnel in Australia can make ADHD referrals to pediatricians but typically do so indirectly, through families. Medication is used in about half of diagnosed cases, in part because the nationalized health insurance system in Australia covers 85% of physician costs related to the assessment and treatment of ADHD. In addition, up to 12 sessions with a psychologist per year are covered. Behavior therapy is often used; it is more available in urban than in rural areas.

Despite this systematic, nationalized funding of ADHD care, Australian leaders have wished for a system of integrated teams, spanning disciplines, involved in providing the optimal treatment for ADHD. To remedy this situation, in 2009 the Australian National Health and Medical Research Council offered draft professional guidelines for ADHD treatment. For preschoolers, medication was not deemed an appropriate first-line intervention. Even for older children and adolescents, medications are not to be used as the first treatment option unless symptoms are severe and the family agrees to such a treatment plan. Although there has been increasing recognition of adult forms of ADHD, few adult medical practitioners are trained adequately, meaning that pediatricians must often extend their care through the early adult years.

Overall, Australia shows clear parallels with the United States in terms of diagnosing and treating ADHD. Much important research on ADHD has come from Australian investigators, meaning that trends there are likely to reflect and perhaps even lead American initiatives in subsequent years.

## Brazil

As highlighted at the beginning of this chapter, a distinctly different set of beliefs and practices regarding ADHD is found in Brazil. This stance is directly related to historical trends of repressive military dictatorships and reliance on psychodynamic theories of the causation of mental illness. As well, the Brazilian educational system is influenced by "constructivism," which does not recognize individual differences like ADHD.

Only recently has Brazil begun to emulate American practices and treatment options, and only for affluent subpopulations. The pace of change in this huge nation will be important to observe as perhaps a harbinger of Latin American trends.

## Canada

In many respects the situation in Canada is close to ideal in terms of systematic coverage of ADHD. Not only is the Canadian medical system nationalized with respect to reimbursement, but systematic sets of guidelines (provincial and national) support comprehensive evaluations and treatment plans. The Canadian Attention Deficit Disorder Resources Alliance (CADDRE) provides an ADHD toolkit and a Web site, at: www.caddra.ca. It updates practice guidelines regularly and advocates for evidence-based care for ADHD within both schools and government agencies. In order to reach out across the nation's huge land mass, centers of excellence, plus e-health and telehealth resources, have been developed.

Medication is used in up to 50% of diagnosed children and adolescents, along with a wide range of evidence-based psychosocial and behavioral treatments. Medical care is initiated with the family doctor, and referrals to community or provincial centers of excellence are available for complex cases. Still, as in the United States, major regional and provincial variation exists regarding diagnosis and medication use.

There is no separate, distinct designation of ADHD within the educational system. As a result, even though individualized education plans may be written for relevant cases, there is no additional funding for their implementation; such funding is available for children with autism-spectrum disorders. Additionally, most teachers do not receive specific training in ADHD. Schools however can offer parent training, in-class aides, specialized summer programs, and other progressive, evidence-based programs.[22] There are no specialized clinics for adults with ADHD, meaning that pediatricians must often extend their care to older populations.

Overall, the Canadian system is highly organized and heavily evidence based. Standards and educational practices promote the view of ADHD as a chronic, impairing, yet treatable neurodevelopmental condition. Multimodal treatments are emphasized. There does not appear to be another national system of care quite like it.

## China

Since the end of the Cultural Revolution tremendous pressure has landed on the (presumed) single child in each Chinese family to perform at high levels in all academic subjects. Accordingly, problems in attention and behavioral control are extremely salient. At the same time, as highlighted earlier, prevailing cultural norms dictate that all youths conform to lecture-oriented, passive learning–style classroom environments. Thus, the provision of individualized accommodations for selected students is directly counter to predominant cultural beliefs. Instead, it is the child who must accommodate to the classroom setting. At the same time, China's economy is rapidly ascending to become one of the world's strongest, with ever-higher values on performance and productivity.

A central issue is that child and adolescent psychologists and psychiatrists, the key personnel for diagnostic and treatment procedures in China, number only a few hundred in the entire country—a tiny amount for a population of over a quarter of a billion youth under the age of 18. In addition, mental illness is highly stigmatized in Chinese society, and there is a dearth of appropriate teacher training for conditions like ADHD. For official diagnosis, the system is the Chinese Classification and Diagnostic Criteria of Mental Disorders (CCMD-3), based on the *ICD-10* international system. Recall that *ICD* guidelines for diagnosing ADHD are stringent, further depressing rates of diagnosis. As a result of these forces, official diagnosis rates are still low. In the views of Chinese scientists and professionals, there is a huge unmet need.[23]

Medications compete with indigenous herbal remedies as primary treatment modalities, especially in rural areas. Furthermore, ADHD medications are often under tight governmental control. For example, in Shanghai, stimulant medication prescriptions must be renewed every 2 weeks, effectively curtailing their use. Still, in many urban regions, diagnosed children are increasingly likely to receive short-acting or even longer-acting stimulant medications. Although clinics may offer individual cognitive-behavioral therapy, parent training, or school consultation, the lack of trained personnel greatly limits the use of such evidence-based psychosocial treatments.

In short, Chinese cultural and historical forces have limited ADHD diagnoses. Yet strong pressures for achievement, performance, and productivity, along with cultural and family socialization practices reflecting core values of sacrifice and conformity, will almost certainly push for increased diagnosis and medication treatment in the coming years. Opportunities for training of relevant professionals are likely to be tremendous.

## Germany

During the first decade of the current millennium, recognition of ADHD among German children and adolescents more than doubled, fueling concerns—not unlike those in the United States—about overdiagnosis and overtreatment. Most cases are detected in urban areas and among lower social-class children and adolescents. At the same time, medical costs for patients with ADHD are more than twice those of nondiagnosed youth, similar to patterns in the United States.[24]

Between a third and a half of youth diagnosed with ADHD or hyperkinetic disorder in Germany (both *DSM* and *ICD* are used) receive stimulant medications, with rates similar to those in Canada and Australia but still short of current rates in the United States. Short-acting ADHD medications have been substantially overtaken by the more expensive longer-acting forms, driving up costs. In terms of non-medication treatments, however, occupational therapy predominates as a preferred treatment modality, with behavior therapy and parent training used by only a minority of families and youth. Most treatment originates in general medical practice, although hospital-based specialized services are now available in some regions. Whereas multimodal treatments are believed to be the most evidence based, medication-only treatment is still common.

Overall, German practices closely resemble those of the United States, with a lag of perhaps a decade. Public concerns about overdiagnosis and overmedication are commonly raised, with strong debate about the validity of ADHD. Tracking such controversy may provide a signal of how other highly industrialized nations respond to and provide services for individuals with ADHD.

## Israel

As noted at the outset of this chapter, cultural norms and expectations are highly relevant with respect to Israeli diagnostic and treatment patterns. First, the generally high activity levels among Israeli schoolchildren cloud distinctions between cases of ADHD and the normative range. This general tolerance for high-activity students, noted by conference participants, may well be problematic for limit-setting. As a result, ADHD is diagnosed in Israel amidst a system with "high background noise." Second, the strong pressure for achievement in Israel means that schools are referring ever-increasing numbers of children for assessment and diagnosis. Third, as highlighted earlier, there are higher rates of diagnosis and treatment in Jewish than in Arab youth in Israel.[25] Unknown is whether these are true ethnic differences, reflections of a greater level of service provision for more affluent Israeli children (along with underrecognition among Arab youth), or products of different value systems in the respective cultures.

Medications are now prescribed for at least half of youth who receive an ADHD diagnosis. In Israel, short-acting stimulants (now generic) are far more used than the more expensive longer-acting, patented formulations, as the latter are typically not covered by health insurance. Schools provide special services and accommodations for youth diagnosed with ADHD. Concerns have been raised that school personnel are in some cases pressuring parents to obtain an ADHD diagnosis and treatment for their child, yielding tensions similar to those in the United States. In fact, Scientologists and other activists have been critical of ADHD diagnoses and medication treatments in Israel.

Overall, Israel includes a potent mix of forces: access to ADHD medications, including recent policy changes related to the dispensing of such pills without need for a diagnosis (and subsequent policies going in the opposite direction, whereby only specialists can diagnose); strong pressures to achieve; high rates of general activity; and critical stances toward diagnosis and medication. Predicting where Israel will end up with respect to ADHD is difficult, but trends there are likely to be influential around the world.

## Netherlands

Like other Northern European nations, the Netherlands features a rate of ADHD diagnosis that is comparable to that of the United States. Whereas medication was seldom used 25 years ago, rates of stimulant and non-stimulant medication have grown rapidly in recent years. Although no formal national data on treatment rates are available, estimates are that between a third and a half of diagnosed children and adolescents end up receiving medication.

The preferred treatment modality is a combination of medication and evidence-based psychosocial treatments (parent training, school consultation, behavior therapy). Both national health insurance and private insurance provide financial coverage. As in nearly all other nations surveyed, the transition from providing treatment to youth to treating adults is not smooth. There are few specialists in the adult forms of the disorder, despite current efforts to remedy this situation. In Dutch schools the category of learning disabilities garners special accommodations and privileges, but the same is not true for youth with ADHD. Overall, in recent years, the Netherlands has mimicked American patterns of diagnosis and treatment quite strongly.

## Norway

From the mid-1990s through 2009, the number of youth in Norway diagnosed with ADHD increased substantially, and the number receiving ADHD medications went up 20-fold. Governmental efforts to enhance awareness and acceptance of ADHD were partly responsible for these changes. However, strong debate in professional and public circles now exists regarding the potential for overzealous labeling. At present, estimates are that perhaps a third of diagnosed youth receive medication prescriptions. Immediate-release stimulants predominate, with medication costs covered primarily by a national social security system. Most youth receive adjunctive psychosocial treatments, including family therapy, parental marital therapy, and individual play therapy. Under the nationalized system, these interventions are largely free of charge.

Major regional differences exist across the counties of Norway with regard to diagnostic rates and treatments used. Even so, Norway's nationalized health care system and its high levels of economic resources have reduced debate over related expenditures. Despite general acceptance of the viability of ADHD, controversy over the numbers of diagnosed and treated youth continues. Recent foci in Norway include the growing numbers of adults with apparent ADHD and the presence of ADHD in females.

## United Kingdom

The history of ADHD diagnosis and treatment in the British Isles is intriguing, as discussed earlier. Although the true rate of hyperactive behavior patterns has remained relatively constant for half a century, as documented in population-based studies, clinicians have typically diagnosed as having "conduct problems" those children who would be considered in the United States as having ADHD. Moreover, there has been a long-standing reluctance to consider medication treatments. The National Health Service funds treatments, but parents must often place pressure on clinicians to diagnose ADHD or treat it with medication or specialized psychosocial services. Parent training is now available, as are behavioral approaches in general. However, psychoanalytically oriented practitioners and some aspects of the media still decry medication treatments.

The British National Institute for Health and Clinical Excellence (NICE) has published extensive clinical guidelines for ADHD.[26] Unlike parallel guidelines from the American Academy of Pediatrics or the American Academy of Child and Adolescent Psychiatry in the United States, medication is not viewed as a first-line treatment except in severe cases. In this document, medication for ADHD is clearly seen as having a role but is recommended only after other, evidence-based psychosocial and behavioral treatments have been tried first.

As with many other nations surveyed, the presence of ADHD, in and of itself, does not grant special services or accommodations in schools. Only a detailed educational assessment can do so. Considerable variation exists across regions within the U.K. regarding rates of diagnosis and treatment.

In sum, despite a long history of failing to consider ADHD as a valid diagnosis, changes in diagnostic standards and a growing willingness to consider medication as a treatment are now apparent in the United Kingdom. Whether marketing of ADHD medicines in this nation will overcome the cultural and historical resistance to pharmacological treatment will be fascinating to follow.

## Summary

Across these nations the bottom line is that, depending on history, culture, educational values, professional training models, and funding mechanisms, patterns of treating ADHD vary greatly across countries. Trends across the past two decades suggest a growing "Americanization" of ADHD models of treatment, with an emphasis on medication as a primary intervention. Clearly, however, not all nations use medication at high rates, and resistance is still strong in some quarters. Behavioral treatments are used in some nations far more than in others. With increasing industrialization and with growing pressures for achievement and performance, patterns of both the recognition of ADHD and its treatment should become more similar globally, with high reliance on medication.

## Economic Development and ADHD

Although our survey and conference did not include any truly underdeveloped countries, such nations would not, in our view, be likely to recognize issues related to ADHD or enact formal policies about this condition. For one thing, subsistence countries may not have adopted (or may not be able to enforce) compulsory education, greatly limiting the settings in which attentional focus and self-regulation are salient for children and adolescents. For another, even with mandatory schooling, the harsh economic realities of these nations would doubtless lead to a prioritization of other, more severe physical and mental health conditions: infant mortality, life-threatening infectious illnesses, HIV, and mental disorders featuring psychotic symptoms. In short, diagnosis and treatment of ADHD require a certain level of economic development. Without it, a nation's priorities will have far more to do with subsistence than performance enhancement.

We are not suggesting that lapses in attention and severe problems in impulse control are absent in economically underdeveloped nations. Indeed, such issues would present themselves in any situations prioritizing a need for concentration on complex tasks or demands for focusing on detailed work. Yet upwardly mobile nations, which place a premium on competitive schooling and job productivity amidst information-rich employment opportunities, are the venues where the constituent symptoms of ADHD rise to the fore.

Thus, when countries attain the types of educational systems and economic structures emphasizing technology, the fast learning of complex information, and industrial and postindustrial means of production, ADHD quickly appears on the radar screen and medications begin to ascend the ladder of treatments. ADHD requires sufficient levels of economic prosperity to set in motion Westernized medical models of mental disorder, requiring, in turn, enough disposable income—and subsidized insurance plans—to fund treatment and care. The undeniable biology underlying ADHD is embedded in economic, political, and educational systems that propel it to the forefront of international attention.

# Beyond White, Middle-Class Boys—Plus the Stigma of ADHD

THE STEREOTYPE THAT ADHD IS A SUBURBAN PROBLEM for fidgety, grade-school boys is a thing of the past. Several important subgroups drive this point home. We begin with consideration of preschoolers. Depending on one's perspective, they offer a real opportunity for early identification and treatment, to prevent years of academic failure, or a group ripe for overdiagnosis and overmedication. At the other end of the age spectrum are adults with attention problems, who were not even believed to exist several decades ago. Now this group constitutes the most rapidly growing area of clinical and research interest and has the most rapid expansion of medication sales. We then proceed to the still-understudied group of females with ADHD, whose potential for major life impairment as they mature is striking. Next, we cover ethnic and racial minority groups, formerly neglected as candidates for ADHD but now diagnosed and treated at high rates in the Unites States. Their all-too-real problems are often compounded by the dual discrimination of minority and ADHD status. Discussion of such groups brings to light a host of contemporary scientific and policy-related issues linked to ADHD and medication.

The final area we consider in this chapter is the stigma that still surrounds mental illness in general and ADHD in particular. ADHD paradoxically receives high castigation, precisely because of the view that the underlying problems are sporadic and controllable. *You— or your child—seem fine most of the time, so what's the matter, anyway?* Moreover, ADHD is highly linked to substandard academic and vocational performance. Wherever economies demand ever-higher output, individuals with problems in attention, focus, and self-regulation are highly likely to be devalued.

## Young Children

We first raise the issue of whether one can make a valid ADHD diagnosis in a preschool-aged child. The issue is complicated because so many young children show high rates of inattention, impulsivity, and hyperactivity as part of normative development. The controversy has increased with the potential diagnosis of even younger children. In fact, published medication trials exist for children as young as 2 1/2![1] Although this entire topic could merit a chapter unto itself, we will restrict our coverage to several key points.

First, the revised guidelines for the assessment and treatment of ADHD, released in late 2011 by the influential American Academy of Pediatrics (AAP), explicitly state that assessment and treatment can extend to children as young as 4 years of age.[2] This set of guidelines could be a cause for celebration, given the need for early identification that might prevent a lifetime of impairment. Yet it might also signal a major concern because of the potential for overdiagnosis and the ever-growing rates of medication in young children and their vulnerable brains.

On the one hand, there is clearly a legitimate case to be made for recognizing behavioral and emotional problems as early in life as possible, before learning is compromised, behavioral and emotional issues accumulate, and demoralization kicks in. Recall once again Becky from Chapter 2, whose life chances sank steadily after her problems were professionally discounted when she was a child.

Indeed, Jose (Chapter 1) began to show benefits from recognition of his ADHD prior to entering grade school. In the autism world, the name of the game is to detect the symptoms as early as possible—that is, during the first several years of life—and engage the child and family in intensive, home-based behavioral treatment. Such intervention is the only evidence-based treatment that has shown major benefit for changing the life trajectory of children with autism-spectrum disorders.[3]

Making the parallel case, it can be argued strongly that the field should concentrate on intervening as early as possible with significant signs of ADHD—not as young as 1 or 2 years of age but certainly by age 3 or 4, when the social world widens and preacademic development is paramount. Yet there are reasons to be cautious. During the preschool years, distinguishing true ADHD from behavior that is simply at the high end of the bell curve is no easy matter (Chapter 3). For severe autism, the signs and symptoms stand out markedly: it is rare for infants and toddlers to refuse to be held, withhold eye contact, ignore parental bids for shared attention ("look at the bird!" as parents eagerly point and the child eagerly joins in), or play repetitively with nonsocial objects and tantrum wildly when their routines are stopped. The constituent behaviors of ADHD, by contrast, are precisely what most young boys and many young girls are doing much of the time.

The bottom line is that it takes an extremely thorough assessment—one revealing that the behaviors in question are truly deviant compared to those of other children of the same age and one ruling out maltreatment, family stress, or neurological conditions as the actual trigger—before a diagnosis should be made. Without such diligence, clinics will be flooded with false positives: children without substantial risk for later problems now branded as having ADHD.

What happens when a thorough evaluation occurs and a diagnosis *is* made? Even then, recall that only half of preschoolers with ADHD continue to meet stringent criteria for a diagnosis at the end of elementary school (Chapter 2). As a result, the doctor who immediately jumps to writing a prescription may be engaging in overtreatment half of the time. At the same time, the doctor who informs the family of a 4-year-old who meets criteria for ADHD that he will "just grow out of it" is likely to be wrong half the time in the other direction, at great cost to the child, family, school, and even community, given lost opportunities for early intervention.[4] No wonder this entire area is contentious. We all pay the price when ADHD is appraised as part of cursory evaluations: the condition is trivialized, overdiagnosis may lead to stigmatization and inappropriate treatment, and underdiagnosis is a possibility as well, potentially leading to a spiral of failure.

For preschool-aged children with accurate diagnoses, the AAP Guidelines from 2011 are extremely clear that the first choice of intervention is behaviorally oriented parent training, not medication.[5] Other countries have made similar recommendations (see Chapter 8). We found no examples in which medications are listed as first-line treatments for young children with ADHD.

A major, cross-site study completed during the past decade revealed that stimulant medications do, in fact, show benefits for preschoolers. But average effects were smaller than for older children. In addition, side effects (decreased appetite, sleep problems) are potentially more troublesome at this age than for school-aged youth. Several years after the trial, those who continued medication from community practitioners still had major problems related to ADHD.[6] Furthermore, it is unknown whether the effects of stimulant medication on young children's brains are harmful or, alternatively, beneficial and even protective against ADHD-related loss of brain volume, as some research has suggested for school-aged children.[7]

Can a 2 1/2-year-old truly have ADHD? Looking back in time, many youth with diagnosed ADHD can be seen to have been holy terrors in toddlerhood, giving new meaning to the "terrible two's." Yet predicting the future from behavioral extremes at this age would inevitably lead to unacceptably high rates of false-positive designations. Separating out difficult temperament, chaotic households, abusive environments, individual differences in maturation, and a host of other factors from the earliest manifestations of lifelong ADHD is a formidable challenge, requiring extremely thorough assessment. At best, it is still an imprecise science.

Think of Tommy (Chapter 3)—and all the others like him in the world—born in highly unfavorable circumstances to substance-abusing parents—whose inattentive and disruptive patterns undoubtedly reflect genetic vulnerability, prenatal drug exposure, and extreme family discord as well as child maltreatment. Explosive children at young ages are now subject to a high risk of being branded with not only ADHD but also juvenile forms of bipolar disorder. With the latter diagnosis, the potential is now strong for receiving potent antipsychotic and mood-stabilizing medications.[8] As long as our understanding of the predictive pathways from early risk to later impairment remains fragmentary, there will be major trade-offs between the benefits and liabilities of early identification and treatment.

Our own belief is that ADHD diagnoses of preschool-aged children are potentially appropriate, but if and only if the stringent assessment practices advocated in Chapter 3 are followed. This is most likely to be the case if the child is observed in a preschool setting, and adults other than the parents are brought into the evaluation. Of course, such thorough evaluations necessitate adequate insurance coverage and reimbursement. (It is intriguing to note that there are now major mandates to compensate adequate evaluations and treatments for young children with autism-spectrum disorders, but none of comparable scope for ADHD.) Still, diagnosing ADHD in a child below the age of 3 is entering a danger zone. Certainly there are toddlers who are "off the charts" in terms of behavioral dysregulation, but specifying a diagnosis at that age is fraught with peril.

The kinds of behaviorally based, skill-building interventions for preschool children with ADHD are likely to promote behavioral regulation and enhanced cognitive development for nearly all children of this age. Thus, psychosocial treatments do not have to be stigmatizing or potentially risky. Rather, it is medication use that's the lightning-rod issue. When medications are initiated for preschoolers, we recommend that only specially trained medical professionals initiate treatment and monitor progress.

In the end, can the promise of early detection outweigh the risks of (1) stigma and labeling and (2) the potential for overzealous medication? The positive side of the coin is that families may avoid disastrous developmental consequences and compromised achievement if their children receive early assessment and preventive intervention. The potential long-term savings to society could be enormous. But it will take well-funded research to understand who is at true risk, along with amply reimbursed and well-trained professionals who can devote the time needed to undertake accurate evaluations.

## Adults

Thirty years ago, anyone discussing hyperactivity, ADD, or ADHD in adults was entering a void. The assumption was that the condition virtually disappeared with the onset of puberty.[9] Yet knowledge is accumulating rapidly with respect to the reality of attention and impulse-control problems for many adults (see Frank in Chapter 6). Even though the most overtly hyperactive symptoms in childhood tend to go underground during adolescence, problems in attention regulation and disinhibition remain salient in the vast majority of children with ADHD through adolescence. Along the way, far too many of these individuals become embroiled in delinquent behavior, peer relationship problems, substance abuse, repeated interpersonal problems, and, eventually, checkered employment histories, all of which incur major costs to the economy (see Chapter 1).

Yet what about the transition from childhood to adulthood? The short answer is that the percentage who still meet criteria for ADHD depends on how adult ADHD is defined. In a crucial investigation, in which the research team followed children (over 90% boys) with well-diagnosed ADHD from childhood into early adulthood, Russell Barkley discovered that if the young adult was asked about adult manifestations of the condition, the answer was vanishingly small: fewer than 5% qualified for an adult ADHD diagnosis. Stopping right there would lead to the conclusion that ADHD almost completely disappears after adolescence. However, the team also asked parents or caregivers questions about the individual's symptoms and problems, even in cases where the young adult no longer lived at home. When these data were added to the mix, the percentage of those meeting criteria for ADHD rose precipitously, to nearly 50%. Furthermore, if the criteria for adult ADHD were relaxed somewhat, so that fewer items were required for diagnosis—as is no doubt appropriate, given that nearly everyone decreases their display of overtly hyperactive behaviors over time—two-thirds of the sample now qualified.[10]

This point raises an important consideration about ADHD's mechanisms: it may involve not just a lack of attention to external information (e.g., teachers or supervisors) but also to one's own behavior and internal processes. In other words, ADHD is linked to deficient *self-monitoring*, the ability to accurately perceive one's behavior and its impact. In short, ADHD goes far beyond fidgeting and squirm-ing—and beyond an "attention deficit" per se—to incorporate defi-cits in appraising one's own performance, evaluating one's actions in terms of self- or other-imposed standards, and changing behavior in mid-stream if regulation is required. A huge problem for many adults with ADHD is the lack of self-recognition of the impact of their issues with time management, self-control, impulsive driving, and flare-ups during interpersonal interactions, leading to negative spirals and the blaming of others for accumulating life problems.[11]

Now that adult forms of ADHD are recognized, individuals wondering about the reasons for their inconsistent performance, troubled relationships, impulse-control problems, and employment disasters may have an answer. At the same time, they may be able to gain access to evidence-based treatments. Both medications and cognitive-behavioral/self-management strategies are effective for adults with ADHD. On the other hand, many of these same symp-toms might be related more specifically to major depression, poor educational background, substance abuse, or poor interpersonal skills. A cursory evaluation may too readily yield an ADHD diagnosis, serv-ing as a convenient yet inaccurate label to explain such concerns.

As noted earlier, a relatively high proportion of young adults taking neuropsychological tests related to ADHD diagnoses may be "faking bad" in order to gain accommodations, receive access to ADHD medications, or both (see Chapter 7).[12] With a growth indus-try like adult ADHD, there is the potential for gaming the system as part of a quick and overzealous diagnosis. The consequences can be disastrous, especially if stimulants are prescribed without careful monitoring, fueling diversion of these medications to those without ADHD. Our hope is that improved professional training and greater public education about what ADHD is (and is not) will allow the millions of individuals who truly deserve help for this condition to receive it.

## Girls, Women, and Minorities

Until relatively recently, there was an utter dearth of scientific litera-ture on females with ADHD. Only boys, most believed, could have

ADHD. Girls might display problems with anxiety, depression, or acting-out behavior, but ADHD just wasn't in their repertoire. Yet the reality of girls and women with ADHD is now apparent to both scientists and clinicians around the world.[13] Furthermore, ADHD used to be thought of as a largely white, middle-class phenomenon. Yet just as with autism and eating disorders, it is now well known that ADHD is an "equal-opportunity condition."

## Females

The best estimate is that there is a 3:1 ratio of boys to girls out in the community who meet official diagnostic criteria for ADHD. This figure may be closer to 2:1 for the Inattentive type, signaling that hyperactivity and impulsivity are the features more likely to appear in boys and men, even though girls and women certainly can display them as well.[14]

ADHD is not alone in this regard. Nearly all early-appearing neurodevelopmental disorders show a strong male preponderance, including autism-spectrum disorders, serious physical aggression, and movement disorders (e.g., Tourette's). With ADHD, however, some have questioned whether higher rates among males might actually be the product of gender bias in our diagnostic system. If we expanded the symptom picture to include female variants of the relevant problems (e.g., hyperverbal behaviors as opposed to hyperactive physical behaviors), according to this argument, there might be an equal rate of ADHD in girls and boys.[15]

Yet this line of reasoning can be carried too far. As a different example, some have argued that major depression, which is well known to show at least a 2:1 female-to-male ratio during and after adolescence, would show equal rates across the sexes if men's antisocial behavior and alcohol problems—so-called male equivalents—were counted as cases of depression. It is an interesting thought: we can probably all think of men with aggressive behavior or drinking problems who have an underlying depression. Yet assuming that all forms of violence or drinking and drug use are actually manifestations of depression is a real leap. It's a bit like the old concept of MBD (minimal brain dysfunction; see Chapter 1): in 1962, a major monograph on that topic listed 99 primary symptoms of this condition, spanning nearly the entire realm of mental disorder. Such global

thinking does little to further the aim of a valid science. We are better off not making the assumption that behaviors and emotions are
interchangeable across disorders.[16]

In sum, there *are* sex differences in mental disorders. Along with
aggression and movement disorders, ADHD actually does predominate in boys, whereas depression, eating disorders, and other "internalizing" conditions are more prevalent in females once adolescence
is reached.

Intriguingly, however, the situation changes across development.
In fact, the limited evidence to date suggests that, by adulthood, the
sex ratio regarding ADHD begins to even out. It may be that women
are more disclosing of life problems than men over time. Or, because
they are more likely to display the Inattentive type, perhaps women
have a form of the condition that is more likely to persist (i.e., hyperactive symptoms fade with time far faster than inattentive symptoms). Whatever the mechanism, female manifestations of ADHD
are increasingly relevant across the lifespan.[17]

In childhood, enough girls with ADHD have now been studied to
yield convincing findings. Girls meeting rigorous criteria for ADHD
show serious behavioral, academic, and interpersonal problems, on
par with those of boys. They are less likely than boys to display
comorbid aggressive behavior but more likely to show depression
and related "internalizing" problems. Through adolescence, girls are
just as likely to persist with major life problems as boys, including
academic underachievement and social and interpersonal difficulties.
Their risk for substance abuse may, however, be lower.[18]

By early adulthood, the results are striking, as shown by the
startling findings of Hinshaw's own research team. In currently
the largest sample of girls with ADHD, initially studied during the
1990s and then followed systematically 5 and 10 years later, their
life patterns over time were tracked. Overall, female rates of academic problems, social and peer issues, and need for special services
rivaled those of males. Yet by early adulthood, the female ADHD
sample showed devastatingly high rates of cutting and other forms
of self-injurious actions, as well as active suicide attempts. This high
risk for self-destruction appeared mainly in the Combined subtype
of ADHD, suggesting that early impulsive behavior and disinhibition play a major role in precipitating these outcomes in young
women. In fact, almost one in four young women with this form of

ADHD had made a suicide attempt by early adulthood, and over half were engaging in cutting and other forms of self-destruction.[19] Thus, ADHD in girls and women signals a pernicious set of problems, with a high potential for self-destructive behavior not seen in boys and men with this diagnosis. Clearly, ADHD in females requires early detection and dedicated efforts toward intervention.

In terms of treatment response, research to date indicates few if any sex differences in response to medication, behavioral intervention, or any other forms of intervention for ADHD.[20] Thus, treatment access for girls and women is a major priority, as evidence-based interventions treatments clearly work for them.

Overall, girls and women represent another growth area in the world of ADHD. By adulthood, medication prescriptions for women now outnumber those for men (see Chapter 6). Far more work is needed to understand female manifestations, including underlying sex differences in how the brain is organized and the pernicious long-term outcomes that girls experience as they mature. No longer can we permit gender biases to make us believe that ADHD somehow bypasses girls and women.

## Ethnic and Racial Minorities

Just as with preschoolers, adults, and females, the situation is changing quickly for ethnic and racial minority groups regarding ADHD. Previously, suburban kids experiencing strong achievement pressures were the main group thought to qualify as either having ADHD diagnoses or needing medications. But this view has changed radically. African-American youth are now just as likely as white youth to receive diagnoses and medication treatment, if not more likely.[21] The stereotype that cultural deprivation is the only explanation for inattentive and disruptive behavior among African-American youth is simply untrue.

ADHD is not alone in this regard. It used to be believed, for example, that autism occurred only in upper-class families, as a function of "emotional refrigeration," or that eating disorders like anorexia and bulimia appeared only in middle-class, Caucasian females, linked to enmeshed family interaction patterns. Both conditions are now known to span the entire socioeconomic and racial and ethnic spectrum. Hispanic youngsters still lag behind both white and African-American children and adolescents in terms of receiving ADHD diagnoses, but they are beginning to catch up, as we have noted.[22]

Whereas recognition that ADHD exists across racial and ethnic lines is a welcome development, it would be hugely problematic if ADHD became a convenient, default medical label for all problems of impoverished minority youth, problems that ought to be ascribed more accurately to deficient prenatal care, inadequate family structure, or substandard housing or schooling. Only via thorough evaluation—in the hands of professionals equipped to sort out issues of within-child versus within-systems problems—can we avoid underdiagnosing or overdiagnosing this condition, whether in majority or minority individuals.

## Stigma: Is ADHD Still a Source of Shame?

*Stigma* is a term that initially denoted a physical brand—a literal "mark of shame"—tattooed or burned into the skin of individuals in harshly devalued groups. In ancient Greece, such marks were placed on slaves or traitors to ensure that citizens would instantly recognize a social outsider.[23] Think, too, of yellow stars, badges, and colored hats of the Middle Ages for identifying Jews—or the literal branding of HIV-positive individuals in some countries. For the most part, however, stigma now conveys a psychological, symbolic indication of infamy and shame rather than a physical brand.

Some stigmatized groups are readily identifiable—for example, by a different skin color, a physical disability, or visible diseases like leprosy (now termed Hansen's disease). Yet other stigmatized attributes are concealable, such as being adopted, being gay or lesbian, or having a history of problem behavior or mental disorder. Concealable stigmas might be thought of as less problematic precisely because they can be hidden. Yet this very ability to conceal the stigma creates major conflicts. *Does anyone know about my history? Whom do I tell, and when? What if, in keeping quiet, my "condition" leaks out anyway?* Concealable stigmas incur high levels of uncertainty and anxiety, producing friction in everyday interactions because of potential "leakage" and betraying the deep shame that may surround the condition or status in question.[24]

Some aspects of stigma are part of everyday social contact and social cognition. Members of all societies must defer to group norms in order to promote cooperation; without doing so, social bonds could not exist. An effective means of enforcing such norms is to notice and punish those who are not members of the "in-group." Still, when degradation denies the basic rights of stigmatized groups for no legitimate reason—and especially when dehumanization ensues— action must be taken to ensure human rights.

If individuals are stigmatized, they are likely to be victims of stereotyping ("all Catholics are [name your trait]"), prejudice ("Catholics are therefore evil"), and discrimination ("in our nation, Catholics don't have full rights"). Moreover, every aspect of their being is filtered through the devalued trait or group membership. Victims of stigma, who typically know full well the aspersions cast on their group, often become demoralized and disenfranchised, through a process known as internalized stigma or *self-stigma*. Self-stigma is likely to be severe when the individual in question believes, at least in part, that he or she is somehow to blame for having the condition or "mark" in question. This is highly likely to be the case with respect to mental illness, given the predominant belief that disturbed behavior is a matter of poor self-control, ineffective parenting, or some kind of moral flaw.[25]

In current American society, the most stigmatized subgroups include individuals with mental disorders, substance abuse, or homelessness. On top of such societal stigma, self-stigma predicts a failure to engage in appropriate evaluation or treatment and early termination from intervention, if it is even sought. Stigma robs people of other life opportunities as well: independent housing, jobs, relationships. Stigmatization is arguably the most important issue facing the entire mental health field, because so many other problems (e.g., a relative lack of funding of mental health research compared to that for research on physical illnesses; the extremely low treatment rates for many forms of mental disorder) emanate from the shame and silence surrounding the entire topic.[26]

Much of the relevant research on stigma has focused on the severe conditions of schizophrenia, major depression, and bipolar disorder. Not surprisingly, they receive heavy loads of castigation. One might hypothesize that ADHD would receive relatively mild stigma, given that individuals with this condition seem intact in many domains and don't show the severe loss of contact with reality associated with psychotic behavior. Paradoxically, however, ADHD may actually incur *high* rates of derogation and stigmatization, precisely because of the predominant belief that individuals with this diagnosis should "get their act together," and that parents are the main cause of the symptoms. A recent review of research findings revealed considerable stigmatization of individuals with ADHD.[27]

*What's the matter: doesn't your kid try hard enough in school? It must be your parenting style, after all.*

*If only our society didn't make so many excuses for poor behavior and underachievement, we wouldn't squander so many resources on wayward youth.*

*For adults with ADHD: how unfair, just another "medical" cover for low effort, a way of getting unneeded accommodations.*

*To think that you're using medication for your kid (or yourself). What are you trying to do, poison his brain so he can conform?*[28]

In addition, the strong value placed on educational and vocational performance in our culture—the main point emphasized throughout this book—means that people who do not perform well in school or the workplace are likely to be recipients of strong moral indignation. The clear tendency for public media to disparage and belittle mental disorders is another driving force behind stigma (Chapter 7).[29]

As a result, despite the clear benefits that accrue from medication and behavioral treatments, many families never get an evaluation for their child or, even if they do, tend to hide the ADHD label from nearly everyone around them. A majority of adolescents with ADHD, along with their parents, are reluctant to pursue treatment because of stigma. Teachers hold back from raising referral questions with teens, also because of stigma.[30] An accurate diagnosis can open the door for appropriate treatment and accommodations and prevent years of academic, social, and behavioral struggles. Yet many would rather avoid the label.

Stigma doesn't occur solely in the United States. In China and other Asian nations, a family's admission that a child has a serious learning or attention disorder produces major shame. South Asian nations, like India, stigmatize mental disorders in part because such symptoms taint the family, potentially delimiting marriage partners.[31]

Biological factors clearly underlie the risk for ADHD (Chapter 2). When an individual exhibits negative behavior patterns, stigma and blame should be reduced if the behavior is thought to be beyond personal control and volition. Biological (and especially genetic) explanations would therefore be expected to reduce stigmatization—after all, in such cases the individual clearly couldn't help it. Many public awareness campaigns intended to reduce stigma are based on branding mental illnesses as diseases like any other—or as "brain diseases."[32]

However, there's a major catch. When mental illness is attributed exclusively to flawed genes or other uncontrollable, biological causal forces, stigma can actually *increase*. First, if the behavior is genetically based, it is assumed to be permanent and treatable only through biological means, such as medication. Second, the exclusively biological view of causation promotes the belief that the individuals in question are flawed at their core, with deviance encoded in their very DNA. Thus, at its extreme, the biological perspective can promote dehumanization. When people are viewed as less than fully human, discrimination, maltreatment, and even extermination are not far behind. Think of Hitler's branding of not only Jews but also gay and lesbian individuals and those with mental illness or mental retardation as vermin.[33]

A major goal in addressing stigma is for the public to understand that disorders like ADHD reflect *both* genetic vulnerability *and* difficult life circumstances (and even elements of personal choice, such as whether treatment is sought). In other words, the goal is to reduce blame while simultaneously promoting responsibility. Clearly, we must transcend the idea that the person in question is a malingerer—a "bad kid" or irresponsible adult. Instead, we must foster the belief that he or she deserves treatment, with the underlying condition involving biology, cultural forces, and personal and family responsibility for getting help.

Recall from Chapter 7 our discussion of direct-to-consumer (DTC) advertisements, with their potential to reduce stigma by promoting discussion of mental illness and treatment. A recent study examined medication ads in high-circulation magazines from 1998 through 2008, analyzing them in terms of certain "stigma-reducing elements." These elements included the views that the condition has biological origins (which at least to some extent removes personal blame), the perspective that actions other than medication might help (e.g., exercising to lose weight), and depictions of a person with a disorder as deserving of social support (e.g., the inclusive message that "you are not alone"). Importantly, however, only 4% of the DTC advertisements included all three stigma-reducing elements, with 21% failing to include any stigma-reducing element. Media ads are still an important target for stigma reduction.[34]

One potential solution is to have sports heroes or celebrities "come out" as having mental disorders like ADHD. Over the past years a number have: Michael Phelps, record-setting Olympic swimmer; Andres Torres, former San Francisco Giant (and 2010 World Series champion, for whom medication led to increased focus and productivity on the field); Shane Victorino, another accomplished major league baseball player; Howie Mandel and Robin Williams, noted and outrageous comics; and CEOs of major corporations. The message is that it is not only okay to have ADHD but also potentially an advantage, via increased energy and outside-the-box thinking. In short, there is a clear movement to reveal hidden strengths related to ADHD. Yet spinning ADHD exclusively as a talent or gift is inaccurate and risky. It is a condition requiring recognition and treatment, despite the energy and divergent thinking it might sometimes engender.

Once Michael J. Fox and Muhammad Ali became spokesmen for Parkinson's disease, donations soared and public acceptance appeared to increase. Could the same be true for mental disorders like ADHD? One thing is clear: reducing stigma will require a multipronged approach, combining public education, personal disclosure and contact, the active thwarting of media stereotypes, and increased access to treatment and services.[35] Despite greatly increased knowledge of mental illness throughout American society, fundamental attitudes toward people with mental disorders are surprisingly resistant to change. There's a long road ahead.

A core solution to stigma is to ensure that children, adolescents, and adults with ADHD (and other mental disorders) can obtain evidence-based treatment, preventing problem behavior from eroding relationships, and enhancing achievement and productivity. Yet stigma must be overcome before treatment is even sought. Among the many potential solutions, we particularly advocate humanization in media coverage, access to quality care, and promotion of empathy through the promotion of truths rather than myths about ADHD.

# The Future of ADHD: Predictions, Confusions, and Conclusions

H OW MANY TIMES HAS EACH OF US, SCHEFFLER AND *Hinshaw, heard phone messages like the ones below—or received e-mails following the same script?*

"Please, Richard, who can evaluate my son? We're frantic! There's talk at school that he's going to fail most of his classes."

"Steve, we know of your work; can you get us an 'in' to see an ADHD specialist? Our daughter has been drifting for years, and things are getting desperate."

*The messages keep arriving: who in the Bay Area...or New York...or Ohio...or virtually anywhere...sees people with ADHD? After we contact a clinician and try to get the family a "push" up the inevitably long wait list, what stays with us is the desperation in the tone of the caller or writer, lingering long after the message has been left. In the lives of such families, these are make-or-break issues.*

*Even in urban centers like the San Francisco Bay Area, with their intensive concentrations of mental health professionals, the number* of ADHD experts is small and the wait for providers with real expertise depressingly long. Why are so few clinicians experts in this condition? With the continuing push for diagnosis and medication, who is doing the evaluations—and who is delivering and monitoring the interventions? As far into the 21st century as we are now, shouldn't things be different?

In China, the pressure to perform well in school has never been stronger, as the nation continues to ride a crest of urbanization, modernization, industrialization, and economic growth. The test scores among Shanghai youth in 2010 were at the top of the world rankings.[1] Any student whose attention flags after hours of intense lessons cannot expect anything like an individual education plan. Still, with the right connections, a given family might find a psychiatrist who can provide a diagnosis of ADHD and prescribe medication, yielding a quick and relatively painless way of stretching attention and handling the huge academic workload.

India, another population giant pushing toward industrialization and modernization, is now showing great interest in ADHD, in part because of low international achievement test scores in 2010. Related Web sites are now appearing in India, describing ADHD and noting a growth of diagnoses, particularly in major cities. When achievement and productivity are in the mix, ADHD diagnoses and medications aren't far behind.[2]

And what about Israel, with its intense academic culture and attendant pressures (Chapter 8)? Getting a diagnosis of ADHD is common for many individuals, and for a time, medicine could be obtained for adults who had not yet received an ADHD diagnosis. Yet Israeli authorities are trying to make it policy that youth with ADHD can receive diagnoses only from specialists with advanced training in this condition.[3]

One thing is clear: in an ever-more competitive world, ADHD is everywhere, confronted by an ever-growing number of schools, families, and cultures, as well as economic pressures.

Throughout these pages, we have conveyed the complexities of ADHD, a condition linked to genetic, biologically driven tendencies toward poor focus, rushed judgments, and a fast-paced cognitive style in today's context of compulsory education, increasing performance demands, and a press for performance in the workplace. In the midst of the current surge of rates of diagnosis and medication, we have emphasized how essential it is to evaluate ADHD and its intervention thoroughly, even though quick and cursory assessments are all too common in clinical practice. We have discussed the huge variation in diagnosis across the United States, with educational policies an essential aspect of such variation, and the vastly different treatment practices that exist around the world. We have also shown that, despite its unprecedented success rates—arguably the highest across the entire field of mental health—medication is rarely enough for those with severe ADHD. Pills alone cannot redress academic and social skills deficits. Behavioral and cognitive-behavior interventions require far more well-trained professionals than currently exist.

We begin this final chapter with a note of optimism. That is, amidst the many wrenching personal and family struggles with ADHD presented in these pages, the major costs incurred by this condition, and the myths and outdated stereotypes that get in the way of sensible thinking about the entire topic, there is real reason for hope. ADHD *can* be evaluated with precision, if the needed time and resources are invested. ADHD *can* be treated effectively, but only if evidence-based treatments are funded and used, and only if well-funded research propels us toward new mechanisms as treatment targets. School settings *can* be adapted to different learning styles, with the potential for lifelong learning. Although such adaptation will not solve every problem linked to ADHD, it can provide a tremendous boost.

Our core question is whether the current increases in rates of ADHD diagnosis and medication treatment will continue. To aid our predictions, we briefly review trends across the past 45 years. Authoritative reviews cited rates of hyperactivity or ADD at 3–5% of the youth population in the 1970s and 1980s, and growing. Following an anti-ADHD tendency during the late 1980s, policy shifts in the early 1990s led to increases in the numbers of children diagnosed, with upward trends apparent over the past 20 years. The current rates of 1 in 9 (ever diagnosed) and nearly 1 in 11 (currently diagnosed), reported from the 2011–2012 National Survey of Children's Health, are all-time highs.[4]

In terms of medication, after increased stimulant use during the 1970s, a short-lived yet significant drop-off took place in the late 1980s, linked to political backlash driven by negative media accounts. Yet medication prescriptions quickly re-escalated, fueled by increases in diagnosis of ADHD, the rapid ascent of direct-to-consumer ads at the end of 1990s, and the success of long-acting medication formulations that began in earnest at the turn of the millennium. Currently, 69% of U.S. youth with current diagnoses of ADHD are medicated. In recent years, the largest increases in medication use have been for adolescents and adults.[5]

Looking at the next 10 years, we raise the question as to whether rates of ADHD diagnosis will climb ever higher—to 15% or more—and whether medications will become the first-line treatment option for three-quarters, four-fifths, or more of those youth who are diagnosed. Table 10–1 summarizes our thinking on both sides of this query. Entries include 10 core reasons for believing that rates of diagnosis and medication will continue to grow, plus 10 major reasons for believing that things will inevitably level off or decline.

## Weighing and Weighting the Evidence

### Trending Upward

On the one hand, there is considerable reason to think that ADHD is still in a growth spurt. Current rates of diagnosis and medication as reported by families were unthinkable a decade or two ago.[6] Autism has also shown an unprecedented and unexpected burst of diagnosis across the past 20 years, with rates far beyond anyone's guess (currently around 1 in 50).[7] The message is that once a diagnostic category generates medical and educational services, its use tends to soar.

But ADHD is different from autism. In fact, it is unique among child and adolescent mental health disorders. Its rates are high enough now that it is not uncommon to see several youth with an ADHD diagnosis in a given school classroom. Moreover, ADHD is linked to a group of medications with extremely high success rates; no such pills exist for autism or for learning disorders. In addition, as we have highlighted throughout the book, because of the major emphasis on performance in the current era, stimulants are increasingly diverted for use by the general population. Spiraling

TABLE 10–1  Reasons for Differing Trends Related to ADHD

*Top 10 reasons for believing that rates of ADHD diagnosis and medication will continue to rise:*

1. New practice guidelines from the American Academy of Pediatrics were released in 2011, which include the explicit statement that the diagnosis and treatment of ADHD may justifiably begin by age 4.
2. Diagnostic criteria for ADHD in *DSM*-5 (2013) make it easier to qualify for a diagnosis, because the age of onset for the display of impairing ADHD symptoms rises from under 7 to under 12 years of age.
3. Ever-narrowing of admissions slots to top universities (with greatest payoff in terms of income potential) fuel ever-stronger pressures to achieve, along with a continued rise in rates of ADHD-linked accommodations for both placement testing and college students.
4. Hispanic rates of ADHD diagnosis and treatment are now heading upward for this fast-growing segment of the U.S. population, potentially fueling higher rates of overall diagnosis.
5. Several ADHD medications are slated to lose patent exclusivity, including the large-selling, long-acting formulations, which would dramatically lower costs in many instances.
6. In parallel with autism, an ADHD diagnosis often leads to accommodations and services; as such, there is a continuing incentive for more diagnoses.
7. A continuing, fast rise in global and international diagnosis and treatment rates may fuel a "boomerang" effect on the United States and lead to a continuing upward spiral here.
8. Increased pressure for achievement and work performance will enhance the desire for neuroenhancement, along with recognition of other examples of medication use outside of diagnosed conditions (e.g., Viagra and Cialis for male sexual performance). Because such medications are now commonplace, the desire for performance enhancement from stimulants may also grow.
9. The potential for reduction of public stigma related to ADHD will fuel greater acceptance and a continued "run" on seeking of the diagnosis.
10. If the Affordable Care Act withstands legislative challenges, its key provisions—e.g., young adults able to remain on parental coverage until age 26; expanded populations being eligible for Medicaid coverage; paying a penalty for not opting in to healthcare coverage; coverage of pre-existing conditions such as ADHD—will be associated with greater healthcare use overall, including treatment of ADHD.

*(continued)*

TABLE 10–1 (Continued)

*Top 10 reasons for believing that rates of ADHD diagnosis and medication will taper off or fall:*

1. Increased media attention given to medication diversion for college and high school students will lead to concern over drug dependence and addiction. Likewise, increased dissemination of information on the variable and rather small stimulant effects on cognition and learning in normal-range samples will dampen enthusiasm for neuroenhancement. See, for example, the American Academy of Neurology's 2013 statement against the use of stimulants in the general population.

2. Stimulant quotas set by the Drug Enforcement Agency (DEA) may not be raised at the same rates as previously, leading to lowered overall usage.

3. More generally, cultural "saturation" may be reached regarding ADHD, fueled by reactionary press accounts in such outlets as *The New York Times,* with the potential to spur a levelling-off of diagnosis and medication treatment.

4. Recognition of the growing costs of diagnosing and treating so many cases of ADHD will serve to reduce rates (as a parallel, see Clinton's welfare reform of 1990s, which stemmed in part from recognition that it was costing too much to continue existing welfare policies).

5. Changes in most health insurance policies—of higher copay rates and higher deductibles—will lead to less "discretionary" medication use.

6. Further spread of laws that restrict schools from suggesting that children with ADHD receive medication could lower rates of diagnosis and treatment.

7. Continuing controversy over the role of stimulants in heart attacks and sudden death may trigger greater caution regarding medication use.

8. The dismantling of No Child Left Behind may reduce pressures on school districts to diagnose as many cases of ADHD as are currently being detected.

9. Continued biomedical research could reveal underlying subtypes of ADHD with observable brain-based anomalies. This discovery could lead to a discounting of the "reality" of ADHD diagnoses for those individuals who do not fit such profiles.

10. The continuing shortage of well-trained providers and clinicians— those who are experts in ADHD diagnosis and treatment—will produce "demand shock," whereby fewer will seek diagnosis and treatment because of inadequate care.

achievement pressures plus rampant job outsourcing will continue to place a premium on achievement and work productivity; the prevalence of ADHD and stimulants escalate when such performance is a priority.[8]

As for professional practices, it is likely that the American Academy of Pediatrics 2011 guidelines, with their emphasis on early identification and treatment for children as young as 4 years of age, will fuel ever-higher rates of ADHD diagnosis (Chapter 9). Furthermore, the *DSM-5* decision to allow youth to receive an ADHD diagnosis if impairing symptoms appear before age 12 (instead of the more restrictive age of 7, from *DSM-IV*) is now in place. The motivation behind this change is that many youth—especially those who present mainly with inattentive problems—do not show major impairments until middle school, yet they are otherwise just as impaired as kids who were easily recognizable before first or second grade. Although existing empirical research does not indicate that major increases in diagnosis automatically occur with this change, we believe that higher rates of diagnosis in community practice may well result.[9]

Furthermore, we should not underestimate the rise of ADHD diagnoses and medication treatment for Hispanic youth. With this group's nationwide surge in population, it makes sense that overall rates of ADHD diagnosis and treatment will head upward.[10]

At a policy level, if the Affordable Care Act continues to survive current legislative and implementation challenges, its (1) extension of coverage for young adults, (2) penalties for not obtaining insurance, (3) provisions for expansion of Medicaid, and (4) lack of exclusion of pre-existing conditions are all likely to result in greater health care usage, with ADHD treatments part of the mix. More specifically related to medications, as long-acting stimulant formulations continue to lose their patent exclusivity protections, prices should drop, providing incentive for their purchase.[11]

Table 10–1 also notes that a global "boomerang" may be operative. That is, given the rapid international spread of ADHD diagnoses and medication treatment, there is ever-greater justification that ADHD is not simply a trumped-up, American phenomenon. In short, the more that ADHD diagnoses and medication treatments diffuse around the globe, the harder it is to contend that it is a condition "made in the USA."

## Leveling Off or Trending Downward

On the other side of the coin, however, current rates of increase for diagnosis and treatment cannot last forever. From an economic perspective, increasing copayments and deductibles in many health insurance policies will provide a disincentive to pursue treatments. In our era of unprecedented federal deficits and a general need for cost-cutting, ADHD may come to be viewed as a discretionary frill rather than an essential medical condition. Intriguingly, as evidence mounts related to the biological reality of certain neural subtypes of this condition, it could be that those individuals who don't clearly fit such profiles will be discounted as posers—individuals without "real" ADHD.

With respect to negative media attention, there might be a parallel with the late 1980s, when negative media portrayals of ADHD and medication treatments spurred a leveling of diagnostic rates and a dramatic (yet short-lived) reduction in medication usage.

Moreover, there is bound to be intensified debate over production quotas for ADHD medications, with pressure to strike a balance between meeting legitimate demand versus fueling oversupply and medication diversion. Indeed, with use of ADHD medications among those undiagnosed increasingly in the news, pressure may build to gradually reduce quotas. Moreover, as noted in Chapter 4, the American Academy of Neurology provided a clear statement in 2013 to the effect that ADHD medications should not be used in the general population. Such increasing pushback may well prompt lower rates of stimulant use in the future.[12]

Regarding legislation and policy, the Obama administration's educational priorities include a dismantling of No Child Left Behind and, in its place, provision of incentives for states to produce better educational outcomes, especially in science, math, and technology. At one level, it is conceivable that removing penalties for schools that fail to produce improved test scores will ease pressure on obtaining more ADHD diagnoses. We would point out, however, that the incentives of the Race to the Top still emphasize a push for performance.[13]

Finally, there is the "demand shock" of more and more people requesting ADHD treatment from a small pool of trained professionals, a pool that is not growing at a sufficient rate to keep up with demand. In fact, a crisis-level shortage of child and adolescent psychiatrists and developmental/behavioral pediatricians exists in the United States.[14] These subspecialties require years of training, and the supply of professional programs is dwindling. Laws of economics predict that an inadequate supply of providers will produce higher fees—and a lack of access to care for families without means.

## Predicting the Future

What is the overall verdict? First, ADHD is here to stay, and so is medication. Despite continued bad press, despite the social stigma that still clings to this diagnosis, and despite the current state of the art related to deficient clinical assessment and treatment monitoring, ADHD is now an established part of child, adolescent, and adult mental health, with more than sufficient scientific evidence for its largely biological underpinnings and major associated impairments, along with a growing public face of ADHD among noted personalities. Stimulants work far too well for individuals with ADHD, at least in the short run, for this diagnosis and such medications to quickly leave the scene.

As for specific predictions, we have just highlighted that the push for performance and productivity in the United States should get more rather than less intense. In addition, the Affordable Care Act's provisions will drive ever-greater access to healthcare; more and more preschoolers are likely to be diagnosed because of changing professional standards; and the loss of patent exclusivity on long-acting stimulants will substantially reduce prices for these medications. For all of these reasons, it is highly likely that across the next 5 years, rates of youth ADHD will climb from the 2011–2012 levels of 11% (ever diagnosed) and 8.8% (currently diagnosed) to perhaps 13% in terms of lifetime diagnoses, or between one in eight and one in seven. This would mean that the rate for boys would be as high as one in six to one in five. In 2007, two-thirds (66%) of currently diagnosed children and adolescents were receiving medication, with a slight increase to 69% by 2011–2012. Thus, the youth medication rate may be reaching saturation. Still, we predict that adult medication rates will continue their current surge.[15]

On the other hand, several of the forces listed in the second part of Table 10–1—negative press attention, official calls to thwart medication-related neuroenhancement, and the potential for reduced stimulant quotas—should lead to a considerable leveling off of rates of diagnosis by 2020. Eventually, both diagnosis rates and medication rates could fall. We would make this prediction, of a leveling off and subsequent decline over the next decade, with more confidence if standards for accurate diagnosis of ADHD were enforced and reimbursed, reducing the quick-and-dirty "evaluations" that are still commonplace.

This may be a favorable turn of events if it signals that higher standards for diagnosing ADHD are actually practiced and if it means that people with legitimate diagnoses can obtain high-quality care from responsive providers. It would be a disaster if the tables turned so far that ADHD became ridiculed and restigmatized as a psychiatric, medicalized excuse for flaky behavior or lack of effort.

The strongest policy recommendation we make in this book is for a revitalized commitment to upgraded professional training in the nature, assessment, diagnosis, and treatment of ADHD. The public simply cannot continue to tolerate diagnoses based on cursory assessment or the dispensing of medication based on a wing and a prayer. It is highly likely that rushed evaluations leading to thoughtless medication prescriptions are just the ones that tend to get diverted to the general population. An additional priority for us is that behavioral and educational (for youth) and cognitive-behavioral (for adults) interventions be made much more available and provided with skill.

Turning around systems of care for ADHD will require several important events and practices: enhanced education and training in medical and professional schools; adequate reimbursements for thorough and accurate evaluations; team approaches spanning medicine, psychology, education, and related fields; and enforcement of the viable professional practice guidelines now in place. A huge boost toward these ends would be provided by an educated populace of consumers who demand optimal care. To that end, busting relevant myths has been a core motivation for writing this book.

## Different Disorder, Different Attitudes and Practices

In September 2012, *The New York Times* published an extremely important editorial on the crisis in treating high blood pressure (hypertension, defined as a reading above 140/90) in the United States. This editorial used a Centers for Disease Control and

Prevention study as its guide. In brief, 67 million Americans have hypertension, a figure well above that of ADHD. This condition is deadly and costly, leading to an estimated $130 billion cost to the economy each year. Hypertension can usually be treated successfully with medications, diet and lifestyle changes, or a combination. Yet over half of people with high blood pressure (36 million) are not receiving adequate healthcare, even though over 80% have health insurance coverage. This group is either unaware of their condition, not receiving medication for it, or receiving poorly monitored and therefore ineffective medication.[16]

Rather than blaming society for overlabeling a quarter of all adults, decrying medication use as poisoning the population, or chastising more and more people for letting their blood pressure levels climb, the *Times* editorial instead called for more efficient medical care for hypertension. A prime example is the kind provided by Kaiser Permanente, which has mounted an aggressive campaign to make sure that medications are taken regularly. Under this program in Northern California, which includes a regional hypertension registry and use of paraprofessionals to assist with medication and healthcare delivery, the number of deaths from strokes has been cut in half in 10 years, with serious heart attacks reduced by over 60%.[17]

There are two essential points to take away from this crucial example. First, the specific targeting of an important health issue, along with major efforts to increase awareness and ensure treatment, can produce dramatic changes in health outcomes, given real interest and investment. Second, if the same tone from the spate of anti-ADHD stories in 2012 and 2013 had been applied to blood pressure, op-ed and opinion pieces on hypertension would have castigated the weak personal will of those with high blood pressure readings and equated medication use with laziness and moral turpitude. That ADHD continues to receive the major-league ridicule it does speaks volumes about the stigma that remains. When it comes to mental disorders in general and ADHD in particular, knowledge and empathy are too often in short supply.

## Global Trends

Regarding the rest of the world, if ADHD exists (and thrives) only in above-subsistence economies, the growth of ADHD globally will be largely contingent on continuing modernization, industrialization, and postindustrialization in more and more nations. Because China and India comprise nearly a third of the world's population—and given the almost frantic push toward education in these nations—it is clear to us that diagnosis of ADHD will gather steam rather than slow down globally. Striving for ever-greater levels of productivity, other nations will not be far behind, as medications continue to find new markets overseas.

## Back to School

Given ADHD's strong linkage to educational practices and policies, along with escalating pressure for enhanced achievement, job performance, and productivity in today's world, it is tempting to think that a different set of philosophies about education and schooling could change the playing field. Many of these are captured in educational objectives like innovation, collaboration, communication, and critical thinking, beyond the accumulation of rote knowledge.[18] In other words, a less rigid, "one-size-fits-all" approach to schooling—via recognition of individual learning styles and a more tailored set of educational processes, objectives, and learning strategies—might be set-breaking. Use of engaging curricula, which ensure that greater numbers of youth will get turned on to discovering their skills, might lower rates of learning and attention disorders.

Along these lines, we note the ever-increasing role of high-tech in education. So long as computers are not viewed as replacing human instructors, high-quality and individualized educational programming via digital notebooks could allow more students with ADHD to attain academic success. The end result could be lowered rates of diagnosed ADHD, which tends to show itself most strongly in environments that emphasize conformity and rote learning.[19]

Still, the United States remains in the middle of the pack with respect to international test score performance.[20] If our nation is to maintain a semblance of competitiveness, much needs to happen. Pulitzer Prize–winning journalist Thomas Friedman points to small nations like Estonia, where it is becoming standard for *first-graders* to learn computer programming. Will China, he wonders out loud—and not entirely tongue in cheek—begin to teach *preschool* students to write "code"? If the United States is to remain competitive, he contends, we can't continue the myth that the Clinton-era ethos of working hard is the sole ticket to the American dream. He offers the following, far more complex formula:

> The truth is, if you want a decent job that will lead to a decent life today, you have to work harder, constantly reinvent yourself, obtain at least some form of postsecondary education, make sure that you're engaged in lifelong learning, and play by the rules. That's not a bumper sticker, but we terribly mislead people by saying otherwise.[21]

In short, within a global, "flat" world, Americans can no longer rely on the pre-Internet, pre-NAFTA world dominated by lower level, unionized jobs. Instead, Friedman contends, the need for a more sophisticated, educated, motivated, and flexible workforce has never been stronger. How to create such a workforce and, at the same time, appreciate individual differences in learning styles and attentional capacities may be the biggest challenge to our entire educational system.

## What Can Be Done? The Bottom Line

Supplementing our top 10 reasons for the continued rise of ADHD plus the top 10 reasons for thinking that things will level off or decline (see Table 10–1), we list below 10 major goals for improving the science and practice related to ADHD in the future. Each corresponds roughly to one of the book's chapters.

(1) *Ensure that ADHD is recognized as both biological and cultural and contextual in nature (Chapter 1).* When ADHD is viewed as either "all biological" or "all cultural," little progress is made. Individual differences in attention and self-regulation clearly exist, but these differences are brought into sharp relief in the context of our current push for performance. Integration is the key to finding answers, transcending the narrow-minded and reductionistic approaches that characterize too much of our past thinking about ADHD.

(2) *Demand that ADHD be diagnosed carefully by profession-als who know their business (Chapters 2 and 3).* This goal will require action on many fronts: upping the scientific lit-eracy of the general public, changing professional training procedures to assure education in evidence-based assessment practices; insisting on insurance reimbursement for full eval-uations; increasing the numbers of well-trained practitioners; and developing integrated assessment and treatment centers (see below).

(3) *Ensure that ADHD be treated by clinicians (and parapro-fessionals) who are versed in evidence-based interventions (Chapter 3).* Society must demand that ADHD-related treat-ments be delivered in accordance with current professional standards by professionals who monitor the efficacy of such interventions. We highlight, once again, Kaiser Permanente's model of evidence-based treatment program for hyperten-sion, which has produced dramatic reductions in heart attacks and death from strokes. Combinations of well-delivered med-ication plus family- and school-based behavioral treatments are typically optimal for ADHD.[22]

(4) *Set realistic national quotas for stimulants, balancing the need for prescriptions for legitimate cases of ADHD with the reality of ever-greater diversion of the medications for neuroenhance-ment or pleasure (Chapter 4).* Diversion of ADHD medications has grown in recent years to levels not seen since the 1970s. Stimulants on every dorm floor—sometimes mail ordered with no monitoring whatsoever—are *not* going to enhance the nation's public health or make us a smarter society.

(5) *Alter educational practices to promote more individualized approaches (Chapter 5).* L. Todd Rose, a Harvard educator with a personal background of severe ADHD, discusses teach-ing procedures (including computer-assisted learning) that could assist youth with ADHD and other learning and behav-ioral problems by turning schools into far more motivating contexts. The goal is not to coddle, or lower expectations for, youth with attentional and learning problems but to enable individuals with divergent learning and attentional styles to thrive. Test scores matter, but so does the fostering of attitudes promoting lifelong achievement and employment success.[23]

(6) *Facilitate partnered systems of care, and coordinated payment mechanisms, across insurers, schools, and employers (Chapter 6).* With the goals of reducing the need for costly special-education procedures and lifting overall achievement, we advocate university–school partnerships. Well-trained college students under close supervision could supplement regular-education teachers by (1) observing potentially troublesome youth in classrooms, thereby aiding the assessment process and (2) serving as aides to coach, prompt, and reinforce targeted youth. At the same time, nurses and medical paraprofessionals could help monitor medication-related gains. The potential to lower the multibillion dollar sinkhole in the economy linked to ADHD-related absenteeism and substandard work performance is great.

(7) *Convey a different set of media images about ADHD, emphasizing the reality of daily struggles and triumphs (Chapter 7).* This recommendation applies to all mental disorders, which should be portrayed in realistic rather than sensationalized terms, to reduce the still-prevalent stigma that exists. There are many procedures needed to reduce stigmatization—legislative change, access to evidence-based treatment, and enhanced empathy from society—with media depictions emphasizing humanization an essential part of the mix.

(8) *Encourage information exchange across scientists and clinicians internationally (Chapter 8).* Global health is a huge enterprise in many aspects of medicine and clinical care (e.g., infectious disease, disaster relief). Along these lines, the sharing of research and clinical information in the domains of behavioral health and mental disorders is essential. ADHD's increasing globalization mandates collaboration.

(9) *Continue to recognize that ADHD exists well beyond white, middle-class boys, revealing itself across gender, race and ethnicity, and the age span (Chapter 9).* To deflate the stereotype that ADHD is an upper-middle-class phenomenon of fidgety male behavior, efforts are needed to reveal its nature as an equal-opportunity condition that yields serious impairment among females, young children, adults, and minority individuals.

(10) *Recognize that fostering human potential, reducing stigma, and enhancing economic productivity go hand in hand.* Better systems of care, supported by an educated public and a responsive health system, will promote humanization, foster academic and social gains, enhance major life chances, and promote economic productivity.

## In the End

Keeping in mind the stark difference between current practices, policies, and attitudes related to hypertension and ADHD, we contend that the essential issues are ones of attitude, positioning, and stigma. Myths about ADHD persist. Too many people continue to believe that it's a cop-out, an unvalidated condition related to society's penchant for overmedicalizing deviance or a convenient label intended to cover over social problems. These myths destroy any hope of providing systematic educational, behavioral, and medical care for the youth, families, and adults who desperately need help. Medications are still viewed suspiciously for behavioral and psychiatric conditions, a position unfortunately fostered by the ease of getting an ADHD diagnosis and securing pills for performance enhancement in too many quarters of society—and by overreliance on medication as the only treatment worth pursuing. To deal with ADHD better than we do now, we must alter our attitudes as well as our educational and healthcare practices. At the same time, the incentives of the largely for-profit healthcare system in the United States may spur innovation and competition, but they can also drive up costs unless professional education, service delivery, and promotion of evidence-based practices are enhanced.

Our hope is that we have stimulated you to think about ADHD in productive, scientifically based, and innovative ways. If society can encourage better "fit" of differing behavioral and attentional styles into productive life pathways, the benefits for human potential, human capital, and the nation's (and even world's) economy should be of major proportions. Accompanying such shifts might be a real reduction in the doubt, shame, and stigma that still cling to individuals and families contending with the often devastating problems linked to ADHD. Aligning economic objectives with the desire for a more educated, humane, and productive society is a goal that all of us should endorse and work to achieve.

If we do not upgrade our fundamental attitudes about ADHD, as well as our standards for its diagnosis and treatment, we will all pay the price for many decades to come. The rewards to individuals, families, and society emanating from integrative thinking—and from doing it right—are potentially enormous.

# Notes

## Introduction

1. Schwarz (2013); for responses, see Hughes (2013) and Kollins (2013). Soon thereafter, additional front-page *Times* headlines were discussing the rising rates of ADHD diagnoses among children and adolescents in the United States (see Schwarz & Cohen, 2013).
2. Schwarz (2012a); see also Smith & Farah (2011) and Swanson et al. (2011). For somewhat earlier data, see Wilens et al. (2008).
3. Hughes (2012). Another side of the story was that the missing medications were not the newer, patented, far more expensive formulations but the less expensive generic forms. Whereas the Office of Diversion Control of the DEA sets yearly manufacturing quotas for medicines deemed potentially dangerous, like stimulants, economic pressures from manufacturers to push consumers toward higher price medicines may have also been involved. See Tkacik (2011), and discussion in Chapter 7.
4. Tkacik (2011); see also Harris (2011).
5. See Smith & Farah (2011) and Swanson et al. (2011); see also Low (2012) and Tkacik (2011). For information on rapid rises in emergency room visits linked to stimulants, see Hamblin (2013).

6. Sroufe (2012); Kureishi (2012).

7. Barkley (2006a); Chronis-Tuscano et al. (2010); Hinshaw (2002a); Hinshaw et al. (2012).

8. Visser et al. (2010); Visser et al. (2013); Schwarz & Cohen (2013). See also Froehlich et al. (2007), Getahun et al. (2013); Polanczyk et al. (2007); and Willcutt (2012).

9. For estimates from past decades, see Safer & Krager (1992); Safer & Malever (2000); and Safer et al. (1996). Note that the 2011–2012 NSCH data reveal that the rate of currently diagnosed youth aged 4–17 years is 8.8%, versus the rate of "ever" having been diagnosed, 11.0%.

10. Visser et al. (2010, 2013). For the 2003 and 2007 surveys, over 100,000 families were contacted. For the 2011–2012 survey, the number was 76,000.

11. Visser et al. (2013); Schwarz & Cohen (2013).

12. Getahun et al. (2013) showed that in California, rates of increase for ADHD diagnoses across the past decade were particularly high among Hispanic and African-American youth (especially girls for the latter). See also Visser et al. (2010, 2013). For additional information, see Garfield et al. (2012) and Zuvekas & Vitiello (2012). For information on adults with ADHD, see Okie (2006). Information on spending for prescription medications in the United States indicates that ADHD medicines ranked 12th (following, in descending order, medicines for cancer, lung conditions, high cholesterol, diabetes, psychosis, ulcers, depression, autoimmune conditions, HIV, high blood pressure, and pain); see IMS Institute for Healthcare Informatics (2012). Other sources of data confirm these trends: in 2000, 6.2 million office visits occurred for evaluating or treating ADHD in youth under 18, but by 2005 that rate had jumped to nearly 10 million per year, as described in Garfield et al. (2012). For adult prescriptions, see Schwarz (2013), who cites data from IMS Health that adult prescription rates increased 141% between 2007 and 2011. See also Connor (2012) for an overview of concerns linked to overdiagnosis and overmedication of ADHD. Note that in the 2003 NSCH related to ADHD, the question on medications inquired about a lifetime diagnosis of ADHD, but in the second (2007) and third (2011–2012) surveys, the question related to medication

was asked only for those families who reported a *current* diagnosis of ADHD in their offspring.
13. See Wakefield (1992).
14. Barkley (2006a); Nigg (2006); Nigg (2013); Thapar et al. (2013).


## Chapter 1

1. Getahun et al. (2013) document the sharp rise in ADHD diagnosis among Hispanic youth.
2. Groening (1994).
3. American Psychiatric Association (1980, 1987). The third edition (*DSM-III*, 1980) listed Attention Deficit Disorder with or without Hyperactivity; 7 years later, *DSM-III-R* changed the name to Attention-Deficit/Hyperactivity Disorder (ADHD), under the assumption that hyperactive/impulsive symptoms were most often present (no subtypes were listed). By 1994, *DSM-IV* (American Psychiatric Association, 1994) kept the name of ADHD but listed subtypes of "Predominantly Inattentive," "Predominantly Hyperactive-Impulsive," and "Combined" (for individuals displaying both symptom areas). If this historical progression seems confusing, we agree.
4. Mayes et al. (2008, 2009). For antipsychiatry, Scientology-backed opinions on ADHD and medication, see, as an example, Breggin (2002, p. 3): "Many children diagnosed with ADHD and treated with stimulants have relatively benign problems. Often they simply daydream in the classroom or dislike school a little more often than other children. Or they may be a little bit more active and energetic than most."
5. American Psychiatric Association (1952).
6. Quay & Werry (1972).
7. Palmer & Finger (2001); see also Barkley (2008).
8. The first U.S. state to enact a compulsory education law was Massachusetts, in 1852; the last (among the 48 states) was Mississippi, in 1917, as described in Wikipedia. Earlier, compulsory education was advocated by Plato in *The Republic*, as well as in the Talmud, in Aztec culture, and during the Reformation.
9. Still (1902); see Barkley (2006b).

10. Bradley (1937); see also Mayes et al. (2009).

11. Strauss & Lehtinen (1947); Clements & Peters (1962).

12. Laufer et al. (1957).

13. American Psychiatric Association (1968); see Chiarello & Cole (1987) for discussion of the Food and Drug Administration's approval of Ritalin earlier in the decade.

14. Iannelli (2011).

15. Swanson et al. (2011); Berman et al. (2009).

16. For a historical review, see Itkonen (2007).

17. Douglas (1972); American Psychiatric Association (1980).

18. American Psychiatric Association (1987); regarding CHADD, see Mayes et al. (2009).

19. See, for example, Sappell & Welkos (1990) and Mieszkowski (2005); for a review see Mayes et al. (2009).

20. Swanson et al. (1995); Mayes et al. (2008, 2009).

21. American Psychiatric Association (1994).

22. See Connor (2012) for commentary; see American Academy of Child and Adolescent Psychiatry Work Group on Quality Issues (1997).

23. See Zametkin et al. (1990), whose investigation was a key starting point for neuroimaging research in regard to ADHD. This body of research is summarized in Chapter 2.

24. MTA Cooperative Group (1999a, 1999b).

25. American Academy of Pediatrics (2000); see also Lenz (2005).

26. Scheffler et al. (2007).

27. See Mann et al. (2006). Gibbons et al. (2012) conducted a review finding no linkage between SSRIs in youth and suicidal behavior, 8 years after the major controversy from 2004 that led to a "black box" warning on prescription labels for these medications.

28. Barry et al. (2012).

29. See Swanson et al. (2011); American Academy of Child and Adolescent Psychiatry (2007).

30. See http://health.harvard.edu/press_releases/the-controversy-over-cardiac-testing-before-ADHD-treatment-begins

31. Volkow et al. (2009); see also Smith & Farah (2011) and Wilens et al. (2008).

32. Visser et al. (2010); see also Elder (2010).

33. Habel et al. (2011); Mayes et al. (2009); Sroufe (2012); Kureishi (2012); see also American Academy of Pediatrics (2011).

34. Schwarz (2013); Visser et al. (2013); American Psychiatric Association (2013).
35. Bradley (1937).
36. See, for example, Swanson et al. (2011).
37. American Psychiatric Association (1987, 1994, 2013).
38. Mayes et al. (2009).
39. MTA Cooperative Group (1999a, 1999b); see also Conners et al. (2001); Swanson et al. (2001).
40. The earliest of the new generation of longer-acting stimulant formulations include Concerta and Adderall XR. Lang et al. (2010) and Scheffler et al. (2007) document the greater increase in costs than in sales volume, related to the high cost of these patented formulations.
41. See Smith & Farah (2011) and Wilens et al. (2008).
42. Dickler (2011).
43. Ray et al. (2006). One implication is that earlier diagnosis might be protective against even higher excess costs later on. See also Ray et al. (2009): mothers of youth with ADHD have higher expenses than those of mothers of children without ADHD. The calculations related to the $20 billion-plus figure are found in notes 6, 7, and 8 for Chapter 6.
44. See Petris Working Paper, at www.petris.org/ADHDExplosion. This working paper incorporates data from the Medical Expenditure Panel Survey (MEPS), which provide a national-level update on the Ray et al. (2006) Kaiser incremental cost data. We highlight that when we controlled for comorbidity in the adult analyses, this factor did account for some of the excess costs for adults. Also, our estimate of 6 million youth emanates from the 2011–2012 NSCH data (see Visser et al., 2013). Using that estimate of the rate of 4- to 17-year-olds who have received an ADHD diagnosis (11%), we initially multiplied that rate by the number of children and adolescents in that age range across the United States. Note, however, that the rate of *current* diagnoses from the 2011–2012 NSCH data was 8.8%, which would provide a lower estimate. We believe that the most accurate estimate would be to split the difference between the two estimates (particularly because the costs of services remain high for previously diagnosed individuals with ADHD). Thus, a 10% rate yields an estimate of 6 million youth with ADHD. We gratefully acknowledge the contributions of Jeffrey Rhoades, PhD,

Social Science Analyst, Agency for Healthcare Research and Quality, regarding data analyses performed for this chapter.

45. See Barkley (2006a) for a summary.
46. Robb et al. (2011). This figure included special education services as well as grade retention and disciplinary incidents. The cost increment, multiplied by the estimated 6 million school-aged youth with ADHD in the United States, comes out to over $30 billion annually.
47. Pelham et al. (2007); see also Doshi et al. (2012).
48. Fletcher (2013).
49. Doshi et al. (2012).
50. Lefley (1989).

## Chapter 2

1. See www.nhlbi.nih.gov/guidelines/hypertension/jnc7full.pdf
2. From another perspective, Pickles & Angold (2003) view the debate as to whether mental health and illness are continuous or categorical as similar to the one asked by physicists regarding whether light is best conceptualized as a continuous wave or discrete photons. The answer is both: depending on one's perspective and framework, either view is potentially valuable. The same is undoubtedly true regarding mental illness.
3. Wakefield (1992).
4. Sobanski et al. (2010); Biederman et al. (2012).
5. American Psychiatric Association (2013).
6. See Barkley (2006a), Lawrence et al. (2002); Gladwell (1999).
7. Pingault et al. (2011); Breslau et al. (2011); Molina & Pelham (2003).
8. American Psychiatric Association (1994, 2013). Whereas these subclassifications were called "types" in *DSM-IV*, they are now viewed as "current presentations" in *DSM-5*, because over time, many youth switch between them. The biggest change between *DSM-IV* and *DSM-5* is that, in the former, one had to have at least some impairing symptoms of ADHD before the age of 7 to qualify for a diagnosis, but the latest edition has changed this "age of onset" criterion to before the age of 12. This change might be expected to promote a major increase in rates of ADHD, even though Polanczyk et al. (2010) report that this was not the case

for a large British cohort. In practice, however, most clinicians who do not follow evidence-based diagnostic practices would be expected to diagnose more children under this relaxed criterion.

9. Barkley (2006a); Hinshaw & Blachman (2005); Lahey et al. (1994).
10. Biederman et al. (2010); Hinshaw et al. (2012).
11. See, for example, Rothbart & Sheese (2007); see also Siegler et al. (2011).
12. Rothbart et al. (2007).
13. Campbell & Ewing (1990).
14. Siegler et al. (2011).
15. See Barkley (2006a).
16. See Barbaresi et al. (2013) for current estimates that the figure might actually be closer to ⅓, if one doesn't relax the diagnostic criteria to account for lower symptom rates in adults (accompanying news story in Healy, 2013). See also Kessler et al. (2010) and Faraone et al. (2006) regarding full versus partial persistence into adulthood. Barkley et al. (2002a) provide information on obtaining "informant" ratings into adulthood. In fact, the self-perceptions of young adults with ADHD begin to match the views of others by the age range of the mid-20s (see Barkley et al., 2008). The *DSM-5* criteria are found in American Psychiatric Association (2013).
17. For information on achievement problems, see Kent et al. (2011); Frazier et al. (2007); and Polderman et al. (2011). For information on the problems accruing from ADHD even in highly intelligent individuals, see Brown et al. (2009); Katusic et al. (2011); and Antshel et al. (2007).
18. Erhardt & Hinshaw (1994); Hinshaw & Melnick (1995); Hoza et al. (2005). Whereas youth with excessive hyperactivity/impulsivity are highly likely to be rejected by peers, those with the Inattentive form may be more likely to generate indifferent responses (i.e., the sociometric category of being ignored). See also Pera (2008).
19. See Barkley (2006a).
20. Hinshaw (2013).
21. Barbaresi et al. (2013); Barkley et al. (2008); Barkley et al. (2002b); Rowe et al. (2004); Swensen et al. (2004).
22. Angold et al. (1999).

23. Lee et al. (2008); Owens et al. (2009).
24. Diller (2011).
25. Douglas (1972).
26. Berger & Posner (2000).
27. See Castellanos et al. (2005) and Castellanos et al. (2006).
28. Barkley (2012); Brown (2013). However, up to half of people with ADHD do not appear to have noteworthy EF deficits as measured by objective tests, signaling that the EF model is not universal for ADHD (or, in the view of Barkley, that the typical means of measuring EF through one-on-one testing may not be valid).
29. Barkley (1997a, 1997b). Barkley once called for a shift in terminology, such that ADHD would be called "inhibitory deficit disorder." Confusing matters is that, in some accounts, response inhibition is branded as an executive function, rather than a precursor to the invoking of other executive functions.
30. Volkow et al. (2009).
31. See Burt (2009); Nikolas & Burt (2010); and Faraone et al. (2005); see also Cross-Disorder Group of the Psychiatric Genomics Consortium (2013).
32. Rutter (2006).
33. See Nesse (2005). In terms of specific genes linked to ADHD, key candidates are those that code for how the neurotransmitter dopamine is handled in the brain. A key dopamine-related gene is called *DRD4*, because it codes for the production of "type 4" dopamine receptors in the brain, which are highly linked to motivation and attention. People with a certain configuration of this gene are prone to try out exciting yet risky behaviors; it is conceivable, then, that the risk for developing ADHD is tied in with a more general tendency to be motivated for high-risk activities or for thinking outside the box. Other relevant genes are linked to important brain processes, such as the growth of neurons and their branching out to connect with other neurons. There is an incredible amount to be learned about the specific genes related to ADHD and how they interact with the environment to yield vulnerability to this condition; see, again, Cross-Disorder Group of the Psychiatric Genomics Consortium (2013). Regarding the genetic underpinnings of learning disorders, see Haworth & Plomin (2010).

34. See Nigg (2006), and Thapar et al. (2013) for an overview. Intriguingly, the data of Thapar et al. (2009) support the contention that maternal smoking during pregnancy predicts ADHD in the child largely through shared genes. See also Yoon et al. (2012).

35. For a definitive meta-analysis, see Nigg et al. (2012), who estimate small effects of restriction diets or dyes and additives on ADHD symptoms; see also Stevenson (2010).

36. Eskenazi et al. (2009); Eskenazi et al. (2010); de Cock et al. (2012); Kuehn (2010).

37. See Nigg et al. (2010).

38. Johnston & Mash (2001).

39. Stevens et al. (2008).

40. See, for example, Nakao et al. (2011).

41. Shaw et al. (2006, 2007, 2009); see also Shaw et al. (2012) regarding the total surface volume of cortex. Also see Ducharme et al. (2012) and Proal et al. (2011).

42. For overviews, see Bush (2010); Bush (2011); Nagel et al. (2011); and Konrad & Eickhoff (2010). See also Castellanos & Proal (2012). Girls show earlier brain maturation than boys, but whether sex differences in brain development are linked to ADHD is still unknown.

43. Even when the brain is at utter rest—as the mind wanders from topic to topic—brain images may be able to track susceptibility to ADHD. In other words, the brain-related "resting state" or "default network" of people with ADHD may intrude upon their task performance, contributing to the huge fluctuation in performance that characterizes people with high levels of inattention. See Castellanos et al. (2006); and Fassbender et al. (2009).

44. Beauchaine & Neuhaus (2008).

45. Hinshaw (2013).

## Chapter 3

1. For an example of a promising objective measure of attention and activity level, see Sumner (2010). In the summer of 2013, the FDA approved a "brain wave" (EEG) test for aiding in the

objective diagnosis of ADHD; see www.nlm.nih.gov/med-lineplus/news/fullstory_138754.html. Critics quickly contended, however, that this device was far from sound as "the" objective indicator of ADHD (e.g., www.medscape.com/view-article/809079; www.childmind.org/en/press/brainstorm/eeg-brainwave-test-ADHD-skips-ahead-science). The lack of objective diagnosis fuels the fire of critics who contend that there is no such thing as ADHD: if it can't be pinpointed via objective lab numbers or through the vivid colors of a brain image, it has no reality. For the antipsychiatry perspective, see Breggin (2001). But see the Web site Quackwatch for a highly critical view of his stances (http://www.quackwatch.org/11Ind/breggin.html). See also DeGrandpre & Hinshaw (2000) for a pro-and-con exchange on the reality of ADHD.

2. Wakefield (1992) presents a view of mental disorder as containing both biological/evolutionary and social/impairment components.

3. See Nigg (2006) and Thapar et al. (2013) for summaries of causal factors for ADHD.

4. Sleator & Ullmann (1981). In this classic study, doctors "missed" the vast majority of previously diagnosed cases of ADHD when they relied solely on their observations in the office.

5. See Hinshaw (2007); Kessler, Berglund et al. (2005).

6. Hinshaw & Zupan (1997).

7. See Chi & Hinshaw (2002).

8. In research settings, these kinds of checklists and rating scales are often supplemented with "structured interviews," which contain lists of questions dealing with the symptoms of ADHD and related disorders. The questions probe for details about when the problems started, how long they have persisted, and the kinds of impairment they engender. Although these interviews provide rich understanding of the individual's problems, they are usually too time-consuming for most clinical use. The astute reader may have noted that our discussion of age norms, which suggests strongly that differing numbers of symptoms should be required for children of different ages, is ignored in the DSM, which has a fixed number of symptoms for diagnosing youth of any age (although there is the requirement for one fewer symptom in adults, per ADHD domain, in DSM-5; American Psychiatric Association [2013]).

9. A medical examination may also include a cardiac examination. Some have contended that such a test is needed before medication treatment, given the slight potential for stimulant medications to propel heart-related problems. Yet recent consensus is that this procedure is usually unnecessary; see Habel et al. (2011); Cooper et al. (2011); Mick et al. (2013); and Olfson et al. (2012). For a review of sleep and ADHD, see Yoon et al. (2012).

10. Angold et al. (1999).

11. See Johnston & Mash (2001); see also Wells et al. (2006).

12. American Academy of Pediatrics (2000, 2011); American Academy of Child and Adolescent Psychiatry Work Group on Quality Issues (1997, 2007); see also Lynch et al. (2010).

13. Angold et al. (2000). Garfield et al. (2012) showed that an increasing number of visits for ADHD in recent years have been performed by psychiatrists, as opposed to pediatricians or general practitioners.

14. For information on complementary and alternative medicine (CAM) see www.nccam.nih.gov, which estimates that 38% of Americans employ CAM in some form. For information on alternative treatments for ADHD, see Arnold (1999) and Hurt et al. (2011).

15. Feingold (1977); Stevenson (2010); McCann et al. (2007); see review of Sonuga-Barke et al. (2013), which includes positive findings from free fatty acid supplementation studies.

16. Lofthouse et al. (2011); Lofthouse et al. (2012); see Arnold et al. (2012) for initial data on the "sham" biofeedback control group.

17. Rutledge et al. (2012); Wass et al. (2012); see also Shipstead et al. (2012).

18. See Bradley (1937) for the initial publication on stimulants for therapeutic use in children.

19. Rapoport (1978); Rapoport (1980).

20. See Swanson et al. (1993); Conners (2002); and Faraone & Buitelaar (2010). For a review of the ways in which stimulants affect brain regions and tracts implicated in ADHD-related behaviors, see Levy (2009) and Volkow et al. (2012). As to whether stimulants can help individuals just below the diagnostic threshold for ADHD, the answer is generally yes, at least to some extent. We address this point in more detail in Chapter 4. Finally, some have questioned whether taking medications might

reduce individuals' beliefs in their own levels of effort. Scientific studies suggest otherwise: see Milich et al. (1989) and Pelham et al. (2002).

21. Lichtenstein et al. (2012).

22. See, for example, Habel et al. (2011); Cooper et al. (2011); Mick et al. (2013); Olfson et al. (2012). For other side effects, see Julien et al. (2011).

23. See Pelham et al. (1995); Balthazor et al. (1991); see also Scheffler et al. (2009); Zoega et al. (2012); Langberg & Becker (2012).

24. Humphreys et al. (2013). See also Lee et al. (2011) and Molina et al. (2013). In all probability, the protective benefits for some individuals are counterbalanced by the fact that, in naturalistic trials, the most severely affected individuals get the most treatment.

25. For evidence related to the potential for neuroprotective effects of stimulant medications, see Castellanos et al. (2002). See also Nakao et al. (2011) and Sobel et al. (2010). For a recent review related to ADHD, see Spencer et al. (2013). For a different example, it is now well known that selective serotonin reuptake inhibitors (SSRIs) exhibit neuroprotective effects in key brain regions for people with depression.

26. Julien et al. (2011).

27. Molina et al. (2009); Molina et al. (2013). See also Riddle et al. (2013) for parallel findings from a long-term follow-up of preschoolers receiving medication for ADHD.

28. See Rappley et al. (1995); Palli et al. (2012).

29. Volkow et al. (2009).

30. Fabiano et al. (2009). Note that because of the strong heritability of ADHD, a sizable proportion of biological parents of youth with ADHD may have the condition themselves, whether diagnosed or not. It's hard enough to parent a child or adolescent with ADHD consistently, but parental inattention, impulse control problems, and/or emotion dysregulation make the task far more difficult.

31. Pfiffner & McBurnett (1997); Mikami et al. (2010); Mikami et al. (2013). For information on deviancy training, see Dishion et al. (1996). Others point out that deviancy training among peers can be minimized with clear contingencies and strong control of the group by its leaders.

32. See Solanto et al. (2010); Knouse & Safren (2010); Pfiffner et al. (2007); Pfiffner & Glasscock (2011).

33. MTA Cooperative Group (1999a); Swanson et al. (2001); Conners et al. (2001).

34. Hinshaw et al. (2000).

35. Singh (2012). The VOICES team interviewed 151 American and British children aged 9 to 14 who were taking medication for ADHD between 2008 and 2010. "On balance," Singh writes, "children report that stimulant drugs improve their capacity for moral agency," explaining that most felt the medications allowed them to make better choices. As an American 11-year-old girl told the researchers, "With medication, it's not that you're a different person; you're still the same person, but you just act a little better. Medication will help you control yourself." A 10-year-old American boy put it this way: "Medication slows my brain down and makes good ideas stay longer." Another 10-year-old boy described his ADHD as a "blocker" that prevented him from going the right way. "[The medicine] opens the blocker so you can go [the right] way. But you still have the choice of going the wrong way," he said.

36. See Lynch et al. (2010); MTA Cooperative Group (1999b); note also Garfield et al. (2012), with growing psychiatrist involvement in ADHD treatment.

37. American Academy of Pediatrics (2000, 2011); American Academy of Child and Adolescent Psychiatry Work Group on Quality Issues (1997, 2007); see also Epstein et al. (2010).

## Chapter 4

1. Sroufe (2012) and Kureishi (2012). See Chapter 7 for detailed coverage of *The New York Times'* stances on ADHD in 2012 and 2013.

2. See Battista (2012); see also Boeck (2012) and Hochman (2011) for stories about baseball players Andres Torres and Shane Victorino.

3. Swanson et al. (2011) assert that stimulant dependence or abuse is negligible for well-monitored prescriptions to viable cases of individuals with ADHD, although hard and fast numbers are hard to come by. See also Schwarz (2013) for the harrowing details of the case of Fee.

4. Smith & Farah (2011).

5. See Mayes et al. (2009); Safer et al. (1996).

6. Lang et al. (2010); Scheffler et al. (2007). See also Fullerton et al. (2012), who analyzed Medicaid data in Florida from 1996 to 2005 and found that costs of stimulants went up at a far higher rate than other prescriptions, linked largely to price increases for the longer-acting formulations. They also noted that during that time, second-generation antipsychotic medication prescriptions (and especially costs) rose dramatically for youth with ADHD, reflecting the trend for the most severely affected cases to be tried on medications to reduce explosiveness and aggression.

7. Visser et al. (2013).

8. Volkow et al. (2009).

9. It would make things clearer if stimulants were called "SDRI,"— that is, selective dopamine reuptake inhibitors, which describes their actions (see the parallel with SSRI medications, which block the serotonin transporter). Note that in addition to blocking dopamine transport/reuptake, amphetamines (unlike methylphenidate) also inhibit monoamine oxidase (MAO) and enhance the release of dopamine into the synaptic cleft; see Julien et al. (2011).

10. Elia et al. (1991); Conners (2002); Wilens (1999).

11. Wilens (1999); Elliott & Kelly (2006); Swanson, Waxmonsky, et al. (2013).

12. See Kroutil et al. (2006) for estimates of rates of substance dependence for individuals without ADHD who use stimulants. The reported range was 10–13%. See also Rasmussen (2008), who provides estimates for levels of general stimulant abuse back in the 1960s and 1970s, as well as Berman et al. (2009) and Swanson et al. (2011). Timothy Wilens (personal communication, August 2013) noted that, in an adolescent/young adult follow-up of medicated boys with ADHD conducted at Massachusetts General Hospital, about 10% admitted to having sold their medications and about 20% to having taken more medication than prescribed on at least some occasions. Nearly all such individuals had co-occurring conduct problems and/or abuse issues with other medications. Thus, even though well-monitored children with ADHD rarely show abuse or dependence, as they mature, close medication monitoring is even more crucial.

13. Although Web sites exist for procuring stimulants via mail order, we intentionally do not include specific links in these notes.

14. For information related to the posing of this question, see Barkley (2006a).
15. Erhardt & Hinshaw (1994). In addition, girls with ADHD receive even more peer rejection than boys with this condition, probably because their behavior patterns are more gender-atypical (see Blachman & Hinshaw, 2005). There is an important clinical implication from this work: if a youth is known to be responsive to a given treatment (medication or behavioral), it would be extremely beneficial to start the school year with that treatment in place—rather than to try and "see how things go," only to have reputations tainted after an unsuccessful start to the school year.
16. See Whalen et al. (1989).
17. For example, Carlson et al. (1991); see also Milich et al. (1991). There has been a long-standing concern that the dosages optimal for such cognitive enhancement are not the same as those for reducing disruptive behavior. Years ago, research revealed that it took relatively low stimulant doses to boost performance on memory tests or other lab measures, with higher doses, which dampened cognitive performance, needed for producing behavioral control (Sprague & Sleator, 1977). Thus, medication might be titrated to the highest dose possible in order to reduce problem behavior, but with compromised learning. In other words, medicine might make kids docile but dull. Yet subsequent work has shown that whereas extremely high doses might well impede learning and laboratory test performance, at low to moderate dose levels, both cognition and behavior improve in tandem. Finally, individual differences in medication response are the rule, so different patterns may well apply to different youth or adults receiving the medications.
18. Advokat et al. (2011); Hellwig-Brida et al. (2011).
19. MTA Cooperative Group (1999a, 1999b).
20. Barbaresi et al. (2007); see also Powers et al. (2008).
21. Scheffler et al. (2009).
22. Zoega et al. (2012).
23. Rapoport (1978); Rapoport (1980).
24. Smith & Farah (2011).
25. Smith & Farah (2011); Swanson et al. (2011). See also Ilieva et al. (2013).
26. See, for example, Rabiner (2013); Swanson et al. (2011); Sahakian & Morein-Zamir (2007); Talbot (2009); and Stix (2012). See also

Singh et al. (2013) for an excellent perspective on neuroenhancement in relation to the globalization of ADHD.

27. Smith & Farah (2011).

28. Kroutil et al. (2006); Rasmussen (2008); see also Swanson et al.
    (2011) and Hamblin (2013). Sweeney et al. (2013) report that
    nomedical use of prescription stimulants (i.e., diversion) is typi-
    cally performed by people already engaging in broader patterns
    of misused medications.

29. Swanson et al. (2011).

30. See Grinspoon & Hedblom (1975); Rasmussen (2008); see also
    Swanson et al. (2011).

31. Swanson et al. (2011); for a critical commentary on diversion, see
    Stein (2012).

32. Haney-Jardine (post-production). Miguel Tejada, a former MVP
    in the American League, was suspended for 105 games in August,
    2013, for using the stimulant Adderall. Tejada claims that he
    has legitimate ADHD and was using Adderall for medical rea-
    sons but hadn't yet received a Therapeutic Use Exemption (see
    http://www.bloomberg.com/news/2013-08-17/royals-tejada-gi
    ven-105-game-suspension-by-mlb-for-amphetamines.html).

33. Stix (2009).

34. Smith & Farah (2011), p. 736.

35. Graf et al. (2013); see story in WebMD, retrieved from http://
    www.webmd.com/add-adhd/childhood-adhd/news/20130313/
    dont-give-adhd-meds-to-undiagnosed-kids-experts-urge

36. See British Pain Society (2010).


## Chapter 5

1. Authors' analysis of data from Visser et al. (2010). For Figures 5–1
   and 5–2, we color-coded a state-by-state map of the United States
   to reflect the rates of "ever diagnosed" with ADHD from the
   2007 National Survey of Children's Health (NSCH). As we have
   discussed, the most recent NSCH reported that the overall rate
   of "ever diagnosed" for children and adolescents in the United
   States had climbed to 11% by 2011–2012, as reported by Visser
   et al. (2013). In this most recent survey, much of the South and

Midwest had continued to grow in terms of rates of ADHD diagnosis and medication treatment, but the West retained its previously low levels. Specifically, North Carolina's rate of ADHD diagnosis dipped slightly (14.4% versus 15.6% in 2007), whereas California's increased slightly (7.3% versus 6.2% in 2007), partially because of the increasing rates in the large Hispanic population there. Because the 2011–2012 NSCH data were released at the time of the final writing of this book, with no opportunity for us to perform detailed analysis of state-by-state patterns, we focus on the dramatic 2007 statewide differences in Figures 5–1 and 5–2. The regional differences highlighted in this chapter would doubtless apply to the newer data as well.

2. Visser et al. (2010); Visser et al. (2013).
3. Wennberg (1984); Wennberg & Gittelsohn (1973, 1982).
4. Wennberg (1984); Wennberg & Gittelsohn (1973, 1982).
5. See Rose (2013).
6. Visser et al. (2010). We used data from the 2007 NSCH to compile the information in Table 5–1, as well as several additional sources. For consequential accountability, see Dee & Jacob (2011); Hanushek & Raymond (2005). For high school exit exams, see Jacob & Dee (2009); Warren et al. (2006); and Center for Education Policy High School Exit Exam Final Reports (2002–2011); for information on providers, see National Center for Health Workforce Analysis.
7. See Petris Working Paper, at www.petris.org/ADHDExplosion
8. Getahun et al. (2013); see also Visser et al. (2013).
9. Rappley et al. (1995).
10. Bokhari et al. (2005); Bruckner et al. (2012); see also Fulton et al. (2009).
11. Petris Working Paper, at www.petris.org/ADHDExplosion
12. Cohen et al. (1996).
13. Visser et al. (2010).
14. Mainous et al. (2008); see also www.euromedinfo.eu/how-culture-influences-health-beliefs/html
15. Hanushek (2003); Hanushek & Raymond (2005). As our colleague Susan Stone has noted, there have been many historical shifts, related to school policy, between output- and standards-based benchmarks and a more individually tailored, personalized set of benchmarks (as John Dewey called for a century ago).

16. No Child Left Behind Act (2002).
17. Kress et al. (2011); Hanushek & Raymond (2005).
18. Stone et al. (2010).
19. Kline (2009).
20. Dee & Jacob (2006, 2011); Jacob & Dee (2009); Hanushek & Raymond (2005); Warren et al. (2006). See also Figlio & Loeb (2011).
21. For full details, see Fulton et al. (2014). We defined low income as within 200% of the federal poverty level. See also Figlio & Loeb (2011); Bokhari & Schneider (2011).
22. For information on consequential accountability and exit exam laws shown in Table 5–2, see Dee & Jacob (2011); Hanushek & Raymond (2005); Jacob & Dee (2009); Warren et al. (2006); and Center for Education Policy High School Exit Exam Final Reports (2002–2011). For information on psychotropic medication laws, see Note 22 below.
23. See Ablechild.org. *Child labeling & drugging bills & resolutions passed*. Retrieved January 28, 2011, from http://ablechild. org/slegislation.htm; see FightForKids.org. *U.S. bills & resolutions introduced or passed against coercive psychiatric labeling & drugging of children*. Retrieved December 2, 2010, from http://www.fightforkids.org/bills_and_resolutions.php; see also American Academy of Child and Adolescent Psychiatry (2005); Curran (2008); Lenz (2005); and Fulton et al. (2014).

## Chapter 6

1. Estimates of how many adults actually have ADHD are complicated by the question of whether the number of required symptoms should be officially reduced in adults, given the normative declines in hyperactivity with age (*DSM-5* now requires five of nine symptoms in either symptom domain, rather than six of nine, as is the case for youth). Substantial evidence exists that even if symptoms are "lost" over time, substantial impairment remains. For estimates, see http://www.webmd.com/add-adhd/ guide/adhd-adults. One way to estimate the number of adults with ADHD is to assume that adult prevalence is 4.4% (around half the "current" prevalence for children and adolescents of 8.8%) and multiplying that number by the approximately 220 million adults in the United States under the age of 65,

arriving at a figure of approximately 9 million. Some, however, contend that the more accurate percentage of child-to-adult rates is closer to one-third—see Barbaresi et al. (2013). For an alternative perspective—namely, that rates are actually higher than 50%—see Barkley et al. (2008). See also Kessler, Adler et al. (2005); and Kessler et al. (2006). For costs related to ADHD in adulthood, see Biederman & Faraone (2006). For information on continuing impairments, see Klein et al. (2012) and Hinshaw et al. (2012).

2. Biederman & Faraone (2006); Doshi et al. (2012).

3. Lichtenstein et al. (2012); Fredriksen et al. (2013); Wilens et al. (2001).

4. Knouse & Safren (2010); Safren et al. (2010); Solanto (2011); Solanto et al. (2010).

5. See Petris Working Paper, at www.petris.org/ADHDExplosion. We gratefully acknowledge the contributions of Jeffrey Rhoades, PhD, Social Science Analyst, Agency for Healthcare Research and Quality, regarding the data analyses performed for this chapter.

6. In terms of calculations, we begin with the 2011–2012 NSCH data (Visser et al., 2013). These reveal a rate of *current* diagnosis of ADHD among 4- to 17-year-olds of 8.8%, with 69% of them receiving medication. Thus, taking 69% of 8.8%, just over 6% of youth in the United States are receiving ADHD medication. With approximately 65 million youth in the United States, between 4 and 4.5 million are currently medicated. Next, incremental costs for treating youth with ADHD were $1500 in 2008 (even controlling for comorbidity). Applying the 9.8% rate of annual increase of such costs (which adjusts for both medical and consumer price inflation) yields a figure of $2,500 per year by 2013, thus totaling nearly $8 billion. Again, overall treatment costs (beyond medication) are estimated to have risen from over $12 billion (2008; see Table 6–1) to $20 billion (2013), applying the 9.8% annual rate of increase to the 2008 figure.

7. In terms of the numbers of youth receiving treatment, the technical term is *use prevalence*, meaning the percent of the entire population of young people who actually use services to treat ADHD, such as visits to medical providers and consuming stimulants. In 2008, the use prevalence for children and adolescents was 6.7%, as compared to 4.2% in 2000 (see Table 6–1,

second row). This signals a greater than 50% increase in less than a decade. We now perform some calculations from 2007, a year for which we have data in Table 6–1 and from the second NSCH survey (Visser et al., 2010). The overall lifetime rate of ADHD for children and adolescents from the 2007 NSCH was 9.5%; the rate of youth with a *current* diagnosis was 7.2%. From Table 6–1, second row under the 2007 column, the use prevalence was 5.4%. Dividing 5.4% by 7.2% reflects the percentage of currently diagnosed youth with ADHD who were actually receiving treatment (or were at least having doctor's office visits in which ADHD was noted as a reason for the visit, which is what the Medical Expenditure Panel Survey [MEPS] data signify). This figure is 75%. Taking the opposite perspective, a quarter of currently diagnosed youth were *not* receiving treatment. As noted in the text, (1) more and more youth being are being treated for ADHD, and (2) the costs for each treated child are steadily increasing (see Note 6).

8. For adults with ADHD, use prevalence is far lower than it is for youth. For the period from 2006 to 2008, MEPS data reveal that only 0.7% of all adults were using services related to ADHD. This figure of 0.7%, when divided by 4.4% (the estimated adult prevalence of ADHD, which is half the NSCH figure for 4- to 17-year olds of 8.8% from Visser et al., 2013), is only 16%. Thus, only a sixth of adults with ADHD were actually receiving treatment. Still, taking an estimate of nearly $10 billion for 2008 adult treatment costs, multiplying by the estimated yearly increase in such costs of 15.7%, the total treatment spending by 2013 would be $20 billion. Again, however, if the numbers of adults treated (about one in six) were closer to the more than two-thirds of youth who are treated, the resultant adult treatment costs would rise to over $85 billion. As highlighted later in the chapter, treatment costs would go up substantially if evidence-based treatments were actually performed, based on higher training costs and a greater number of sessions to monitor treatment outcome carefully.

9. Swanson, Lakes et al. (2013).

10. See calculations in Notes 7 and 8.

11. The MTA Cooperative Group (1999b) found that, among children with ADHD from the United States and Canada in the 1990s, those receiving medication in the community had a low

standard of care. See also Epstein et al. (2010) and Lynch et al. (2010).

12. Foster et al. (2007).

13. See, for example, Anderson & Estee (2002) and Blount et al. (2007).

14. U.S. Department of Commerce (2012).

15. See Becker (1975).

16. See Barro & Lee (2001); Helliwell (2006); Lange & Topel (2006); Olaniyan & Okemakinde (2008); Pissarides (2000).

17. Levy & Kochan (2012). We are extremely grateful for Frank Levy's sharing of these most important data.

18. Friedman, T. (2012).

19. Hanushek & Raymond (2005).

20. Jacob (2007).

21. Krueger & Whitmore (2001). The question, however, is whether the increased cost nationwide of smaller class sizes pays off in terms of eventual academic productivity.

22. Currie & Stabile (2006); Knapp et al. (2011).

23. Fletcher (2013).

24. Scheffler et al. (2009).

25. See Zoega et al. (2012).

26. MTA Cooperative Group (1999a); Conners et al. (2001).

27. Lange & Topel (2006); Olaniyan & Okemakinde (2008).

28. Different federal statutes, including the Americans with Disabilities Act (ADA), underlie such accommodations, which apply to physical, developmental, and mental disabilities. Signed into law in 1990, the ADA was amended by Congress in 2008, with the result that the standard for documenting a substantial disability was lowered. Thus, it is now easier to assert impairment and be granted accommodations.

29. Vickers (2010).

30. Vickers (2010).

31. See the Educational Testing Service Web site for entrance exam accommodations: http://www.ets.org/disabilities/

32. Vickers (2010) makes the case for this means of disclosing or "flagging" accommodations.

33. Rose (2013). The claim is that so-called noncognitive factors (e.g., motivation, executive functions) are as essential for achievement as "smarts" per se.

34. Allen & Seaman (2010); Pappano (2012); Friedman (2013a); Lewin (2012); Wallis (2013).
35. Psacharopoulos & Patrinos (2004); Vandal & Education Commission of the States (2011).

## Chapter 7

1. Gonon et al. (2012).
2. Lillard & Peterson (2011); Christakis et al. (2004). For a media account, see Park (2012).
3. See http://adultaddstrengths.com/2005/5/11/the-gifts-of-adhd/ and http://www.attitudemag.com/adhd/article/754.html. See also Beck (2010) and Katusic et al. (2011).
4. See Barkley (2006a); Chronis-Tuscano et al. (2010); Hinshaw et al. (2012).
5. Elder (2010); see also Morrow et al. (2012). See media story in Szalavitz (2012).
6. American Academy of Pediatrics (2011).
7. Schwarz (2012a); Battista (2012). See also Stein (2012).
8. For provocative perspectives on neuroenhancement, see Sahakian & Morein-Zamir (2007); see also Greely et al. (2008); Larriviere et al. (2009).
9. Lake (2010).
10. For example, see Habel et al. (2011); Cooper et al. (2011); Mick et al. (2013); Olfson et al. (2012).
11. Jasinski et al. (2011).
12. Hinshaw (2007); Wahl (1995).
13. Whitley & Berry (2013); Coverdale et al. (2002); O'Hara & Hinshaw (2013); Wahl (2003); Wilson et al. (2000).
14. Pescosolido et al. (2010); Phelan et al. (2000, 2002).
15. Schrag & Divoky (1975); Conrad & Schneider (1980); see also Singh (2002). For background related to the role of Scientology along these lines, see also Wright (2013) and McGrath (2013).
16. See Singh (2002).
17. Ray & Hinnant (2009).
18. Merrow (1995); DeGrandpre (2000); Diller (1998).
19. Gladwell (1999); see also Hallowell & Ratey (1995).

20. Gonon et al. (2012). It is undoubtedly true that parallel "over-selling" has occurred for many other conditions as well.

21. Wikipedia: http://en.wikipedia.org/wiki/Attention_deficit_hyperactivity_disorder; WebMD: http://www.webmd.com/add-adhd/default.htm; Centers for Disease Control and Prevention (CDC): http://www.cdc.gov/ncbddd/adhd/; National Institute of Mental Health (NIMH): http://www.nimh.nih.gov/health/publications/attention-deficit-hyperactivity-disorder/complete-index.shtml; KidsHealth for teens: http://kidshealth.org/teen/school_jobs/school/adhd.html; KidsHealth for adults: http://kidshealth.org/parent/medical/learning/adhd.html; Children and Adults with Attention-Deficit/Hyperactivity Disorder (CHADD): http://www.chadd.org/Understanding-ADHD.aspx; Lilly: http://www.adhd.com/index.html; PsychCentral: http://psychcentral.com/disorders/adhd/; Mayo Clinic: http://www.mayoclinic.com/health/adhd/DS00275

22. Barry et al. (2012).

23. http://www.webmd.com/add-adhd/news/20120103/adhd-drug-shortages-why

24. Fields (2012).

25. Tkacik (2011).

26. See Sroufe (2012) and Kureishi (2012).

27. Kristof (2012).

28. Sroufe (2012). For relevant research emanating from Sroufe's team, see Carlson et al. (1995).

29. Kureishi (2012).

30. Friedman, R (2012).

31. Brooks (2012).

32. Hruska (2012).

33. O'Neil (2012).

34. Dell'Antonia (2012).

35. Schwarz (2012a).

36. Schwarz (2012b); Schwarz (2013); Schwarz & Cohen (2013); "Worry over attention deficit cases" (2013); Gup (2013); Thakkar (2013). The latter, dealing with sleep and ADHD, was based on extremely small numbers of research participants.

37. Hallowell (2012).

38. ALZA Corporation (2003). ALZA, the initial manufacturer of Concerta, was subsequently acquired by Johnson & Johnson.

39. Shire US Inc. (2007).

40. Shire US Inc. (2012).

41. Huh et al. (2010); Mogull (2008).

42. Gilbody et al. (2005).

43. Feldman & Begun (1978); Comanor & Wilson (1979); Folland (1985); Masson & Rubin (1985).

44. Calfee (2002); Cregan & Magazine Publishers of America (2002); Federal Trade Commission (2004).

45. Dave & Saffer (2010); See also Kaiser Family Foundation (2003).

46. Avery et al. (2012).

47. We thank Sharanjit Sandhu for her work on these data, which were compiled from a search of magazine advertisement databases and an examination of actual copies of the relevant magazines in Figure 7–4.

48. Frank et al. (2002).

49. Handlin et al. (2003); Donohue et al. (2007). We thank Christopher Adalio and his unpublished synthesis of information on the topic of direct-to-consumer advertising.

50. For a thorough description of patents and patent exclusivity, see Eisenberg (2003). We thank Howard Goldman for penetrating comments along these lines.

51. Gilbody et al. (2005).

52. Mintzes et al. (2003).

53. World Health Organization (2009); Agency for Healthcare Research and Quality (2009).

## Chapter 8

1. Retrieved from http://onejerusalem.com/2011/02/09/medical-histadrut-permits-over-the-counter-ritalin/. The Medical Federation in Israel is called Histadrut. As stated by the head of the Ethics Board, Professor Avinoam Reches, in defense of the policy change: "Everyone has the right to make the most of themselves so long as it doesn't hurt or endanger others...Though a person may not suffer from Attention Deficit Disorder, if Ritalin helps him concentrate then it is allowed. It is the same for memory-improvement drugs. If they help a person

with slightly worsened cognitive skills then there is no reason not to give them to him." The policy was clarified by Professor Avi Sadeh, Tel Aviv University, August, 2011, personal communication; Professors Yoel Elizur and Or-Noy further clarified actual policy via personal communication, August 2012.

2. Hinshaw et al. (2011).
3. For a cultural perspective on ADHD, see Timimi & Taylor (2004).
4. Faraone et al. (2003). There are ADHD support groups in Saudi Arabia, for example.
5. Polanczyk et al. (2007). These authors note, however, that the relatively low sample sizes in Africa and the Middle East make contrasts of these regions with North America less than robust statistically.
6. Hinshaw et al. (2011).
7. World Health Organization (2009); see http://www.who.int/classifications/icd/en/
8. Prendergast et al. (1988).
9. Polanczyk et al. (2007).
10. Getahun et al. (2013); see also Visser et al. (2010).
11. Polanczyk et al. (2008).
12. Schwab (2012).
13. Lu et al. (2006); Sun et al. (2009); Norvilitis et al. (2010); Hinshaw et al. (2011).
14. See, for example, Burt (2009).
15. Scheffler et al. (2007).
16. These findings on global medication include data provided courtesy of IMS Health, but do not necessarily reflect views of IMS Health. License: IMS Institute for Healthcare Informatics (IHI) customized therapy class definition: ADHD (N6B & Strattera, Intuniv) totalSource: MIDAS™ 2000–2010, IMS Health Incorporated. All Rights Reserved. See Petris Working Paper, at www.petris.org/ADHDExplosion. We thank Peter Levine, MD, for his work on creating standard units of different stimulant medications.
17. See, once again, Petris Working Paper, at www.petris.org/ADHDExplosion
18. Scheffler et al. (2007).
19. Hinshaw et al. (2011).
20. We thank all conference participants, named in the Acknowledgments: Brent Fulton, Brad Berman, Peter Jensen, Glen Elliott, Howard Goldman, Amy Nuttbrock, Heidi Aase,

Tobias Banaschewski, Wenhong Cheng, Paulo Mattos, Arne Holte, Florence Levy, Avi Sadeh, Joe Sergeant, Eric Taylor, and Margaret Weiss. For recent and enlightened work on the globalization of ADHD, particularly related to neuroenhancement and ethical challenges for clinicians, see Singh et al. (2013).

21. Sawyer et al. (2001); Royal Australasian College of Physicians (2009).
22. See www.teachADHD.ca
23. Hinshaw et al. (2011).
24. See Ray et al. (2006) for comparable U.S. figures.
25. See Farbstein et al. (2010); Fogelman et al. (2003); Mansbach-Kleinfeld et al. (2010).
26. National Institute for Health and Clinical Excellence (2009).

## Chapter 9

1. Barkley (1988).
2. American Academy of Pediatrics (2011).
3. Dawson et al. (2012); Warren et al. (2011).
4. Campbell & Ewing (1990).
5. American Academy of Pediatrics (2011).
6. Greenhill et al. (2006); Riddle et al. (2013).
7. See, for example, Castellanos et al. (2002) and Spencer et al. (2013).
8. Carey (2006, 2011); Harris et al. (2007). We note that second-generation antipsychotic medications have a clear role in psychiatry. The question, however, is whether the major increases in their prescription for children are justified.
9. See, for example, Wood et al. (1976) for a very early study of ADHD in adults.
10. Barkley et al. (2002a). Partly on the basis of data like those from this investigation, *DSM-5* has reduced the criteria for diagnosis of adults from six to five symptoms of either inattention or hyperactivity/impulsivity, as noted earlier.
11. Barkley (1997a, 1997b); Barkley (2012); Barkley et al. (2008).
12. Jasinski et al. (2011).
13. See, for example, Hinshaw (2002b); Hinshaw & Blachman (2005); Rucklidge (2010).

14. American Psychiatric Association (2000), Hinshaw & Blachman (2005).
15. Quinn (2005).
16. Clements & Peters (1962).
17. Kessler et al. (2006); see also Swanson, Lakes, et al. (2013).
18. Hinshaw et al. (2012); see also Babinski et al. (2011); Biederman et al. (2012).
19. Hinshaw et al. (2012); see also Chronis-Tuscano et al. (2010).
20. MTA Cooperative Group (1999b).
21. Visser et al. (2010).
22. Getahun et al. (2013); Visser et al. (2013).
23. Hinshaw (2007); Hinshaw & Stier (2008).
24. Pachankis (2007).
25. Major & O'Brien (2005).
26. See Hinshaw (2007); Sartorius (1998, 2002); Sirey et al. (2001).
27. Lebowitz (2013).
28. Again, stigma of mental illness is usually strongest for the most severe and chronic mental disorders (see Crisp et al., 2000), but paradoxically, stigma may be particularly severe for conditions that are milder and more variable, about which observers believe that the individual should have been able to show self-control. Another essential issue is what Goffman (1963) originally called "courtesy stigma"—the stigma that extends to those associated with individuals in stigmatized groups, particularly family members.
29. See Wahl (1995) and Hinshaw (2007).
30. Bussing et al. (2011); Quinn & Wigal (2004); Mueller et al. (2012).
31. Loya et al. (2010).
32. This branch of social psychology is termed attribution theory; see Weiner et al. (1988); Hinshaw (2007); and Phelan et al. (2002).
33. Martinez et al. (2011).
34. An & Kang (2011). Given the discussion in the text, we would caution that ads featuring the message of onset non-controllability (i.e., those conveying a biological/genetic cause of ADHD as the sole message) could inadvertently lead to increased stigmatization.
35. Hinshaw (2007).

## Chapter 10

1. Dillon (2010); see also Graham (2010). Scores from youth in the United States on these PISA (Program for International Student Assessment) tests were not in the top 15 internationally.
2. See Baria (2011); Ravichandran (2011); Lahiri (2011).
3. See Chapter 8.
4. We contemplated providing a graph of trends in diagnosis rates and medication rates from 1970 to the present. But there were major problems in doing so accurately. There are no truly national-level, representative data on rates of ADHD diagnosis using state-of-the-art assessment procedures with a consistent set of diagnostic criteria. Thus, it is not possible to estimate the "true prevalence" of ADHD versus what is termed the "diagnostic prevalence" or "administrative prevalence," referring to rates of diagnosis by community practitioners. See American Psychiatric Association (1980, 1987) for earlier estimates. Nigg (2006) expertly summarized rigorous evidence through the early part of the last decade with respect to the actual prevalence of ADHD in the United States and arrived at an "upper bound" estimate of 6.8%. Moreover, Polanczyk and colleagues (2007) have estimated an international prevalence of 5% (with somewhat higher rates in the United States). A recent analysis by Willcutt (2012) placed the international rate at 6%, which was fairly constant across regions of the world. Yet the NSCH data (Visser et al., 2010, 2013) reveal that rates of professional ADHD diagnoses, as reported by parents, are now 11% for "ever diagnosed" and 8.8% for "currently diagnosed." ADHD clearly appears to be *diagnosed* more and more frequently, despite the impossibility of knowing whether its *actual* rates have gone up as well. Psychiatrist Allen Frances, who was head of the *DSM-IV* Task Force but who has since become a critic of rising prevalence rates of many *DSM* disorders, lists 12 reasons why ADHD diagnostic rates have increased in recent years, which overlap to some extent with the reasons we subsequently provide in Table 10–1 (e.g., direct-to-consumer ads, ADHD's role as a trigger for special services, increasing academic pressures, etc.). See Pacana (2011).

5. In terms of rates of youth medication, ADHD medication rates were relatively low in the 1970s, doubled in the early part of the 1980s, retreated in the late 1980s related to negative media attention, and then tripled during the 1990s (e.g., Safer et al., 1996). Estimates were that perhaps half of youth with ADHD received medication a decade ago (see review in Nigg, 2006). Since then, rates have climbed, such that 69% of currently diagnosed youth are now reported to receive medication prescriptions (Visser et al., 2013). Yet youth medication rates are leveling off, whereas adult rates are rising sharply (see, for example, Schwarz, 2013, who recently analyzed IMS data on adult rates).

6. Visser et al. (2010); Visser et al. (2013).

7. See Baio (2012); Hoffman (2013). The stretching of the bounds of autism-spectrum disorders has played a major role in such increases, although it is conceivable that the actual prevalence of the disorder has increased (especially for milder cases).

8. Rich (2012). See also Dillon (2010); Graham (2010); and Hinshaw (2009).

9. American Academy of Pediatrics (2011); American Psychiatric Association (2013). See also Polanczyk et al. (2010).

10. Getahun et al. (2013); see also Visser et al. (2010).

11. Patient Protection and Affordable Care Act (2010).

12. Graf et al. (2013).

13. Rich (2013).

14. See the feature in *Medical News Today*, April 5, 2009: "Shortage of child and adolescent psychiatrists reaches crisis point, USA," retrieved from http://medicalnewstoday.com/releases/144968.php.

15. Our calculations are as follows: the rate of lifetime ADHD diagnosis for children and adolescents climbed 22% from 2003 to 2007 (i.e., from 7.8% to 9.5%) and another 16% from 2007 to 2011–2012 (i.e., from 9.5% to 11.0%). Another 12% increase by 2015–2016—a reasonable estimate for the next NSCH survey—would place the lifetime diagnosis rate at 13% by then. As noted in other chapters, the adult prescription rate continues to climb (see, for example, Schwarz, 2013).

16. "Simple treatments, ignored" (2012); Valderrama et al. (2012).

17. "Simple treatments, ignored" (2012).

18. See Friedman (2013b) and Rose (2013). Rose emphasizes a human and personalized technology that could allow individual differences in learning, sensation seeking, attentional styles, and the like to be channeled into creative output. See also Hanushek et al. (2008) and Eggers & Hagel (2012).

19. Again, see Rose (2013).

20. Rich (2012). This article noted an interesting contrast between the United States and Finland, a nation in which youth scored quite high. Finland features strong teacher preparation but does not have high-stakes testing. The United States still lags behind other nations that do feature such testing. See also Hanushek et al. (2008), regarding the need for fundamental reform of our education system if the U.S. economy is to prosper. Additional perspective is provided by Eggers & Hagel (2012).

21. Friedman, T. (2012).

22. See Conners et al. (2001), as well as MTA Cooperative Group (1999a, 1999b). We note that most states have now mandated coverage of early and intensive treatments for autism (see National Conference of State Legislatures, 2012, and American Speech-Language-Hearing Association, n.d.). If the ADHD world were as well-organized and coordinated as the autism world, considerably better treatments might well be in place.

23. Rose (2013); see also Pfiffner & Glasscock (2011). We thank our colleague Susan Stone for noting the historical battles between responsive versus standards-based educational policies and practices over the past decades. Specifically, we note that low-cost strategies for youth with ADHD include using a child's name to prompt him or her, seating kids with attention problems up front in class, reducing working memory requirements by providing multiple cues and avoiding long and overly complex directions, and frequent assessments of learning progress (as opposed to once-per-year or all-or-none standardized tests). At another level, education researchers are devising creative video learning games that can assess students' level of understanding of important concepts in such topics as biology; see http://www.wcer.wisc.edu/news/coverStories/2013/games_based_assessment.php

# References

Advokat, C., Lane, S. M., & Luo, C. (2011). College students with and without ADHD: Comparison of self-report of medication usage, study habits, and academic achievement. *Journal of Attention Disorders, 15*(8), 656–666.

Agency for Healthcare Research and Quality. (2009). *Impact of direct-to-consumer advertising on drug use varies depending on the drug, scope of advertising, and culture.* Retrieved from http://www.ahrq.gov/legacy/research/mar09/0309RA16.htm

Allen, I. E., & Seaman, J. (2010). *Learning on Demand: Online Education in the United States, 2009.* Retrieved from ERIC database. (ED529931)

ALZA Corporation. (2003, November). I see Jason. Not his ADHD [Advertisement]. *Working Mother,* p. 37.

American Academy of Child and Adolescent Psychiatry. (2005). *AACAP state psychotropic medication and screening update.* Retrieved from http://www.aacap.org/galleries/LegislativeAction/psychotropicMeds_102005.pdf

American Academy of Child and Adolescent Psychiatry Work Group on Quality Issues. (1997). Practice parameter for the assessment and treatment of children, adolescents, and adults with attention-deficit/hyperactivity disorder. *Journal of the American Academy of Child & Adolescent Psychiatry, 36,* 85S–121S.

American Academy of Child and Adolescent Psychiatry Work Group on Quality Issues. (2007). Practice parameter for the assessment and treatment of children and adolescents with attention-deficit/ hyperactivity disorder. *Journal of the American Academy of Child and Adolescent Psychiatry, 46,* 894–921.

American Academy of Pediatrics. (2000). Clinical practice guideline: Diagnosis and evaluation of the child with attention-deficit/ hyperactivity disorder. *Pediatrics, 105,* 1158–1170.

American Academy of Pediatrics. (2011). ADHD: Clinical practice guideline for the diagnosis, evaluation, and treatment of attention-deficit/hyperactivity disorder in children and adolescents. *Pediatrics, 128*(5), 1007–1022.

American Psychiatric Association. (1952). *Diagnostic and statistical manual of mental disorders.* Washington, DC: Author.

American Psychiatric Association. (1968). *Diagnostic and statistical manual of mental disorders* (2nd ed.). Washington, DC: Author.

American Psychiatric Association. (1980). *Diagnostic and statistical manual of mental disorders* (3rd ed.). Washington, DC: Author.

American Psychiatric Association. (1987). *Diagnostic and statistical manual of mental disorders* (3rd ed., revised). Washington, DC: Author.

American Psychiatric Association. (1994). *Diagnostic and statistical manual of mental disorders* (4th ed.). Washington, DC: Author.

American Psychiatric Association. (2000). *Diagnostic and statistical manual of mental disorders* (4th ed., text rev.). Washington, DC: Author.

American Psychiatric Association. (2013). *Diagnostic and statistical manual of mental disorders* (5th ed.). Washington, DC: Author.

American Speech-Language-Hearing Association. (n.d.). *State insurance mandates for autism spectrum disorder.* Retrieved from http:// www.asha.org/Advocacy/state/States-Specific-Autism-Mandates/

An, S., & Kang, H. (2011). Stigma-reducing components in direct-to-consumer prescription ads: Onset controllability, offset controllability, and recategorization. *Health Communication, 26*(5), 468–478.

Anderson, N., & Estee, S. (2002, December). *Medical cost offsets associated with mental health care: A brief review.* Retrieved from Washington State Department of Social and Health Services Web site: http://www.dshs.wa.gov/pdf/ms/rda/research/3/28.pdf

Angold, A., Costello, E. J., & Erkanli, A. (1999). Comorbidity. *Journal of Child Psychology and Psychiatry, 40*(1), 57–87.

Angold, A., Erkanli, A., Egger, H. L., & Costello, E. J. (2000). Stimulant treatment for children: A community perspective. *Journal of the American Academy of Child & Adolescent Psychiatry, 39*(8), 975–984.

Antshel, K. M., Faraone, S. V., Stallone, K., Nave, A., Kaufmann, F. A., Doyle, A.,...Biederman, J. (2007). Is attention deficit hyperactivity disorder a valid diagnosis in the presence of high IQ? Results from the MGH longitudinal family studies of ADHD. *Journal of Child Psychology and Psychiatry, 48*(7), 687–694.

Arnold, L. E. (1999). Treatment alternatives for attention-deficit/ hyperactivity disorder (ADHD). *Journal of Attention Disorders, 3*(1), 30–48.

Arnold, L. E., Lofthouse, N., Hersch, S., Pan, X., Hurt, E., Bates, B.,...Grantier, C. (2012). EEG neurofeedback for ADHD: Double-blind sham-controlled randomized pilot feasibility trial. *Journal of Attention Disorders, 17*(5), 410–419.

Avery, R. J., Eisenberg, M. D., & Simon, K. I. (2012). The impact of direct-to-consumer television and magazine advertising on antidepressant use. *Journal of Health Economics, 31*(5), 705–718.

Babinski, D. E., Pelham, W. E. J., Molina, B. S., Gnagy, E. M., Waschbusch, D. A., Yu, J., Maclean, M. G.,...Karch, K. M. (2011). Late adolescent and young adult outcomes of girls diagnosed with ADHD in childhood: An exploratory investigation. *Journal of Attention Disorders, 15*(3), 204–214.

Baio, J. (2012). Prevalence of autism spectrum disorders—Autism and Developmental Disabilities Monitoring Network, 14 sites, United States, 2008. *Morbidity and Mortality Weekly Report, Surveillance Summaries, 61*(SS03), 1–19. Retrieved from the Centers for Disease Control and Prevention Web site: http:// www.cdc.gov/mmwr/preview/mmwrhtml/ss6103a1.htm

Balthazor, M. J., Wagner, R. K., & Pelham, W. E. (1991). The specificity of the effects of stimulant medication on classroom learning-related measures of cognitive processing for attention deficit disorder children. *Journal of Abnormal Child Psychology, 19*(1), 35–52.

Barbaresi, W. J., Colligan, R. C., Weaver, A. L., Voigt, R. G., Killian, J. M., & Katusic, S. K. (2013). Mortality, ADHD, and psychosocial adversity in adults with childhood ADHD: A prospective study. *Pediatrics, 131*(4), 637–644.

Barbaresi, W. J., Katusic, S. K., Colligan, R. C., Weaver, A. L., & Jacobsen, S. J. (2007). Long-term school outcomes for children with attention-deficit/hyperactivity disorder: A population-based perspective. *Journal of Developmental and Behavioral Pediatrics, 28*(4), 265–273.

Baria, Z. F. (2011, September 15). Does your child suffer from ADHD? The Times of India. Retrieved from http://articles.time-sofindia.indiatimes.com/ 2011-09-15/parenting/30115743_1_adhd-behaviour-attention-deficit- hyperactivity-disorder

Barkley, R. A. (1988). The effects of methylphenidate on the interactions of preschool ADHD children with their mothers. *Journal of the American Academy of Child & Adolescent Psychiatry, 27*(3), 336–341.

Barkley, R. A. (1997a). *ADHD and the nature of self-control.* New York: Guilford Press.

Barkley, R. A. (1997b). Behavioral inhibition, sustained attention, and executive functions: Constructing a unifying theory of ADHD. *Psychological Bulletin, 121*(1), 65–94.

Barkley, R. A. (2006a). *Attention deficit hyperactivity disorder: A handbook for diagnosis and treatment* (3rd ed.). New York: Guilford Press.

Barkley, R. A. (2006b). The relevance of the Still lectures to attention-deficit/hyperactivity disorder: A commentary. *Journal of Attention Disorders, 10*(2), 137–140.

Barkley, R. A. (2008). Commentary on excerpt of Crichton's chapter, on attention and its diseases. *Journal of Attention Disorders, 12*(3), 205–206.

Barkley, R. A. (2012). *Executive functions: What they are, how they work, and why they evolved.* New York: Guilford Press.

Barkley, R. A., Fischer, M., Smallish, L., & Fletcher, K. (2002a). The persistence of attention-deficit/hyperactivity disorder into young adulthood as a function of reporting source and definition of disorder. *Journal of Abnormal Psychology, 111*(2), 279–289.

Barkley, R. A., Murphy, K., Dupaul, G., & Bush, T. (2002b). Driving in young adults with attention deficit hyperactivity disorder: Knowledge, performance, adverse outcomes, and the role of executive functioning. *Journal of the International Neuropsychological Society, 8*(5), 655–672.

Barkley, R. A., Murphy, K. R., & Fischer, M. (2008). *ADHD in adults: What the science says.* New York: Guilford Press.

Barro, R. J., & Lee, J. W. (2001). International data on educational attainment: Updates and implications. *Oxford Economic Papers, 53*(3), 541–563.

Barry, C. L., Martin, A., & Busch, S. H. (2012). ADHD medication use following FDA risk warnings. *Journal of Mental Health Policy and Economics, 15*(3), 119–125.

Battista, J. (2012, December 1). Drug of focus is at center of suspensions. *The New York Times.* Retrieved from http://www.nytimes.com/2012/12/02/ sports/football/adderall-a-drug-of-increased-focus-for-nfl-players.html

Beauchaine, T. P., & Neuhaus, E. (2008). Impulsivity and vulnerability to psychopathology. In T. P. Beauchaine & S. P. Hinshaw (Eds.), *Child and adolescent psychopathology* (pp. 129–156). Hoboken, NJ: Wiley.

Beck, M. (2010, April 6). Attention-deficit disorder isn't just for kids. Why adults are now being diagnosed, too. *The Wall Street Journal.* Retrieved from http://online.wsj.com/article/SB1000142 405270230462030457516590293305907076.html

Becker, G. S. (1975). *Human capital: A theoretical and empirical analysis, with special reference to education* (2nd ed.). New York: Columbia University Press.

Berger, A., & Posner, M. I. (2000). Pathologies of brain attentional networks. *Neuroscience and Biobehavioral Reviews, 24*(1), 3–5.

Berman, S. M., Kuczenski, R., McCracken, J. T., & London, E. D. (2009). Potential adverse effects of amphetamine treatment on brain and behavior: A review. *Molecular Psychiatry, 14*(2), 123–142.

Biederman, J., & Faraone, S. V. (2006). The effects of attention-deficit/hyperactivity disorder on employment and household income. *Medscape General Medicine, 8*(3), 12.

Biederman, J., Petty, C. R., Monuteaux, M. C., Fried, R., Byrne, D., Mirto, T.,…Faraone, S. V. (2010). Adult psychiatric outcomes of girls with attention deficit hyperactivity disorder: 11-year follow-up in a longitudinal case-control study. *American Journal of Psychiatry, 167*(4), 409–417.

Biederman, J., Spencer, T., Lomedico, A., Day, H., Petty, C. R., & Faraone, S. V. (2012). Deficient emotional self-regulation and pediatric attention deficit hyperactivity disorder: A family risk analysis. *Psychological Medicine, 42*(3), 639–646.

Blachman, D., & Hinshaw, S. P. (2005, April). *Predictors of peer acceptance, rejection, and victimization among girls with and without ADHD.* Poster presented at the biennial meeting of the Society for Research in Child Development, Atlanta.

Blount, A., Schoenbaum, M., Kathol, R., Rollman, B. L., Thomas, M., O Donohue, W., & Peek, C. J. (2007). The economics of behavioral health services in medical settings: A summary of the evidence. *Professional Psychology: Research and Practice, 38*(3), 290–297.

Boeck, S. (2012, November 30). MLB drug report: Nearly 1 in 10 get ADD exemption. *USA Today.* Retrieved from http://www. usatoday.com/story/sports/mlb/2012/11/30/ mlbs-annual-drug-report-adderall/1738371/

Bokhari, F., Mayes, R., & Scheffler, R. M. (2005). An analysis of the significant variation in psychostimulant use across the US. *Pharmacoepidemiology and Drug Safety, 14*(4), 267–275.

Bokhari, F. A. S., & Schneider, H. (2011). School accountability laws and the consumption of psychostimulants. *Journal of Health Economics, 30,* 355–372.

Bradley, C. (1937). The behavior of children receiving benzedrine. *American Journal of Psychiatry, 94,* 577–585.

Breggin, P. R. (2001). *Talking back to Ritalin: What doctors aren't telling you about stimulants and ADHD* (rev. ed.). Cambridge, MA: Perseus Publishing.

Breggin, P. R. (2002). *The Ritalin fact book: What doctors won't tell you about ADHD and stimulant drugs.* Cambridge, MA: Perseus Publishing.

Breslau, J., Miller, E., Chung, W.- J., & Schweitzer, J. B. (2011). Childhood and adolescent onset psychiatric disorders, substance use, and failure to graduate high school on time. *Journal of Psychiatric Research, 45*(3), 295–301.

British Pain Society. (2010). *Opioids for persistent pain: Good practice.* Retrieved from http://www.britishpainsociety.org/book_opioid_main.pdf

Brooks, D. (2012, July 5). Honor code. *The New York Times.* Retrieved from http://www.nytimes.com/2012/07/06/opinion/honor-code.html

Brown, T. E., Reichel, P. C., & Quinlan, D. M. (2009). Executive function impairments in high IQ adults with ADHD. *Journal of Attention Disorders, 13*(2), 161–167.

Brown, T. L. (2013). *A new understanding of ADHD in children and adults: Executive function impairments.* New York: Routledge.

Bruckner, T. A., Hodgson, A., Mahoney, C. B., Fulton, B. D., Levine, P., & Scheffler, R. M. (2012). Health care supply and county-level variation in attention-deficit hyperactivity disorder prescription medications. *Pharmacoepidemiology and Drug Safety, 21*(4), 442–449.

Burt, S. A. (2009). Rethinking environmental contributions to child and adolescent psychopathology: A meta-analysis of shared environmental influences. *Psychological Bulletin, 135*(4), 608–637.

Bush, G. (2010). Attention-deficit/hyperactivity disorder and attention networks. *Neuropsychopharmacology, 35*(1), 278–300.

Bush, G. (2011). Cingulate, frontal, and parietal cortical dysfunction in attention-deficit/hyperactivity disorder. *Biological Psychiatry, 69*(12), 1160–1167.

Bussing, R., Zima, B. T., Mason, D. M., Porter, P. C., & Garvan, C. W. (2011). Receiving treatment for attention-deficit hyperactivity disorder: Do the perspectives of adolescents matter? *Journal of Adolescent Health, 49*(1), 7–14.

Calfee, J. E. (2002, July 8). Public policy issues in direct-to-consumer advertising of prescription drugs. *American Enterprise Institute.* Retrieved from Federal Trade Commission Web site: http://www.ftc.gov/ogc/healthcare/calfeedtcjppm.pdf

Campbell, S. B., & Ewing, L. J. (1990). Follow-up of hard-to-manage preschoolers: Adjustment at age 9 and predictors of continuing symptoms. *Journal of Child Psychology and Psychiatry, 31*(6), 871–889.

Carey, B. (2006, June 5). Antipsychotic drug use is climbing, study finds. *The New York Times.* Retrieved from http://www.nytimes.com/2006/06/05/health/05cnd-psych.html?pagewanted=all

Carey, B. (2011, November 20). Drugs used for psychotics go to youths in foster care. *The New York Times.* Retrieved from http://www.nytimes.com/2011/11/21/health/research/ study-finds-foster-children-often- given-antipsychosis-drugs.html

Carlson, C. L., Pelham, W. E., Swanson, J. M., & Wagner, J. L. (1991). A divided attention analysis of the effects of methylphenidate on the arithmetic performance of children with attention-deficit hyperactivity disorder. *Journal of Child Psychology and Psychiatry, 32*(3), 463–471.

Carlson, E. A., Jacobvitz, D., & Sroufe, L. A. (1995). A developmental investigation of inattentiveness and hyperactivity. *Child Development, 66*(1), 37–54.

Castellanos, F. X., Lee, P. P., Sharp, W., Jeffries, N. O., Greenstein, D. K., Clasen, L. S.,…Rapoport, J. L. (2002). Developmental trajectories of brain volume abnormalities in children and adolescents with attention-deficit/hyperactivity disorder. *JAMA: Journal of the American Medical Association, 288*(14), 1740–1748.

Castellanos, F. X., & Proal, E. (2012). Large-scale brain systems in ADHD: Beyond the prefrontal–striatal model. *Trends in Cognitive Sciences, 16*(1), 17–26.

Castellanos, F. X., Sonuga-Barke, E., Milham, M. P., & Tannock, R. (2006). Characterizing cognition in ADHD: Beyond executive dysfunction. *Trends in Cognitive Sciences, 10*(3), 117–123.

Castellanos, F. X., Sonuga-Barke, E., Scheres, A., Di Martino, A., Hyde, C., & Walters, J. R. (2005). Varieties of attention-deficit/hyperactivity disorder-related intra-individual variability. *Biological Psychiatry, 57*(11), 1416–1423.

Center for Education Policy High School Exit Exam Final Reports (2002–2011). Washington, DC: Center for Education Policy. Retrieved from http://www.cep-dc.org/index.cfm?DocumentSub TopicID=8

Chi, T. C., & Hinshaw, S. P. (2002). Mother-child relationships of children with ADHD: The role of maternal depressive symptoms and depression-related distortions. *Journal of Abnormal Child Psychology, 30,* 387–400.

Chiarello, R. J., & Cole, J. O. (1987). The use of psychostimulants in general psychiatry: A reconsideration. *Archives of General Psychiatry, 44*(3), 286–295.

Christakis, D. A., Zimmerman, F. J., DiGiuseppe, D. L., & McCarty, C. A. (2004). Early television exposure and subsequent attentional problems in children. *Pediatrics, 113*(4), 708–713.

Chronis-Tuscano, A., Molina, B. S. G., Pelham, W. E, Applegate, B., Dahlke, A., Overmeyer, M., & Lahey, B. B. (2010). Very early predictors of adolescent depression and suicide attempts in children with attention-deficit/hyperactivity disorder. *Archives of General Psychiatry, 67*, 1044–1051.

Clements, S. D., & Peters, J. E. (1962). Minimal brain dysfunction in the school-age child: Diagnosis and treatment. *Archives of General Psychiatry, 6*(3), 185–197.

Cohen, D., Nisbett, R. E., Bowdle, B. F., & Schwarz, N. (1996). Insult, aggression, and the Southern culture of honor: An "experimental ethnography." *Journal of Personality and Social Psychology, 70*(5), 945–959.

Comanor, W. S., & Wilson, T. A. (1979). The effect of advertising on competition: A survey. *Journal of Economic Literature, 17*(2), 453–476.

Conners, C. K. (2002). Forty years of methylphenidate treatment in attention-deficit/hyperactivity disorder. *Journal of Attention Disorders, 6*, S-17–S-30.

Conners, C. K., Epstein, J. N., March, J. S., Angold, A., Wells, K. C., Klaric, J.,…Wigal, T. (2001). Multimodal treatment of ADHD in the MTA: An alternative outcome analysis. *Journal of the American Academy of Child & Adolescent Psychiatry, 40*(2), 159–167.

Connor, D. (2012, August 11). Problems of overdiagnosis and overprescribing in ADHD. *Psychiatric Times*. Retrieved from http://www.psychiatrictimes.com/ display/article/10168/1926348

Conrad, P., & Schneider, J. W. (1980). *Deviance and medicalization: From badness to sickness*. St. Louis, MO: Mosby.

Cooper, W. O., Callahan, S. T., Fish, F. A., Arbogast, P. G., Ray, W. A., Murray, K. T.,…Connell, F. A. (2011). ADHD drugs and serious cardiovascular events in children and young adults. *New England Journal of Medicine, 365*(20), 1896–1904.

Coverdale, J., Nairn, R., & Claasen, D. (2002). Depiction of mental illness in print media: A prospective national sample. *Australian and New Zealand Journal of Psychiatry, 36*, 697–700.

Cregan, J. R., & Magazine Publishers of America. (2002, September 30). *Re: Comments regarding competition law and policy & health care*. Retrieved from Federal Trade Commission Web site: http://www.ftc.gov/os/comments/healthcarecomments/mpa.pdf

Crisp, A. H., Gelder, M. G., Rix, S., Meltzer, H. I., & Rowlands, O. J. (2000). Stigmatisation of people with mental illnesses. *British Journal of Psychiatry, 177*, 4–7.

Cross-Disorder Group of the Psychiatric Genomics Consortium. (2013). Identification of risk loci with shared effects on five major psychiatric disorders: A genome-wide analysis. *Lancet, 381*(9875), 1360.

Curran, K. M. (2008). Mental health screening in schools: An analysis of recent legislative developments and the legal implications for parents, children, and the state. *Quinnipiac Health Law Journal, 11*(2), 87–143.

Currie, J., & Stabile, M. (2006). Child mental health and human capital accumulation: The case of ADHD. *Journal of Health Economics, 25*(6), 1094–1118.

Dave, D., & Saffer, H. (2010, May). *The impact of direct-to-consumer advertising on pharmaceutical prices and demand* (NBER Working Paper No 15969). Retrieved from National Bureau of Economic Research Web site: http://www.nber.org/papers/w15969

Dawson, G., Jones, E. J., Merkle, K., Venema, K., Lowy, R., Faja, S.,...Webb, S. J. (2012). Early behavioral intervention is associated with normalized brain activity in young children with autism. *Journal of the American Academy of Child & Adolescent Psychiatry, 51*(11), 1150–1159.

de Cock, M., Maas, Y. G. H., & van de Bor, M. (2012). Does perinatal exposure to endocrine disruptors induce autism spectrum and attention deficit hyperactivity disorders? Review. *Acta Paediatrica, 101*(8), 811–818.

Dee, T. S., & Jacob, B. A. (2006, May). *Do high school exit exams influence educational attainment or labor market performance?* (NBER Working Paper No 12199). Retrieved from National Bureau of Economic Research Web site: http://www.nber.org/papers/w12199

Dee, T. S., & Jacob, B. A. (2011). The impact of No Child Left Behind on student achievement. *Journal of Policy Analysis and Management, 30*(3), 418–446.

DeGrandpre, R. (2000). *Ritalin nation: Rapid-fire culture and the transformation of human consciousness.* New York: W. W. Norton & Co.

DeGrandpre, R., & Hinshaw, S. P. (2000). Attention-deficit hyperactivity disorder: Psychiatric problem or American cop-out? *Cerebrum: The Dana Foundation Journal on Brain Sciences, 2*, 12–38.

Dell'Antonia, K. J. (2012, May 4). How many people believe A.D.H.D is caused by poor parenting? *The New York Times.* Retrieved from http://parenting.blogs.nytimes.com/2012/05/04/how-many-people-believe-a-d-h-d-is-caused-by-poor-parenting/

Dickler, J. (2011, September 21). The rising cost of raising a child. *CNN Money.* Retrieved from http://money.cnn.com/2011/09/21/pf/cost_raising_child/index.htm

Diller, L. H. (1998). *Running on Ritalin: A physician reflects on children, society, and performance in a pill.* New York: Bantam Books.

Diller, L. H. (2011). *Remembering Ritalin: A doctor and generation Rx reflect on life and psychiatric drugs.* New York: Penguin Group.

Dillon, S. (2010, December 7). Top test scores from Shanghai stun educators. *The New York Times.* Retrieved from http://www.nytimes.com/2010/12/07/education/07education.html?pagewanted=all

Dishion, T. J., Spracklen, K. M., Andrews, D. W., & Patterson, G. R. (1996). Deviancy training in male adolescent friendships. *Behavior Therapy, 27*(3), 373–390.

Donohue, J. M., Cevasco, M., & Rosenthal, M. B. (2007). A decade of direct-to-consumer advertising of prescription drugs. *New England Journal of Medicine, 357*(7), 673–681.

Doshi, J. A., Hodgkins, P., Kahle, J., Sikirica, V., Cangelosi, M. J., Setyawan, J.,...Neumann, P. J. (2012). Economic impact of childhood and adult attention-deficit/hyperactivity disorder in the United States. *Journal of the American Academy of Child & Adolescent Psychiatry, 51*(10), 990–1002.

Douglas, V. I. (1972). Stop, look, and listen: The problem of sustained attention and impulse control in hyperactive and normal children. *Canadian Journal of Behavioural Science, 4*(4), 259–282.

Ducharme, S., Hudziak, J. J., Botteron, K. N., Albaugh, M. D., Nguyen, T., Karama, S., & Evans, A. C. (2012). Decreased regional cortical thickness and thinning rate are associated with inattention symptoms in healthy children. *Journal of the American Academy of Child & Adolescent Psychiatry, 51*(1), 18–27.

Eggers, W. D., & Hagel, J., III. (2012, September 27). *Brawn from brains: Talent, policy, and the future of American competitiveness.* Retrieved from Deloitte University Press Web site: http://dupress.com/articles/brawn-from-brains-talent-policy-and-the-future-of-american-competitiveness/

Eisenberg, R. S. (2003). Patents, product exclusivity, and information dissemination: How law directs biopharmaceutical research and development. *Fordham Law Review, 72,* 477–491.

Elder, T. E. (2010). The importance of relative standards in ADHD diagnoses: Evidence based on exact birth dates. *Journal of Health Economics, 29*(5), 641–656.

Elia, J., Borcherding, B. G., Rapoport, J. L., & Keysor, C. S. (1991). Methylphenidate and dextroamphetamine treatments of hyperactivity: Are there true nonresponders? *Psychiatry Research, 36*(2), 141–155.

Elliott, G. R., & Kelly, K. (2006). *Medicating young minds: How to know if psychiatric drugs will help or hurt your child.* New York: Stewart, Tabori & Chang.

Epstein, J. N., Langberg, J. M., Lichtenstein, P. K., Kolb, R. C., & Stark, L. J. (2010). Sustained improvement in pediatricians' ADHD practice behaviors in the context of a community-based quality improvement initiative. *Children's Health Care, 39*(4), 296–311.

Erhardt, D., & Hinshaw, S. P. (1994). Initial sociometric impressions of attention-deficit hyperactivity disorder and comparison boys: Predictions from social behaviors and from nonbehavioral variables. *Journal of Consulting and Clinical Psychology, 62*(4), 833–842.

Eskenazi, B., Chevrier, J., Rosas, L. G., Anderson, H. A., Bornman, M. S., Bouwman, H.,…Stapleton, D. (2009). The Pine River statement: Human health consequences of DDT use. *Environmental Health Perspectives, 117*(9), 1359–1367.

Eskenazi, B., Huen, K., Marks, A., Harley, K. G., Bradman, A., Barr, D. B., & Holland, N. (2010). PON1 and neurodevelopment in children from the CHAMACOS study exposed to organophosphate pesticides in utero. *Environmental Health Perspectives, 118*(2), 1775–1781.

Fabiano, G. A., Pelham, W. E., Coles, E. K., Gnagy, E. M., Chronis-Tuscano, A., & O'Connor, B. C. (2009). A meta-analysis of behavioral treatments for attention-deficit/hyperactivity disorder. *Clinical Psychology Review, 29*(2), 129–140.

Faraone, S. V., Biederman, J., & Mick, E. (2006). The age-dependent decline of attention deficit hyperactivity disorder: A meta-analysis of follow-up studies. *Psychological Medicine, 36*(2), 159–165.

Faraone, S. V., & Buitelaar, J. (2010). Comparing the efficacy of stimulants for ADHD in children and adolescents using meta-analysis. *European Child & Adolescent Psychiatry, 19*(4), 353–364.

Faraone, S. V., Perlis, R. H., Doyle, A. E., Smoller, J. W., Goralnick, J. J., Holmgren, M. A., & Sklar, P. (2005). Molecular genetics of attention-deficit/hyperactivity disorder. *Biological Psychiatry*, *57*(11), 1313–1323.

Faraone, S. V., Sergeant, J., Gillberg, C., & Biederman, J. (2003). The worldwide prevalence of ADHD: Is it an American condition? *World Psychiatry: Official Journal of the World Psychiatric Association*, *2*(2), 104–113.

Farbstein, I., Mansbach-Kleinfeld, I., Levinson, D., Goodman, R., Levav, I., Vograft, I.,…Apter, A. (2010). Prevalence and correlates of mental disorders in Israeli adolescents: Results from a national mental health survey. *Journal of Child Psychology and Psychiatry*, *51*(5), 630–639.

Fassbender, C., Zhang, H., Buzy, W. M., Cortes, C. R., Mizuiri, D., Beckett, L., & Schweitzer, J. B. (2009). A lack of default network suppression is linked to increased distractibility in ADHD. *Brain Research*, *1273*, 114–128.

Federal Trade Commission. (2004, May 12). *FTC staff provides comments to FDA on direct-to-consumer drug and device ads: Agency encouraged to make disclosure of risk information more consumer-friendly to promote increased public understanding* (FTC File No. V040016). Retrieved from http://www.ftc.gov/opa/2004/05/dtcdrugs.shtm

Feingold, B. F. (1977). Behavioral disturbances linked to the ingestion of food additives. *Delaware Medical Journal*, *49*(2), 89–94.

Feldman, R., & Begun, J. W. (1978). The effects of advertising: Lessons from optometry. *Journal of Human Resources*, *13*, 247–262.

Fields, L. (2012, April 5). FDA says ADHD drug shortage to end in April. *Consumer Reports*. Retrieved from http://news.consumerreports.org/health/2012/04/fda-says-adhd-drug-shortage-to-end-in-april.html

Figlio, D., & Loeb, S. (2011). School accountability. In E. A. Hanushek, S. Macklin, & L. Woessner (Eds.), *Handbook in economics* (Vol. 3, pp. 383–421). North-Holland, Netherlands: Elsevier.

Fletcher, J. M. (2013). The effects of childhood ADHD on adult labor market outcomes. *Health Economics*. Advance online publication. doi:10.1002/hec.2907

Fogelman, Y., Vinker, S., Guy, N., & Kahan, E. (2003). Prevalence of and change in the prescription of methylphenidate in Israel over a 2-year period. *CNS Drugs*, *17*(12), 915–919.

Folland, S. T. (1985). The effects of health care advertising. *Journal of Health Politics, Policy and Law, 10*(2), 329–345.

Foster, E. M., Jensen, P. S., Schlander, M., Pelham, W. E., Hechtman, L., Arnold, L. E.,…Wigal, T. (2007). Treatment for ADHD: Is more complex treatment cost-effective for more complex cases? *Health Services Research, 42*(1), 165–182.

Frank, R., Berndt, E. R., Donohue, J., Epstein, A., Rosenthal, M. (2002, February 14). *Trends in direct-to-consumer advertising of prescription drugs* (Publication No. 3162). Retrieved from Kaiser Family Foundation Web site: http://www.researchgate.net/publication/24927320_Direct-to-consumer_advertising_of_prescription_drugs/file/79e415134d69703553.pdf

Frazier, T. W., Youngstrom, E. A., Glutting, J. J., & Watkins, M. W. (2007). ADHD and achievement: Meta-analysis of the child, adolescent, and adult literatures and a concomitant study with college students. *Journal of Learning Disabilities, 40*(1), 49–65.

Fredriksen, M., Halmøy, A., Faraone, S. V., & Haavik, J. (2013). Long-term efficacy and safety of treatment with stimulants and atomoxetine in adult ADHD: A review of controlled and naturalistic studies. *European Neuropsychopharmacology, 23*(6), 508–527.

Friedman, R. A. (2012, April 21). Why are we drugging our soldiers? *The New York Times.* Retrieved from http://www.nytimes.com/2012/04/22/opinion/sunday/why-are-we-drugging-our-soldiers.html

Friedman, T. L. (2012, September 8). New rules. *The New York Times.* Retrieved from http://www.nytimes.com/2012/09/09/opinion/sunday/friedman-new-rules.html

Friedman, T. L. (2013a, January 26). Revolution hits the universities. *The New York Times.* Retrieved from http://www.nytimes.com/2013/01/27/opinion/sunday/friedman-revolution-hits-the-universities.html?smid=pl-share

Friedman, T. L. (2013b, March 30). Need a job? Invent it. *The New York Times.* Retrieved from http://www.nytimes.com/2013/03/31/opinion/sunday/friedman-need-a-job-invent-it.html?smid=pl-share

Froehlich, T. E., Lanphear, B. P., Epstein, J. N., Barbaresi, W. J., Katusic, S. K., & Kahn, R. S. (2007). Prevalence, recognition, and treatment of attention-deficit/hyperactivity disorder in a national sample of US children. *Archives of Pediatrics & Adolescent Medicine, 161*(9), 857–864.

Fullerton, C. A., Epstein, A. M., Frank, R. G., Normand, S. T., Fu, C. X., & McGuire, T. G. (2012). Medication use and spending trends among children with ADHD in Florida's Medicaid program, 1996–2005. *Psychiatric Services, 63*(2), 115–121.

Fulton, B., Scheffler, R. M., & HInshaw, S. P. (2014). *ADHD diagnostic prevalence changes across states in the U.S. from 2003 to 2011: An examination of school accountability standards and psychotropic medication laws.* School of Public Health, University of California, Berkeley. Manuscript submitted for publication.

Fulton, B. D., Scheffler, R. M., Hinshaw, S. P., Levine, P., Stone, S., Brown, T. T., & Modrek, S. (2009). National variation of ADHD diagnostic prevalence and medication use: Health care providers and education policies. *Psychiatric Services, 60*(8), 1075–1083.

Garfield, C. F., Dorsey, E. R., Zhu, S., Huskamp, H. A., Conti, R., Dusetzina, S. B.,...Alexander, G. C. (2012). Trends in attention deficit hyperactivity disorder ambulatory diagnosis and medical treatment in the United States, 2000–2010. *Academic Pediatrics, 12*(2), 110–116.

Getahun, D., Jacobsen, S. J., Fassett, M. J., Chen, W., Demissie, K., & Rhoads, G. G. (2013). Recent trends in childhood attention-deficit/ hyperactivity disorder. *JAMA Pediatrics, 167*(3), 282–288.

Gibbons, R. D., Brown, C. H., Hur, K., Davis, J. M., & Mann, J. J. (2012). Suicidal thoughts and behavior with antidepressant treatment: Reanalysis of the randomized placebo-controlled studies of fluoxetine and venlafaxine. *Archives of General Psychiatry, 69*(6), 580–587.

Gilbody, S., Wilson, P., & Watt, I. (2005). Benefits and harms of direct to consumer advertising: A systematic review. *Quality & Safety in Health Care, 14*(4), 246–250.

Gladwell, M. (1999, February 15). Running from Ritalin. *The New Yorker.* Retrieved from http://www.newyorker.com/ archive/1999/02/15/1999_02_15_ 080_TNY_LIBRY_000017548

Goffman, E. (1963). *Stigma: Notes on the management of spoiled identity.* Englewood Cliffs, NJ: Prentice-Hall.

Gonon, F., Konsman, J., Cohen, D., & Boraud, T. (2012). Why most biomedical findings echoed by newspapers turn out to be false: The case of attention deficit hyperactivity disorder. *PLoS ONE, 7*(9): e44275.

Goodman, A., Joyce, R., & Smith, J. P. (2011). The long shadow cast by childhood physical and mental problems on adult life. *Proceedings of the National Academy of Sciences of the United States of America, 108*(15), 6032–6037.

Graf, W. D., Nagel, S. K., Epstein, L. G., Miller, G., Nass, R., & Larriviere, D. (2013). Pediatric neuroenhancement. Ethical, legal, social, and neurodevelopmental implications. *Neurology, 80*(13), 1251–1260.

Graham, E. (2010, December 9). International test scores: U.S. not in top 10. *CBN News*. Retrieved from http://www.cbn.com/cbnnews/world/2010/December/International-Test-Scores-US-Not-in-Top-10-/

Greely, H., Sahakian, B., Harris, J., Kessler, R. C., Gazzaniga, M., Campbell, P., & Farah, M. J. (2008). Towards responsible use of cognitive-enhancing drugs by the healthy. *Nature, 456*(7223), 702–705.

Greenhill, L., Kollins, S., Abikoff, H., McCracken, J., Riddle, M., Swanson, J.,…Cooper, T. (2006). Efficacy and safety of immediate-release methylphenidate treatment for preschoolers with ADHD. *Journal of the American Academy of Child & Adolescent Psychiatry, 45*(11), 1284–1293.

Grinspoon, L., & Hedblom, P. (1975). *The speed culture: Amphetamine use and abuse in America.* Cambridge, MA: Harvard University Press.

Groening, M. (1994). *Life in hell* [Comic strip]. Sheridan, OR: Acme Features Syndicate.

Gup, T. (2013, April 3). Diagnosis: Human. *The New York Times*. Retrieved from http://www.nytimes.com/2013/04/03/opinion/diagnosis-human.html

Habel, L. A., Cooper, W. O., Sox, C. M., Chan, K. A., Fireman, B. H., Arbogast, P. G.,…Selby, J. V. (2011). ADHD medications and risk of serious cardiovascular events in young and middle-aged adults. *JAMA: Journal of the American Medical Association, 306*(24), 2673–2683.

Hallowell, E. (2012, January 31). Dr. Hallowell's response to NY Times piece "Ritalin gone wrong" [Web log post]. Retrieved from http://www.drhallowell.com/blog/2012/01/

Hallowell, E. M., & Ratey, J. J. (1995). *Driven to distraction: Recognizing and coping with attention deficit disorder from childhood through adulthood.* New York: Simon & Schuster.

Hamblin, J. (2013, August 12). ER visits related to brain stimulants have quadrupled. *The Atlantic*. Retrieved from www.theatlantic.com/health/archive/2013/08/er-visits-related-to-brain-stimulants-have-quadrupled/278568

Handlin, A., Mosca, J. B., Forgione, D. A., & Pitta, D. (2003). DTC pharmaceutical advertising: The debate's not over. *Journal of Consumer Marketing, 20*(3), 227–237.

Haney-Jardine, C. (Producer, Director). *Gigante* [Documentary]. USA: Plan A Films.

Hanushek, E. A. (2003). The failure of input-based schooling policies. *Economic Journal, 113*(485), F64–F98.

Hanushek, E. A., & Raymond, M. E. (2005). Does school accountability lead to improved student performance? *Journal of Policy Analysis and Management, 24*(2), 297–327.

Hanushek, E. A., Woessmann, L., Jamison, E. A., & Jamison, D. T. (2008). Education and economic growth. *Education next, 8*(2). Retrieved from http://educationnext.org/education-and-economic-growth/

Harris, G. (2011, November 17). FDA finds short supply of attention deficit drugs. *The New York Times.* Retrieved from http://www.nytimes.com/2012/01/01/health/policy/fda-is-finding-attention-drugs-in- short-supply.html

Harris, G., Carey, B., & Roberts, J. (2007, May 10). Psychiatrists, children and drug industry's role. *The New York Times.* Retrieved from http://www.nytimes.com/2007/05/10/health/10psyche.html

Haworth, C. M., & Plomin, R. (2010). Quantitative genetics in the era of molecular genetics: Learning abilities and disabilities as an example. *Journal of the American Academy of Child & Adolescent Psychiatry, 49*(8), 783–793.

Healy, M. (2013, March 4). Childhood ADHD often can linger into adulthood. *USA Today.* Retrieved from http://www.usatoday.com/story/news/nation/2013/03/04/adhd-adults-childhood/1953789/

Helliwell, J. F. (2006). Well-being, social capital and public policy: What's new? *Economic Journal, 116*(510), C34–C45.

Hellwig-Brida, S., Daseking, M., Keller, F., Petermann, F., & Goldbeck, L. (2011). Effects of methylphenidate on intelligence and attention components in boys with attention-deficit/hyperactivity disorder. *Journal of Child and Adolescent Psychopharmacology, 21*(3), 245–253.

Hinshaw, S. P. (2002a). Is ADHD an impairing condition in childhood and adolescence? In P.S. Jensen & J. R. Cooper (Eds.), *Attention-deficit hyperactivity disorder: State of the science, best practices* (pp. 5-1–5-21). Kingston, NJ: Civic Research Institute.

Hinshaw, S. P. (2002b). Preadolescent girls with attention-deficit/hyperactivity disorder: I. background characteristics, comorbidity, cognitive and social functioning, and parenting practices. *Journal of Consulting and Clinical Psychology, 70*(5), 1086–1098.

Hinshaw, S. P. (2007). *The mark of shame: Stigma of mental illness and an agenda for change.* New York: Oxford University Press.

Hinshaw, S. P., with Kranz, R. (2009). *The triple bind: Saving our teenage girls from today's pressures.* New York: Ballantine.

Hinshaw, S. P. (2013). Developmental psychopathology as a scientific discipline: Rationale, principles, and recent advances. In T. P. Beauchaine & S. P. Hinshaw (Eds.), *Child and adolescent psychopathology* (2nd ed., pp. 1–18). Hoboken, NJ: Wiley.

Hinshaw, S. P., & Blachman, D. R. (2005). Attention-deficit/hyperactivity disorder. In D. Bell-Dolan, S. Foster, & E. J. Mash (Eds.), *Handbook of behavioral and emotional problems in girls* (pp. 117–147). New York: Kluwer Academic/Plenum.

Hinshaw, S. P., & Melnick, S. M. (1995). Peer relationships in boys with attention-deficit hyperactivity disorder with and without comorbid aggression. *Development and Psychopathology, 7*(4), 627–647.

Hinshaw, S. P., Owens, E. B., Wells, K. C., Kraemer, H. C., Abikoff, H. B., Arnold, L. E.,…Wigal, T. (2000). Family processes and treatment outcome in the MTA: Negative/ineffective parenting practices in relation to multimodal treatment. *Journal of Abnormal Child Psychology, 28*(6), 555–568.

Hinshaw, S. P., Owens, E. B., Zalecki, C., Huggins, S. P., Montenegro-Nevado, A., Schrodek, E., & Swanson, E. N. (2012). Prospective follow-up of girls with attention-deficit/hyperactivity disorder into early adulthood: Continuing impairment includes elevated risk for suicide attempts and self-injury. *Journal of Consulting and Clinical Psychology, 80*(6), 1041–1051.

Hinshaw, S. P., Scheffler, R. M., Fulton, B. D., Aase, H., Banaschewski, T., Cheng, W.,…Weiss, M. D. (2011). International variation in treatment procedures for ADHD: Social context and recent trends. *Psychiatric Services, 62*(5), 459–464.

Hinshaw, S. P., & Stier, A. (2008). Stigma in relation to mental disorders. *Annual Review of Clinical Psychology, 4,* 269–293.

Hinshaw, S. P., & Zupan, B. A. (1997). Assessment of antisocial behavior in children and adolescents. In D. M. Stoff, J. Breiling, &

J. D. Maser (Eds.), *Handbook of antisocial behavior* (pp. 36–50). Hoboken, NJ: Wiley.

Hochman, S. (2011, May 5). Victorino's positive spirit has helped him deal with ADD. *Philly.com*. Retrieved from http://articles.philly.com/2011-05-05/sports/29513110_1_attention-deficit-disorder-parents-kid/

Hoffman, J. (2013, March 20). Parental study shows rise in autism spectrum cases. *The New York Times*. Retrieved from http://www.nytimes.com/2013/03/21/health/parental-study-shows-rise-in-autism-spectrum-cases.html

Hoza, B., Mrug, S., Gerdes, A. C., Hinshaw, S. P., Bukowski, W. M., Gold, J. A.,…Arnold, L. E. (2005). What aspects of peer relationships are impaired in children with attention-deficit/hyperactivity disorder? *Journal of Consulting and Clinical Psychology, 73*(3), 411–423.

Hruska, B. (2012, August 18). Raising the Ritalin generation. *The New York Times*. Retrieved from www.nytimes.com/2012/08/19/opinion/sunday/raising-the-ritalin-generation.html

Hughes, R. (2012, June 25). *Stimulant medication shortages update: You helped CHADD to make a difference* [Web log post]. Retrieved from http://www.chaddleadershipblog.blogspot.com/2012_06_01_archive.html

Hughes, R. (2013, February 4). *Substance abuse, ADHD, and medications: The real issues* [Web log post]. Retrieved from http://www.chaddleadershipblog.blogspot.com/2013_02_04_archive.html

Huh, J., DeLorme, D. E., Reid, L. N., & An, S. (2010). Direct-to-consumer prescription drug advertising: History, regulation, and issues. *Minnesota Medicine, 93*(3), 50–52.

Humphreys, K. L., Eng, T., & Lee, S. S. (2013). Stimulant medication and substance use outcomes: A meta-analysis. *JAMA Psychiatry, 70*(7), 740–749.

Hurt, E. A., Arnold, L. E., & Lofthouse, N. (2011). Dietary and nutritional treatments for attention-deficit/hyperactivity disorder: Current research support and recommendations for practitioners. *Current Psychiatry Reports, 13*(5), 323–332.

Iannelli, V. (2011, March 14). ADHD—history of ADHD. *About.com*. Retrieved from http://pediatrics.about.com/od/adhd/a/history_adhd.htm

Ilieva, I., Boland, J., & Farah, M. J. (2013). Objective and subjective cognitive enhancing effects of mixed amphetamine salts in healthy people. *Neuropharmacology, 64,* 496–505.

IMS Institute for Healthcare Informatics. (2012, April). *The use of medicines in the United States: Review of 2011.* Retrieved from http://www.imshealth.com/portal/site/ims/

Itkonen, T. (2007). PL 94-142: Policy, evolution, and landscape shift. *Issues in Teacher Education 16*(2), 7–17.

Jacob, B. A. (2007, January). *Test-based accountability and student achievement: An investigation of differential performance on NAEP and state assessments* (NBER Working Paper No. 12817). Retrieved from National Bureau of Economic Research Web site: http://www.nber.org/papers/w12817

Jacob, B. A., & Dee, T. S. (2009, February). *Do high school exit exams influence educational attainment or labor market performance?* [CLOSUP Working Paper Series No. 18]. Retrieved from University of Michigan, Center for Local, State, and Urban Policy Web site: http://closup.umich.edu/files/closup-wp-18-hs-exit-exams.pdf

Jasinski, L. J., Harp, J. P., Berry, D. T. R., Shandera-Ochsner, A., Mason, L. H., & Ranseen, J. D. (2011). Using symptom validity tests to detect malingered ADHD in college students. *Clinical Neuropsychologist, 25*(8), 1415–1428.

Johnston, C., & Mash, E. J. (2001). Families of children with attention-deficit/ hyperactivity disorder: Review and recommendations for future research. *Clinical Child and Family Psychology Review, 4*(3), 183–207.

Julien, R. M., Advokat, C. D., & Comaty, J. E. (2011). *A primer of drug action* (12th ed.). New York: Worth.

Kaiser Family Foundation. (2003, June 10). *Impact of direct-to-consumer advertising on prescription drug spending* (Publication No. 6084). Retrieved from http://www.kff.org/rxdrugs/6084-index.cfm

Katusic, M. Z., Voigt, R. G., Colligan, R. C., Weaver, A. L., Homan, K. J., & Barbaresi, W. J. (2011). Attention-deficit hyperactivity disorder in children with high intelligence quotient: Results from a population-based study. *Journal of Developmental and Behavioral Pediatrics, 32*(2), 103–109.

Kent, K. M., Pelham, W. E., Molina, B. S. G., Sibley, M. H., Waschbusch, D. A., Yu, J.,…Karch, K. M. (2011). The academic experience of male high school students with ADHD. *Journal of Abnormal Child Psychology, 39*(3), 451–462.

Kessler, R. C., Adler, L., Ames, M., Barkley, R. A., Birnbaum, H., Greenberg, P.,…Üstün, T. B. (2005). The prevalence and effects of adult attention deficit/hyperactivity disorder on work performance in a nationally representative sample of workers. *Journal of Occupational and Environmental Medicine, 47*(6), 565–572.

Kessler, R. C., Adler, L., Barkley, R., Biederman, J., Conners, C. K., Demler, O.,…Zaslavsky, A. M. (2006). The prevalence and correlates of adult ADHD in the United States: Results from the National Comorbidity Survey Replication. *American Journal of Psychiatry, 163,* 716–723.

Kessler, R. C., Berglund, P., Demler, O., Jin, R., Merikangas, K. R., & Walters, E. E. (2005). Lifetime prevalence and age-of-onset distributions of DSM-IV disorders in the National Comorbidity Survey Replication. *Archives of General Psychiatry, 62*(6), 593–602.

Kessler, R. C., Green, J. G., Adler, L. A., Barkley, R. A., Chatterji, S., Faraone, S. V.,…Van Brunt, D. L. (2010). Structure and diagnosis of adult attention-deficit/hyperactivity disorder: Analysis of expanded symptom criteria from the adult ADHD clinical diagnostic scale. *Archives of General Psychiatry, 67*(11), 1168–1178.

Klein, R. G., Ramos, O. M. A., Castellanos, F. X., Lashua, E. C., Roizen, E., Hutchison, J. A., & Mannuzza, S. (2012). Clinical and functional outcome of childhood attention-deficit/hyperactivity disorder 33 years later. *Archives of General Psychiatry, 69*(12), 1295–1303.

Kline, M. (2009, September 25). ADHD case grabs attention. *The Tennessean,* p. NaN.

Knapp, M., King, D., Healey, A., & Thomas, C. (2011). Economic outcomes in adulthood and their associations with antisocial conduct, attention deficit and anxiety problems in childhood. *Journal of Mental Health Policy and Economics, 14*(3), 137–147.

Knouse, L. E., & Safren, S. A. (2010). Current status of cognitive behavioral therapy for adult attention-deficit hyperactivity disorder. *Psychiatric Clinics of North America, 33*(3), 497–509.

Kollins, S. H. (2013, February 16). AHDH story not the norm. *The News and Observer.* Retrieved from http://www.newsobserver.com/2013/02/16/2683543/scott-h-kollins-adhd-story-not.html

Konrad, K., & Eickhoff, S. B. (2010). Is the ADHD brain wired differently? A review on structural and functional connectivity in attention deficit hyperactivity disorder. *Human Brain Mapping,* *31*(6), 904–916.

Kress, S., Zechmann, S., & Schmitten, M. J. (2011). When performance matters: The past, present, and future of consequential accountability in public education. *Harvard Journal on Legislation, 48*(1), 185–234.

Kristof, N. D. (2012, August 10). War wounds. *The New York Times.* Retrieved from http://www.nytimes.com/2012/08/12/opinion/sunday/war-wounds.html?pagewanted=all

Kroutil, L. A., Van Brunt, D. L., Herman-Stahl, M., Heller, D. C., Bray, R. M., & Penne, M. A. (2006). Nonmedical use of prescription stimulants in the United States. *Drug and Alcohol Dependence,* *84*(2), 135–143.

Krueger, A. B., & Whitmore, D. M. (2001). The effect of attending a small class in the early grades on college-test taking and middle school test results: Evidence from project STAR. *Economic Journal, 111*(468), 1–28.

Kuehn, B. M. (2010). Increased risk of ADHD associated with early exposure to pesticides, PCBs. *JAMA: Journal of the American Medical Association, 304*(1), 27–28.

Kureishi, H. (2012, February 18). The art of distraction. *The New York Times.* Retrieved from http://www.nytimes.com/2012/02/19/opinion/sunday/the-art-of-distraction.html

Lahey, B. B., Applegate, B., McBurnett, K., & Biederman, J. (1994). DSM-IV field trials for attention deficit hyperactivity disorder in children and adolescents. *American Journal of Psychiatry, 151*(11), 1673–1685.

Lahiri, T. (2011, June 1). Study to map India's neurological disorders. *The Wall Street Journal.* Retrieved from http://blogs.wsj.com/indiarealtime/2011/06/01/study-to-map-india s-neurological-disorders/

Lake, T. (2010, December 6). The boy who died of football. *Sports Illustrated.* Retrieved from http://sportsillustrated.cnn.com/vault/article/magazine/MAG1180379/index.htm

Lang, H., Scheffler, R. M., & Hu, T. (2010). The discrepancy in attention deficit hyperactivity disorder (ADHD) medications diffusion 1994-2003: A global pharmaceutical data analysis. *Health Policy,* *97*(1), 71–78.

Langberg, J. M., & Becker, S. P. (2012). Does long-term medication use improve the academic outcomes of youth with attention-deficit/hyperactivity disorder? *Clinical Child and Family Psychology Review, 15*(3), 215–233.

Lange, F., & Topel, R. (2006). The social value of education and human capital. In E. A. Hanushek & F. Welch, *Handbook of the economics of education* (pp. 459–509). Amsterdam: North-Holland.

Larriviere, D., Williams, M. A., Rizzo, M., & Bonnie, R. J. (2009). Responding to requests from adult patients for neuroenhancements: Guidance of the ethics, law and humanities committee. *Neurology, 73*(17), 1406–1412.

Laufer, M. W., Denhoff, E., & Solomons, G. (1957). Hyperkinetic impulse disorder in children's behavior problems. *Psychosomatic Medicine, 19,* 38–49.

Lawrence, V., Houghton, S., Tannock, R., Douglas, G., Durkin, K., & Whiting, K. (2002). ADHD outside the laboratory: Boys' executive function performance on tasks in videogame play and on a visit to the zoo. *Journal of Abnormal Child Psychology, 30*(5), 447–462.

Lebowitz, M. S. (2013). Stigmatization of ADHD: A developmental review. *Journal of Attention Disorders.* Advance online publication. doi: 10.1177/1087054712475211

Lee, S. S., Humphreys, K. L., Flory, K., Liu, R., & Glass, K. (2011). Prospective association of childhood attention-deficit/hyperactivity disorder (ADHD) and substance use and abuse/dependence: A meta-analytic review. *Clinical Psychology Review, 31*(3), 328–341.

Lee, S. S., Lahey, B. B., Owens, E. B., & Hinshaw, S. P. (2008). Few preschool boys and girls with ADHD are well-adjusted during adolescence. *Journal of Abnormal Child Psychology, 36*(3), 373–383.

Lefley, H. P. (1989). Family burden and family stigma in major mental illness. *American Psychologist, 44*(3), 556–560.

Lenz, C. (2005). Prescribing a legislative response: Educators, physicians, and psychotropic medication for children. *Journal of Contemporary Health Law & Policy 22*(72).

Levy, F. (2009, August). Dopamine and noradrenaline theories of ADHD and drug response. *ADHD Report, 17*(4), 9–11, 16.

Levy, F., & Kochan, T. (2012). Addressing the problem of stagnant wages. *Comparative Economic Studies, 54*(4), 739–764.

Lewin, T. (2012, July 17). Universities reshaping education on the Web. *The New York Times*. Retrieved from http://www.nytimes.com/2012/07/17/education/consortium-of-colleges-takes-online-education-to-new-level.html?smid=pl-share

Lichtenstein, P., Halldner, L., Zetterqvist, J., Sjölander, A., Serlachius, E., Fazel, S.,...Larsson, H. (2012). Medication for attention deficit-hyperactivity disorder and criminality. *New England Journal of Medicine, 367*(21), 2006–2014.

Lillard, A. S., & Peterson, J. (2011). The immediate impact of different types of television on young children's executive function. *Pediatrics, 128*(4), 644–649.

Lofthouse, N., Arnold, L. E., Hersch, S., Hurt, E., & DeBeus, R. (2012). A review of neurofeedback treatment for pediatric ADHD. *Journal of Attention Disorders, 16*(5), 351–372.

Lofthouse, N., McBurnett, K., Arnold, L. E., & Hurt, E. (2011). Biofeedback and neurofeedback treatment for ADHD. *Psychiatric Annals, 41*(1), 42–48.

Low, K. (2012). Have you experienced stimulant medication shortages in your area? *About.com*. Retrieved from http://add.about.com/od/treatmentoptions/f/Stimulant-Medication-Shortage.htm

Loya, F., Hinshaw, S. P., & Reddy, R. (2010). Mental illness stigma and mediation of differences in South Asian and Caucasian students' attitudes toward psychological counseling. *Journal of Counseling Psychology, 57*, 484–490.

Lu, L., Shi, Q., & Tao, F. (2006). Epidemiological study on subtypes of ADHD of children aged 4–16 years old in Wuhan. *Chinese Mental Health Journal, 20*(4), 221–225.

Lynch, S., Sood, R., & Chronis-Tuscano, A. (2010, October). The implementation of evidence-based practices for ADHD in pediatric primary care. *ADHD Report, 18*(5), 1–6.

Mainous, A. G., Diaz, V. A., & Carnemolla, M. (2008). Factors affecting Latino adults' use of antibiotics for self-medication. *Journal of the American Board of Family Medicine, 21*(2), 128–134.

Major, B., & O'Brien, L. T. (2005). The social psychology of stigma. *Annual Review of Psychology, 56*, 393–421.

Mann, J. J., Emslie, G., Baldessarini, R. J., Beardslee, W., Fawcett, J. A., Goodwin, F. K., ...Wagner, K. D. (2006). ACNP task force report on SSRIs and suicidal behavior in youth. *Neuropsychopharmacology, 31*(3), 473–492.

Mansbach-Kleinfeld, I., Palti, H., Farbstein, I., Geraisy, N., Levinson, D., Brent, D. A., ...Levav, I. (2010). Service use for mental disorders and unmet need: Results from the Israel survey on mental health among adolescents. *Psychiatric Services, 61*(3), 241–249.

Martinez, A., Piff, P. K., Mendoza-Denton, R., & Hinshaw, S. P. (2011). The power of a label: Mental illness diagnoses, ascribed humanity, and social rejection. *Journal of Social and Clinical Psychology, 30,* 1–23.

Masson, A., & Rubin, P. H. (1985). Matching prescription drugs and consumers: The benefit of direct advertising. *New England Journal of Medicine, 313,* 513–515.

Mayes, R., Bagwell, C., & Erkulwater, J. (2008). ADHD and the rise in stimulant use among children. *Harvard Review of Psychiatry, 16*(3), 151–166.

Mayes, R., Bagwell, C., & Erkulwater, J. (2009). *Medicating children: ADHD and pediatric mental health.* Cambridge, MA: Harvard University Press.

McCann, D., Barrett, A., Cooper, A., Crumpler, D., Dalen, L., Grimshaw, K., ...Stevenson, J. (2007). Food additives and hyperactive behaviour in 3-year-old and 8/9-year-old children in the community: A randomised, double-blinded, placebo-controlled trial. *Lancet, 370*(9598), 1560–1567.

McGrath, C. (2013, January 2). A careful writer stalks the truth about Scientology. *The New York Times.* Retrieved from http://www.nytimes.com/2013/01/03/books/scientology-fascinates-the-author-lawrence-wright.html

Merrow, J. (Writer, Executive Producer). (1995). ADD—A dubious diagnosis. [Television series episode]. In J. D. Tulenko (Producer), *The Merrow Report.* Arlington, VA: Public Broadcasting Service.

Mick, E., McManus, D. D., & Goldberg, R. J. (2013). Meta-analysis of increased heart rate and blood pressure associated with CNS stimulant treatment of ADHD in adults. *European Neuropsychopharmacology, 23*(6), 534–541.

Mieszkowski, K. (2005, July 1). Scientology's war on psychiatry. *Salon.* Retrieved from http://www.salon.com/2005/07/01/sci_psy/

Mikami, A. Y., Griggs, M. S., Lerner, M. D., Emeh, C. C., Reuland, M. M., Jack, A., & Anthony, M. R. (2013). A randomized trial of a classroom intervention to increase peers' social inclusion of children with attention-deficit/hyperactivity disorder. *Journal of Consulting and Clinical Psychology, 81*(1), 100–112.

Mikami, A. Y., Lerner, M. D., Griggs, M. S., McGrath, A., & Calhoun, C. D. (2010). Parental influence on children with attention-deficit/hyperactivity disorder: II. Results of a pilot intervention training parents as friendship coaches for children. *Journal of Abnormal Child Psychology, 38*(6), 737–749.

Milich, R., Carlson, C. L., Pelham, W. E., & Licht, B. G. (1991). Effects of methylphenidate on the persistence of ADHD boys following failure experiences. *Journal of Abnormal Child Psychology, 19*(5), 519–536.

Milich, R., Licht, B. G., Murphy, D. A., & Pelham, W. E. (1989). Attention-deficit hyperactivity disordered boys' evaluations of and attributions for task performance on medication versus placebo. *Journal of Abnormal Psychology, 98*(3), 280–284.

Mintzes, B., Barer, M. L., Kravitz, R. L., Bassett, K., Lexchin, J., Kazanjian, A., . . . Marion, S. A. (2003). How does direct-to-consumer advertising (DTCA) affect prescribing? A survey in primary care environments with and without legal DTCA. *Canadian Medical Association Journal, 169*(5), 405–412.

Mogull, S. A. (2008). Chronology of direct-to-consumer advertising regulation in the United States. *American Medical Writers Association Journal, 23*(3), 106–109.

Molina, B. S. G., Hinshaw, S. P., Arnold, L. E., Swanson, J. M., Pelham, W. E., Hechtman, L., Hoza, B., . . . Marcus, S. (2013). Adolescent substance use in the multimodal treatment study of attention-deficit/hyperactivity disorder (ADHD) (MTA) as a function of childhood ADHD, random assignment to childhood treatments, and subsequent medication. *Journal of the American Academy of Child & Adolescent Psychiatry, 52*(3), 250–263.

Molina, B. S. G., Hinshaw, S. P., Swanson, J. M., Arnold, L. E., Vitiello, B., Jensen, P. S., . . . Houck, P. R. (2009). The MTA at 8 years: Prospective follow-up of children treated for combined-type ADHD in a multisite study. *Journal of the American Academy of Child & Adolescent Psychiatry, 48*(5), 484–500.

Molina, B. S. G., & Pelham, W. E. (2003). Childhood predictors of adolescent substance use in a longitudinal study of children with ADHD. *Journal of Abnormal Psychology, 112*(3), 497–507.

Morrow, R. L., Garland, E. J., Wright, J. M., Maclure, M., Taylor, S., & Dormuth, C. R. (2012). Influence of relative age on diagnosis and treatment of attention-deficit/hyperactivity disorder in children. *CMAJ: Canadian Medical Association Journal, 184*(7), 755–762.

MTA Cooperative Group. (1999a). A 14-month randomized clinical trial of treatment strategies for attention-deficit/hyperactivity disorder. *Archives of General Psychiatry, 56,* 1073–1086.

MTA Cooperative Group. (1999b). Moderators and mediators of treatment response for children with ADHD: The MTA Study. *Archives of General Psychiatry, 56,* 1088–1096.

Mueller, A. K., Fuermaier, B. M., Koerts, J., & Tucha, L. (2012). Stigma in attention deficit hyperactivity disorder. *Attention Deficit and Hyperactivity Disorders, 4*(3), 101–114.

Nagel, B. J., Bathula, D., Herting, M., Schmitt, C., Kroenke, C. D., Fair, D., & Nigg, J. T. (2011). Altered white matter microstructure in children with attention-deficit/hyperactivity disorder. *Journal of the American Academy of Child & Adolescent Psychiatry, 50*(3), 283–292.

Nakao, T., Radua, J., Rubia, K., & Mataix-Cols, D. (2011). Gray matter volume abnormalities in ADHD: Voxel-based meta-analysis exploring the effects of age and stimulant medication. *American Journal of Psychiatry, 168*(11), 1154–1163.

National Center for Health Workforce Analysis (2007). *Health Resources and Services Administration user documentation for the Area Resource File (ARF).* Washington, DC: Health Resources and Services Administration. Retrieved from http://arf.hrsa.gov/

National Conference of State Legislatures. (2012, August). *Insurance coverage for autism* (Go 18246). Retrieved from http://www.ncsl.org/issues-research/health/autism-and-insurance-coverage-state-laws.aspx

National Institute for Health and Clinical Excellence. (2009). *Attention deficit hyperactivity disorder: Diagnosis and management of ADHD in children, young people, and adults.* London: British Psychological Society and Royal College of

Psychiatrists. Retrieved from http://publications.nice.org.uk/attention-deficit-hyperactivity-disorder-cg72

Nesse, R. M. (2005). Evolutionary psychology and mental health. In D. M. Buss (Ed.), *The handbook of evolutionary psychology* (pp. 903–927). Hoboken, NJ: Wiley.

Nigg, J. T. (2006). *What causes ADHD? Understanding what goes wrong and why*. New York: Guilford Press.

Nigg, J. T. (2013). Attention-deficit/hyperactivity disorder. In T. P. Beauchaine & S. P. Hinshaw (Eds.), *Child and adolescent psychopathology* (2nd ed.). Hoboken, NJ: Wiley.

Nigg, J. T., Lewis, K., Edinger, T., & Falk, M. (2012). Meta-analysis of attention-deficit/hyperactivity disorder or attention-deficit/hyperactivity disorder symptoms, restriction diet, and synthetic food color additives. *Journal of the American Academy of Child & Adolescent Psychiatry, 51*(1), 86–97.

Nigg, J., Nikolas, M., & Burt, S. A. (2010). Measured gene-by-environment interaction in relation to attention-deficit/hyperactivity disorder. *Journal of the American Academy of Child & Adolescent Psychiatry, 49*(9), 863–873.

Nikolas, M. A., & Burt, S. A. (2010). Genetic and environmental influences on ADHD symptom dimensions of inattention and hyperactivity: A meta-analysis. *Journal of Abnormal Psychology, 119*(1), 1–17.

No Child Left Behind Act of 2001, Pub. L. No. 107-110, 115 Stat. 1425 (2002).

Norvilitis, J. M., Sun, L., & Zhang, J. (2010). ADHD symptomatology and adjustment to college in China and the United States. *Journal of Learning Disabilities, 43*(1), 86–94.

O'Hara, M., & Hinshaw, S. P. (2013). *Newspaper portrayals of mental illness across 25 years in the United States and United Kingdom: Little evidence for fundamental change*. Manuscript in preparation, University of California, Berkeley.

Okie, S. (2006). ADHD in adults. *New England Journal of Medicine, 354*(25), 2637–2641.

Olaniyan, D. A., & Okemakinde, T. (2008). Human capital theory: Implications for educational development. *European Journal of Scientific Research, 24*(2), 157–162.

Olfson, M., Huang, C., Gerhard, T., Winterstein, A. G., Crystal, S., Allison, P. D., & Marcus, S. C. (2012). Stimulants and cardiovascular events in youth with attention-deficit/hyperactivity disorder. *Journal of the American Academy of Child & Adolescent Psychiatry, 51*(2), 147–156.

O'Neil, J. (2012, March 26). Learning to drive with A.D.H.D. *The New York Times*. Retrieved from http://www.nytimes.com/2012/03/27/health/add-and-adhd-challenge-those-seeking-drivers-license.html?pagewanted=all

Owens, E. B., Hinshaw, S. P., Lee, S. S., & Lahey, B. B. (2009). Few girls with childhood attention-deficit/hyperactivity disorder show positive adjustment during adolescence. *Journal of Clinical Child and Adolescent Psychology, 38*(1), 132–143.

Pacana, G. (2011, May 24). ADHD on the rise, or is it? *Examiner.com*. Retrieved from http://www.examiner.com/article/adhd-on-the-rise-or-is-it

Pachankis, J. E. (2007). The psychological implications of concealing a stigma: A cognitive-affective-behavioral model. *Psychological Bulletin, 133*(2), 328–345.

Palli, S. R., Kamble, P. S., Chen, H., & Aparasu, R. R. (2012). Persistence of stimulants in children and adolescents with attention-deficit/hyperactivity disorder. *Journal of Child and Adolescent Psychopharmacology, 22*(2), 139–148.

Palmer, E. D., & Finger, S. (2001). An early description of ADHD (inattentive subtype): Dr. Alexander Crichton and "mental restlessness" (1798). *Child Psychology & Psychiatry Review, 6*(2), 66–73.

Pappano, L. (2012, November 4). The year of the MOOC. *The New York Times*. Retrieved from http://query.nytimes.com/gst/fullpage.html?res=9906E0D91F3EF937A35752C1A9649D8B63&smid=pl-share

Park, A. (2012, March 06). ADHD: Why the youngest kids in a class are most likely to be diagnosed. *Time*. Retrieved from http://healthland.time.com/2012/03/06/adhd-why-the-youngest-students-in-a-class-are-most-likely-to-be-diagnosed/

Patient Protection and Affordable Care Act of 2010, Pub. L. No. 111-148, §2702, 124 Stat. 119, 318-319 (2010).

Pelham, W. E., Foster, E. M., & Robb, J. A. (2007). The economic impact of attention-deficit/ hyperactivity disorder in children and adolescents. *Journal of Pediatric Psychology, 32*(6), 711–727.

Pelham, W. E., Hoza, B., Pillow, D. R., Gnagy, E. M., Kipp, H. L., Greiner, A. R.,...Fitzpatrick, E. (2002). Effects of methyphenidate and expectancy on children with ADHD: Behavior, academic performance, and attributions in a summer treatment program and regular classroom settings. *Journal of Consulting and Clinical Psychology, 70*(2), 320–335.

Pelham, W. E., Swanson, J. M., Furman, M. B., & Schwindt, H. (1995). Pemoline effects on children with ADHD: A time-response by dose-response analysis on classroom measures. *Journal of the American Academy of Child & Adolescent Psychiatry, 34*(11), 1504–1513.

Pera, G. (2008). *Is it you, me, or adult A.D.D.?: Stopping the roller coaster when someone you love has attention deficit disorder.* San Francisco: 1201 Alarm Press.

Pescosolido, B. A., Martin, J. K., Long, J. S., Medina, T. R., Phelan, J. C., & Link, B. G. (2010). "A disease like any other"? A decade of change in public reactions to schizophrenia, depression, and alcohol dependence. *American Journal of Psychiatry, 167*(11), 1321–1330.

Pfiffner, L. J., & Glasscock, S. (2011). *All about ADHD: The complete practical guide for classroom teachers* (2nd ed.). New York: Scholastic Professional Books.

Pfiffner, L. J., & McBurnett, K. (1997). Social skills training with parent generalization: Treatment effects for children with attention deficit disorder. *Journal of Consulting and Clinical Psychology, 65*(5), 749–757.

Pfiffner, L. J., Mikami, A. Y., Huang-Pollock, C., Easterlin, B., Zalecki, C., & McBurnett, K. (2007). A randomized, controlled trial of integrated home-school behavioral treatment for ADHD, predominantly inattentive type. *Journal of the American Academy of Child & Adolescent Psychiatry, 46*(8), 1041–1050.

Phelan, J. C., Cruz-Rojas, R., & Reiff, M. (2002). Genes and stigma: The connection between perceived genetic etiology and attitudes and beliefs about mental illness. *Psychiatric Rehabilitation Skills, 6*(2), 159–185.

Phelan, J. C., Link, B. G., Stueve, A., & Pescosolido, B. A. (2000). Public conceptions of mental illness in 1950 and 1996: What is mental illness and is it to be feared? *Journal of Health and Social Behavior, 41*(2), 188–207.

Pickles, A., & Angold, A. (2003). Natural categories or fundamental dimensions: On carving nature at the joints and the rearticulation of psychopathology. *Development and Psychopathology, 15*(3), 529–551.

Pingault, J., Tremblay, R. E., Vitaro, F., Carbonneau, R., Genolini, C., Falissard, B., & Côté, S. M. (2011). Childhood trajectories of inattention and hyperactivity and prediction of educational attainment in early adulthood: A 16-year longitudinal population-based study. *American Journal of Psychiatry, 168*(11), 1164–1170.

Pissarides, C. A. (2000, November). *Human capital and growth: A synthesis report* (Working Paper No. 168). Retrieved from the Organisation for Economic Cooperation and Development Web site: http://www.oecd-ilibrary.org/content/workingpaper/372502181227

Polanczyk, G., Caspi, A., Houts, R., Kollins, S. H., Rohde, L. A., & Moffitt, T. E. (2010). Implications of extending the ADHD age-of-onset criterion to age 12: Results from a prospectively studied birth cohort. *Journal of the American Academy of Child & Adolescent Psychiatry, 49*(3), 210–216.

Polanczyk, G., de Lima, M. S., Horta, B. L., Biederman, J., & Rohde, L. A. (2007). The worldwide prevalence of ADHD: A systematic review and meta-regression analysis. *American Journal of Psychiatry, 164*(6), 942–948.

Polanczyk, G., Rohde, L. A., Szobot, C., Schmitz, M., Montiel-Nava, C., & Bauermeister, J. J. (2008). ADHD treatment in Latin America and the Caribbean. *Journal of the American Academy of Child and Adolescent Psychiatry, 47*(6), 721–722.

Polderman, T. J. C., Huizink, A. C., Verhulst, F. C., van Beijsterveldt, Catherina E. M., Boomsma, D. I., & Bartels, M. (2011). A genetic study on attention problems and academic skills: Results of a longitudinal study in twins. *Journal of the Canadian Academy of Child and Adolescent Psychiatry, 20*(1), 22–34.

Powers, R. L., Marks, D. J., Miller, C. J., Newcorn, J. H., & Halperin, J. M. (2008). Stimulant treatment in children with attention-deficit/hyperactivity disorder moderates adolescent academic outcome. *Journal of Child and Adolescent Psychopharmacology, 18*(5), 449–459.

Prendergast, M., Taylor, E., Rapoport, J. L., Bartko, J., Donnelly, M., Zametkin, A., . . . Wieselberg, H. M. (1988). The diagnosis of childhood hyperactivity: A U.S.–U.K. cross-national study of DSM-III and ICD-9. *Journal of Child Psychology and Psychiatry, 29*(3), 289–300.

Proal, E., Reiss, P. T., Klein, R. G., Mannuzza, S., Gotimer, K., Ramos-Olazagasti, M., ...Castellanos, F. X. (2011). Brain gray matter deficits at 33-year follow-up in adults with attention-deficit/ hyperactivity disorder established in childhood. *Archives of General Psychiatry, 68*(11), 1122–1134.

Psacharopoulos, G., & Patrinos, H. A. (2004). Returns to investment in education: A further update. *Education Economics, 12*(2), 111–134.

Quay, H. C., & Werry, J. S. (1972). *Psychopathological disorders of childhood.* Oxford, England: John Wiley & Sons.

Quinn, P. O. (2005). Treating adolescent girls and women with ADHD: Gender-specific issues. *Journal of Clinical Psychology, 61*(5), 579–587.

Quinn, P., & Wigal, S. (2004). Perceptions of girls and ADHD: Results from a national survey. *Medscape General Medicine, 6*(2), 2.

Rabiner, D. (2013, March). Misuse & abuse of ADHD meds—An updated review [Electronic mailing list message]. Retrieved from http://www.helpforadd.com/

Rapoport, J. L. (1978). Dextroamphetamine: Cognitive and behavioral effects in normal prepubertal boys. *Science, 199*(4328), 560–563.

Rapoport, J. L. (1980). Dextroamphetamine: Its cognitive and behavioral effects in normal and hyperactive boys and normal men. *Archives of General Psychiatry, 37*(8), 933–943.

Rappley, M. D., Gardiner, J. C., Jetton, J. R., & Houang, R. T. (1995). The use of methylphenidate in Michigan. *Archives of Pediatrics & Adolescent Medicine, 149*(6), 675–679.

Rasmussen, N. (2008). America's first amphetamine epidemic 1929–1971: A quantitative and qualitative retrospective with implications for the present. *American Journal of Public Health, 98*(6), 974–985.

Ravichandran, N. (2011, November 18). ADHD: Getting back the focus. *India Today.* Retrieved from http://indiatoday.intoday.in/story/attention-deficit-hyperactivity-disorder-and-kids/1/159151.html

Ray, G. T., Croen, L. A., & Habel, L. A. (2009). Mothers of children diagnosed with attention-deficit/ hyperactivity disorder: Health conditions and medical care utilization in periods before and after birth of the child. *Medical Care, 47*(1), 105–114.

Ray, G. T., Levine, P., Croen, L. A., Bokhari, F. A., Hu, T. W., & Habel, L. A. (2006). Attention-deficit/hyperactivity disorder in children: Excess costs before and after initial diagnosis and treatment cost differences by ethnicity. *Archives of Pediatrics & Adolescent Medicine, 160*(10), 1063–1069.

Ray, L. & Hinnant, A. (2009). Media representation of mental disorders: A study of ADD and ADHD coverage in magazines from 1985–2008. *Journal of Magazine and New Media Research, 11*(1).

Rich, M. (2012, December 11). U.S. students still lag globally in math and science, tests show. *The New York Times.* Retrieved from http://www.nytimes.com/2012/12/11/education/us-students-still-lag-globally-in-math-and-science-tests-show.html

Rich, M. (2013, February 9). Holding states and schools accountable. *The New York Times.* Retrieved from http://www.nytimes.com/2013/02/10/education/debate-over-federal-role-in-public-school-policy.html

Riddle, M. A., Yershova, K., Lazzaretto, D., Paykina, N., Yenokyan, G., Greenhill, L.,...Posner, K. (2013). The preschool attention-deficit/hyperactivity disorder treatment study (PATS) 6-year follow-up. *Journal of the American Academy of Child & Adolescent Psychiatry, 52*(3), 264–278.

Robb, J. A., Sibley, M. H., Pelham, W. E., Foster, E. M., Molina, B. S. G., Gnagy, E. M., & Kuriyan, A. B. (2011). The estimated annual cost of ADHD to the US education system. *School Mental Health, 3*(3), 169–177.

Rose, L. T., with Ellison, K. (2013). *Square peg: My story and what it means for raising innovators, visionaries, and out-of-the-box thinkers.* New York: Hyperion.

Rothbart, M. K., & Sheese, B. E. (2007). Temperament and emotion regulation. In J. J. Gross (Ed.), *Handbook of emotion regulation* (pp. 331–250). New York: Guilford Press.

Rothbart, M. K., Sheese, B. E., & Posner, M. I. (2007). Executive attention and effortful control: Linking temperament, brain networks, and genes. *Child Development Perspectives, 1*(1), 2–7.

Rowe, R., Maughan, B., & Goodman, R. (2004). Childhood psychiatric disorder and unintentional injury: Findings from a national cohort study. *Journal of Pediatric Psychology, 29*(2), 119–130.

Royal Australasian College of Physicians. (2009, June). *Draft Australian guidelines on attention deficit hyperactivity disorder* (Ref. No. CH54). Retrieved from Australian Government

National Health and Medical Research Council Web site: http://www.nhmrc.gov.au/guidelines/publications/ch54

Rucklidge, J. J. (2010). Gender differences in attention-deficit/hyperactivity disorder. *Psychiatric Clinics of North America, 33*(2), 357–373.

Rutledge, K. J., van den Bos, W., McClure, S. M., & Schweitzer, J. B. (2012). Training cognition in ADHD: Current findings, borrowed concepts, and future directions. *Neurotherapeutics, 9,* 542–558.

Rutter, M. (2006). *Genes and behavior: Nature-nurture interplay explained.* Oxford, England: Blackwell.

Safer, D. J., & Krager, J. M. (1992). Effect of a media blitz and a threatened lawsuit on stimulant treatment. *JAMA: Journal of the American Medical Association, 268*(8), 1004–1007.

Safer, D. J., & Malever, M. (2000). Stimulant treatment in Maryland public schools. *Pediatrics, 106*(3), 533–539.

Safer, D. J., Zito, J. M., & Fine, E. M. (1996). Increased methylphenidate usage for attention deficit disorder in the 1990s. *Pediatrics, 98*(6), 1084–1088.

Safren, S. A., Sprich, S., Mimiaga, M. J., Surman, C., Knouse, L., Groves, M., & Otto, M. W. (2010). Cognitive behavioral therapy vs relaxation with educational support for medication-treated adults with ADHD and persistent symptoms. *JAMA: Journal of the American Medical Association, 304*(8), 875–880.

Sahakian, B., & Morein-Zamir, S. (2007). Cognitive enhancement: Professor's little helper. *Nature, 450*(7173), 1157–1159.

Sappell, J., & Welkos, R. W. (1990, June 29). Suits, protests fuel a campaign against psychiatry. *Los Angeles Times.* Retrieved from http://www.latimes.com/news/local/la-scientology062990a,1,60 85874,full.story?coll=la-news-comment

Sartorius, N. (1998). Stigma: What can psychiatrists do about it? *Lancet, 352*(9133), 1058–1059.

Sartorius, N. (2002). Iatrogenic stigma of mental illness. *British Medical Journal, 324*(7352), 1470–1471.

Sawyer, M. G., Arney, F. M., Baghurst, P. A., Clark, J. J., Graetz, B. W., Kosky, R. J.,…Zubrick, S. R. (2001). The mental health of young people in Australia: Key findings from the child and adolescent component of the national survey of mental health and well-being. *Australian and New Zealand Journal of Psychiatry, 35*(6), 806–814.

Scheffler, R. M., Brown, T. T., Fulton, B. D., Hinshaw, S. P., Levine, P., & Stone, S. (2009). Positive association between attention-deficit/hyperactivity disorder medication use and academic achievement during elementary school. *Pediatrics, 123*(5), 1273–1279.

Scheffler, R. M., Hinshaw, S. P., Modrek, S., & Levine, P. (2007). The global market for ADHD medications. *Health Affairs, 26*(2), 450–457.

Schrag, P., & Divoky, D. (1975). *The myth of the hyperactive child: And other means of child control.* New York: Pantheon Books.

Schwab, D. (2012, December 13). China's growing economic problems. *Examiner.com*. Retrieved from http://www.examiner.com/article/china-s-growing-economic-problems

Schwarz, A. (2012a, June 9). Risky rise of the good-grade pill. *The New York Times*. Retrieved from http://www.nytimes.com/2012/06/10/education/seeking-academic-edge-teenagers-abuse-stimulants.html

Schwarz, A. (2012b, October 9). Attention disorder or not, pills to help in school. *The New York Times*. Retrieved from http://www.nytimes.com/2012/10/09/health/attention-disorder-or-not-children-prescribed-pills-to-help-in-school.html?pagewanted=all

Schwarz, A. (2013, February 3). Drowned in a stream of prescriptions. *The New York Times*. Retrieved from http://www.nytimes.com/2013/02/03/us/concerns-about-adhd-practices-and-amphetamine-addiction.html

Schwarz, A., & Cohen, S. (2013, April 1). A.D.H.D seen in 11% of U.S. children as diagnoses rise. *The New York Times*. Retrieved from http://www.nytimes.com/2013/04/01/health/more-diagnoses-of-hyperactivity-causing-concern.html?smid=pl-share

Shaw, P., Eckstrand, K., Sharp, W., Blumenthal, J., Lerch, J. P., Greenstein, D.,...Rapoport, J. L. (2007). Attention-deficit/hyperactivity disorder is characterized by a delay in cortical maturation. *Proceedings of the National Academy of Sciences of the United States of America, 104*(49), 19649–19654.

Shaw, P., Lalonde, F., Lepage, C., Rabin, C., Eckstrand, K., Sharp, W.,...Rapoport, J. (2009). Development of cortical asymmetry in typically developing children and its disruption in attention-deficit/hyperactivity disorder. *Archives of General Psychiatry, 66*(8), 888–896.

Shaw, P., Lerch, J., Greenstein, D., Sharp, W., Clasen, L., Evans, A.,…Rapoport, J. (2006). Longitudinal mapping of cortical thickness and clinical outcome in children and adolescents with attention-deficit/hyperactivity disorder. *Archives of General Psychiatry, 63*(5), 540–549.

Shaw, P., Malek, M., Watson, B., Sharp, W., Evans, A., & Greenstein, D. (2012). Development of cortical surface area and gyrification in attention-deficit/hyperactivity disorder. *Biological Psychiatry, 72*(3), 191–197.

Shipstead, Z., Redick, T. S., & Engle, R. W. (2012). Is working memory training effective? *Psychological Bulletin, 138*(4), 628–654.

Shire US Inc. (2007, March 2). Broken promises [Advertisement]. *Psychiatric News, 42*(5).

Shire US Inc. (2012, July 23). I didn't outgrow my ADHD. That's why I'm telling my story [Advertisement]. *Newsweek, 160*(5).

Siegler, R. S., DeLoache, J. S., & Eisenberg, N. (2011). *How children develop* (3rd ed.). New York: Worth.

Simple treatments, ignored. [Editorial]. (2012, September 8). *The New York Times.* Retrieved from http://www.nytimes.com/2012/09/09/opinion/sunday/simple-treatments-ignored.html

Singh, I. (2002). Bad boys, good mothers, and the "miracle" of Ritalin. *Science in Context, 15*(4), 577–603.

Singh, I. (2012). *VOICES study: Final report.* Retrieved from ADHD Voices Project Web site: http://www.adhdvoices.com/documents/12_0819_Voices_Report_LR-72dpi-GREY_V4.pdf

Singh, I., Filipe, A. M., Bard, I., Bergey, M., & Baker, L. (2013). Globalization and cognitive enhancement: Emerging social and ethical challenges for ADHD clinicians. *Current Psychiatry Reports, 15*(9), 385.

Sirey, J. A., Bruce, M. L., Alexopoulos, G. S., Perlick, D. A., Raue, P., Friedman, S. J., & Meyers, B. S. (2001). Perceived stigma as a predictor of treatment discontinuation in young and older outpatients with depression. *American Journal of Psychiatry, 158*(3), 479–481.

Sleator, E. K., & Ullmann, R. K. (1981). Can the physician diagnose hyperactivity in the office? *Pediatrics, 67,* 13–17.

Smith, M. E., & Farah, M. J. (2011). Are prescription stimulants "smart pills"? The epidemiology and cognitive neuroscience of prescription stimulant use by normal healthy individuals. *Psychological Bulletin, 137*(5), 717–741.

Sobanski, E., Banaschewski, T., Asherson, P., Buitelaar, J., Chen, W., Franke, B.,…Faraone, S. V. (2010). Emotional lability in children and adolescents with attention deficit/hyperactivity disorder (ADHD): Clinical correlates and familial prevalence. *Journal of Child Psychology and Psychiatry, 51*(8), 915–923.

Sobel, L. J., Bansal, R., Maia, T. V., Sanchez, J., Mazzone, L., Durkin, K.,…Peterson, B. S. (2010). Basal ganglia surface morphology and the effects of stimulant medications in youth with attention deficit hyperactivity disorder. *American Journal of Psychiatry, 167*(8), 977–986.

Solanto, M. V. (2011). *Cognitive-behavioral therapy for adult ADHD: Targeting executive dysfunction.* New York: Guilford Press.

Solanto, M. V., Marks, D. J., Wasserstein, J., Mitchell, K., Abikoff, H., Alvir, J. M. J., & Kofman, M. D. (2010). Efficacy of meta-cognitive therapy for adult ADHD. *American Journal of Psychiatry, 167*(8), 958–968.

Sonuga-Barke, E. J., Brandeis, D., Cortese, S., Daley, D., Ferrin, M., Holtmann, M.,…& Sergeant, J. (2013). Nonpharmacological interventions for ADHD: Systematic review and meta-analyses of randomized controlled trials of dietary and psychological treatments. *American Journal of Psychiatry, 170*(3), 275–289.

Spencer, T. J., Brown, A., Seidman, L. J., Valera, E. M., Makris, N., Lomedico, A.,…& Biederman, J. (2013). Effect of psychostimulants on brain structure and function in ADHD: A qualitative literature review of magnetic resonance imaging-based neuroimaging studies. *Journal of Clinical Psychiatry, 74,* 902–917.

Sprague, R. L., & Sleator, E. K. (1977). Methylphenidate in hyperkinetic children: Differences in dose effects on learning and social behavior. *Science, 198*(4323), 1274–1276.

Sroufe, L. A. (2012, January 28). Ritalin gone wrong. *The New York Times.* Retrieved from http://www.nytimes.com/2012/01/29/opinion/sunday/childrens-add-drugs-dont-work-long-term.html

Stein, M. T. (2012). Stimulants to enhance academic achievement. *Journal of Developmental and Behavioral Pediatrics, 33*(7), 589.

Stevens, S. E., Sonuga-Barke, E., Kreppner, J. M., Beckett, C., Castle, J., Colvert, E.,…Rutter, M. (2008). Inattention/overactivity following early severe institutional deprivation: Presentation and associations in early adolescence. *Journal of Abnormal Child Psychology, 36*(3), 385–398.

Stevenson, J. (2010). Recent research on food additives: Implications for CAMH. *Child and Adolescent Mental Health, 15*(3), 130–133.

Still, G. F. (1902). The Goulstonian lectures on some abnormal psychical conditions in children. *Lancet, 159*(4102), 1008–1013.

Stix, G. (2009). Turbocharging the brain. *Scientific American, 301*(4), 46–55.

Stix, G. (2012, June 13). Should Ritalin be distributed to everyone taking the SATs? [Web log post]. *Scientific American.* Retrieved from http://blogs.scientificamerican.com/observations/2012/06/13/should-ritalin-be-distributed-to-everyone-taking-the-sats/

Stone, S., Brown, T. T., & Hinshaw, S. P. (2010). ADHD-related school compositional effects: An exploration. *Teachers College Record, 112*(5), 1275–1299.

Strauss, A. A., & Lehtinen, L. E. (1947). *Psychopathology and education of the brain-injured child.* Oxford, England: Grune & Stratton.

Sumner, C. (2010, October). New tool for objective assessments of ADHD: The quotient ADHD system. *ADHD Report, 18*(5), 6–9.

Sun, D. F., Yi, M. J., Li, M., & Li, Y. L. (2009). An investigation of ADHD and family environment in 8235 school children aged 4–16 years in Northern Shandong. *Chinese Journal or Nervous and Mental Diseases, 35*(11), 650–654.

Swanson, J. M., Kraemer, H. C., Hinshaw, S. P., Arnold, L. E., Conners, C. K., Abikoff, H. B.,...Wu, M. (2001). Clinical relevance of the primary findings of the MTA: Success rates based on severity of ADHD and ODD symptoms at the end of treatment. *Journal of the American Academy of Child & Adolescent Psychiatry, 40*(2), 168–179.

Swanson, J. M., Lakes, K. D., Wigal, T. L., & Volkow, N. D. (2013). Multiple origins of sex differences in attention deficit hyperactivity disorder. In Y. Christen & D. W. Pfaff (Eds.), *Multiple origins of sex differences in brain: Neuroendocrine functions and their pathologies* (pp. 103–122). Berlin: Springer.

Swanson, J. M., Lerner, M., & Williams, L. (1995). More frequent diagnosis of attention deficit-hyperactivity disorder. *New England Journal of Medicine, 333*(14), 944.

Swanson, J. M., McBurnett, K., Wigal, T., & Pfiffner, L. J. (1993). Effect of stimulant medication on children with attention deficit disorder: A "review of reviews." *Exceptional Children, 60*(2), 154–161.

Swanson, J. M., Waxmonsky, J. G., Wigal, T., Stehli, A., Arnold, L. E., Greenhill, L. L.,...& MTA Cooperative Group (2013). *Long-term effects of extended exposure to stimulant medication for ADHD on mature adult stature.* Manuscript submitted for publication.

Swanson, J. M., Wigal, T. L., & Volkow, N. D. (2011). Contrast of medical and nonmedical use of stimulant drugs, basis for the distinction, and risk of addiction: Comment on Smith and Farah (2011). *Psychological Bulletin, 137*(5), 742–748.

Sweeney, C. T., Sembower, M. A., Ertischek, M. D., Shiffman, S., & Schnoll, S. H. (2013). Nonmedical use of prescription ADHD stimulants and preexisting patterns of drug abuse. *Journal of Addictive Disorders, 32*(1), 1–10.

Swensen, A., Birnbaum, H. G., Hamadi, R. B., Greenberg, P., Cremieux, P., & Secnik, K. (2004). Incidence and costs of accidents among attention-deficit/hyperactivity disorder patients. *Journal of Adolescent Health, 35*(4), 346–347.

Szalavitz, M. (2012, November 26). ADHD medications improve decision-making, but are they being over used? *Time.* Retrieved from http://healthland.time.com/2012/11/26/adhd-medications-improve-decision-making-but-are-they-being-used-properly/

Talbot, M. (2009). Brain gain. The underground world of "neuroenhancing" drugs. *The New Yorker.* Retrieved from http://www.newyorker.com/reporting/2009/04/27/090427fa_fact_talbot

Thakkar, V. G. (2013, April 27). Diagnosing the wrong deficit. *The New York Times.* Retrieved from http://www.nytimes.com/2013/04/28/opinion/sunday/diagnosing-the-wrong-deficit/html

Thapar, A., Cooper, M., Eyre, O., & Langley, K. (2013). Practitioner review: What have we learnt about the causes of ADHD? *Journal of Child Psychology and Psychiatry, 54*(1), 3–16.

Thapar, A., Rice, F., Hay, D., Boivin, J., Langley, K., van den Bree, M.,…Harold, G. (2009). Prenatal smoking might not cause attention-deficit/hyperactivity disorder: Evidence from a novel design. *Biological Psychiatry, 66*(8), 722–727.

Timimi, S., & Taylor, E. (2004). ADHD is best understood as a cultural construct. *British Journal of Psychiatry, 184,* 8–9.

Tkacik, M. (2011, December 31). Why big pharma is causing the Adderall shortage. *The Fix.* Retrieved from http://www.thefix.com/content/pay-attention-adderall-add-big-pharma7004

U. S. Department of Commerce (2012). *The competitiveness and innovative capacity of the United States.* Washington, DC: U.S. Government Printing Office.

Vandal, B., & Education Commission of the States. (2011). *Higher education reform: Next-generation models to increase success and control costs*. Retrieved from ERIC database. (ED524012)

Valderrama, A. L., Gillespie, C., King, S. C., George, M. G., Hong, Y., & Gregg, E. (2012). Vital signs: Awareness and treatment of uncontrolled hypertension among adults—United States, 2003–2010. *Morbidity and Mortality Weekly Report, 61*(35), 703–709. Atlanta, GA: Centers for Disease Control and Prevention.

Vickers, M. Z. (2010, March). *Accommodating college students with learning disabilities: ADD, ADHD, and dyslexia*. Retrieved from John William Pope Center for Higher Education Policy Web site: http://www.popecenter.org/acrobat/vickers-mar2010.pdf

Visser, S. N., Bitsko, R. H., Danielson, M. L., & Perou, R. (2010). Increasing prevalence of parent-reported attention-deficit/ hyperactivity disorder among children—United States, 2003 and 2007. *Morbidity and Mortality Weekly Report, 59*(44), 1439–1443.

Visser, S. N., Danielson, M. L., Bitsko, R. H., Holbrook, M., Kogan, R., Ghandour, R., Perou, R., & Blumberg, S. (2013). Trends in the prevalence of parent-reported ADHD diagnosis and medication treatment by a health care professional: United States, 2003-2011. *Journal of the American Academy of Child and Adolescent Psychiatry*, epub ahead of print.

Volkow, N. D., Wang, G., Kollins, S. H., Wigal, T. L., Newcorn, J. H., Telang, F., ... Swanson, J. M. (2009). Evaluating dopamine reward pathway in ADHD: Clinical implications. *JAMA: Journal of the American Medical Association, 302*(10), 1084–1091.

Volkow, N. D., Wang, G., Tomasi, D., Kollins, S. H., Wigal, T. L., Newcorn, J. H., ... Swanson, J. M. (2012). Methylphenidate-elicited dopamine increases in ventral striatum are associated with long-term symptom improvement in adults with attention deficit hyperactivity disorder. *Journal of Neuroscience, 32*(3), 841–849.

Wahl, O. F. (1995). *Media madness: Public images of mental illness*. New Brunswick, NJ: Rutgers University Press.

Wahl, O. F. (2003). Depictions of mental illnesses in children's media. *Journal of Mental Health, 12*, 249–258.

Wakefield, J. C. (1992). The concept of mental disorder. On the boundary between biological facts and social values. *American Psychologist, 47*(3), 373–388.

Wallis, D. (2013, March 18). Colleges assess cost of free online-only courses. *The New York Times*. Retrieved from http://www.nytimes.com/2013/03/19/education/colleges-assess-cost-of-free-online-only-courses.html?smid=pl-share

Warren, J. R., Jenkins, K. N., & Kulick, R. B. (2006). High school exit examinations and state-level completion and GED rates, 1975 through 2002. *Educational Evaluation and Policy Analysis, 28,* 131–152.

Warren, Z., McPheeters, M. L., Sathe, N., Foss-Feig, J., Glasser, A., & Veenstra-VanderWeele, J. (2011). A systematic review of early intensive intervention for autism spectrum disorders. *Pediatrics, 127*(5), e1303–e1311.

Wass, S. V., Scerif, G., & Johnson, M. H. (2012). Training attentional control and working memory—Is younger, better? *Developmental Review, 32*(4), 360–387.

Weiner, B., Perry, R. P., & Magnusson, J. (1988). An attributional analysis of reactions to stigmas. *Journal of Personality and Social Psychology, 55*(5), 738–48.

Wells, K. C., Chi, T. C., Hinshaw, S. P., Epstein, J. N., Pfiffner, L., Nebel-Schwalm, M.,...Wigal, T. (2006). Treatment-related changes in objectively measured parenting behaviors in the multimodal treatment study of children with attention-deficit/hyperactivity disorder. *Journal of Consulting and Clinical Psychology, 74*(4), 649–657.

Wennberg, J. (1984). Dealing with medical practice variations: A proposal for action. *Health Affairs, 3*(2), 6–32.

Wennberg, J., & Gittelsohn, A. (1973). Small area variations in health care delivery. *Science, 182*(4117), 1102–1108.

Wennberg, J., & Gittelsohn, A. (1982). Variations in care among small areas. *Science, 246,* 120–134.

Whalen, C. K., Henker, B., Buhrmester, D., Hinshaw, S. P., Huber, A., & Laski, K. (1989). Does stimulant medication improve the peer status of hyperactive children? *Journal of Consulting and Clinical Psychology, 57*(4), 545–549.

Whitley, R., & Berry, S. (2013). Trends in newspaper coverage of mental illness in Canada: 2005–2010. *Canadian Journal of Psychiatry*. *58*(2), 107–112.

Wilens, T. E. (1999). *Straight talk about psychiatric medications for kids*. New York: Guilford Press.

Wilens, T. E., Adler, L. A., Adams, J., Sgambati, S., Rotrosen, J., Sawtelle, R.,...Fusillo, S. (2008). Misuse and diversion of stimulants prescribed for ADHD: A systematic review of the literature. *Journal of the American Academy of Child & Adolescent Psychiatry*, *47*(1), 21–31.

Wilens, T. E., Spencer, T. J., & Biederman, J. (2001). A review of the pharmacotherapy of adults with attention-deficit/hyperactivity disorder. *Journal of Attention Disorders*, *5*(4), 189–202.

Willcutt, E. G. (2012). The prevalence of DSM-IV attention-deficit/hyperactivity disorder: A meta-analytic review. *Neurotherapeutics*, *9*(3), 490–499.

Wilson, C., Nairn, R., Coverdale, J., & Panapa, A. (2000). How mental illness is portrayed in children's television: A prospective study. *British Journal of Psychiatry*, *176*, 440–443.

Wood, D. R., Reimherr, F. W., Wender, P. H., & Johnson, G. E. (1976). Diagnosis and treatment of minimal brain dysfunction in adults: A preliminary report. *Archives of General Psychiatry*, *33*(12), 1453–1460.

World Health Organization. (2009, August). Direct-to-consumer advertising under fire. *Bulletin of the World Health Organization*, *87*(8).

Worry over attention deficit cases [Editorial] (2013, April 10). *The New York Times*. Retrieved from http://www.newyork-times.com/2013/04/10/opinion.worr-over-attention-deficit-hyperactivity-disorder.html

Wright, L. (2013). *Going clear: Scientology, Hollywood, and the prison of belief*. New York: Alfred A. Knopf.

Yoon, S. Y. R., Jain, U., & Shapiro, C. (2012). Sleep in attention-deficit/hyperactivity disorder in children and adults: Past, present, and future. *Sleep Medicine Reviews*, *16*, 371–388.

Zametkin, A. J., Nordahl, T. E., Gross, M., & King, A. C. (1990). Cerebral glucose metabolism in adults with hyperactivity of childhood onset. *New England Journal of Medicine*, *323*(20), 1361–1366.

Zoega, H., Valdimarsdóttir, U. A., & Hernández-Díaz, S. (2012). Age, academic performance, and stimulant prescribing for ADHD: A nationwide cohort study. *Pediatrics, 130*(6), 1012–1018.

Zuvekas, S. H., & Vitiello, B. (2012). Stimulant medication use in children: A 12-year perspective. *American Journal of Psychiatry, 169*(2), 160–166.

# Index

Page numbers followed by t or f indicate a reference to a table or figure, respectively, on the specified page. Page numbers followed by n and number indicate a specific note.